"A WOMAN OF FLORENCE."

*After the painting variously ascribed to Piero della Francesca, Verocchio and
Pollaiuolo, and marked on the reverse " Uxor James de' Bardi."*

WOMEN FLOR OF ENCE
BY · ISIDORO · DEL · LVNGO
TRANSLATED · BY · MARY · C STEEGMANN
WITH · PREFACE · BY · DOCTOR GVIDO · BIAGI

: 1908 :
DOVBLEDAY · PAGE
& C°: NEW · YORK

The binding of this volume
is adapted from a late Cinquecento Example.

" Per molti, donna, anzi per mille amanti
creata fusti, e d'angelica forma.
Or par che 'n ciel si dorma,
s'un sol s'apropia quel ch'è dato a tanti."

Michaelangelo Buonarotti.

The title, on reverse of this
page, is adapted from Cotton
MS., Dom. A XVII., f. 49,
in the British Museum.
Date 1425–1430.

PREFACE

THE book which I now have the honour of presenting to the English-speaking public is really the first to deal seriously with a subject of especial interest, and singular attraction to readers of the present day. Modern historical studies have left the highroad of politics—a road trodden by kings and popes and emperors, by armies marching out to war, by clerks and courtiers—to penetrate into the lanes and by-ways, where, obscure and unknown, abides the great throng of those who live and love, suffer and work and die unknown to, as they never knew, history, glory or renown. Modern history seeks to reconstruct the imposing background before which, in the full glare of the footlights, or as in the orchestra of an antique theatre, speak and move the famous actors in the great human drama called history. The origin, the deeds, exploits and vicissitudes, of these prominent personages are well known, but it is a matter of no less importance that we should obtain an intimate knowledge of their relations with the men of their own times—that nameless multitude of the obscure chorus behind the stage of the great tragedy.

The researches of that new science called political economy, and the application of sociological
methods to the study of the past, have imported a
vigorous impulse to these new critical investiga-
tions, and have invested with great importance
certain events hitherto scorned by the historian as
almost beneath his notice. For a very long time
history was written only for the benefit and glorification of the conquerors, the gratification of a class
which had attained to political or civil supremacy.
Until now, again, history has been written from the
point of view of man alone, and only quite lately
has it come to be thought just and right to study
also the cause, and the party, of those who found
no favour with the gods and with Fortune, to tell
the story of the vanquished and the humble, the
host whose vanguard is woman—neither saint nor
heroine, virago nor warrior, but woman, the half of
the race.

As far as Italy is concerned, what may be termed
the lesser, but certainly the most lifelike branch,
of history has yet to be written. With the exception of Venice, which can boast of studies by
Romanin, B. Cecchetti, and P. Molmenti; of Genoa,
which possesses an admirable work upon this subject by L. T. Belgrano; and of Bologna, well described by Ludovico Frati; the inner histories of
Italian cities, of the daily life of the different classes
and their relations to each other, still await investi-

gation. This investigation must be carried out, and these stories compiled, from the less known and less easily accessible sources—the domestic chronicles, mercantile books, private papers and records, legal contracts, inventories of wedding outfits and household property, all those endless masses of documents which, forgotten in the garrets of old palaces, have now inestimable interest and value as witnesses to the manners and customs of a bygone age.

All these researches into the very bosom of the family, into the remotest corners of the house, lead us to woman, ever the centre and mainspring of the house and family. Here we find her as she really was then, with all her prejudices, her modest virtues, her vices and her passions, her deeds of courage and of sacrifice, her jealousies and fears, her hatreds and her long-cherished and concealed loves. The women portrayed in aulic history are all princesses or queens or dames of high lineage, who appear with crowns or halos, in rich apparel and wondrous robes adorned with gems and lace; or they are the women of the poets, figures of tale and legend whom we recognise in the pictures and frescoes, the busts and statues of famous artists. But those other more humble figures, who, whether citizen or gentle, within their own houses, played their modest parts in the simple comedy devoid of exciting intrigue or heroic adventure, inspired no songs or

madrigals, still less a famous epic.   Their utmost
recognition was a brief if affectionate mention in
the memorials of the family, or upon the cold stone
which covered their forgotten bones.   It is not the
heroines, however, the prominent figures of history,
who arouse our keenest sympathy and curiosity, for
we are already wearied with the tales of their virtues
and their fortunes ; our interest now centres round
those wives and mothers and maidens, the mystery
surrounding whom we are endeavouring to penetrate, whose customs and tastes and daily life we
are seeking to reconstruct.   We want to know their
thoughts, their feelings and their affections ; and if
we can trace but one passage in those lives, one
throb of those hearts long since dust, one gleam
of love or vitality in those long-closed eyes, we are
as proud of our success as of some great scientific
discovery.   Henceforth the scholar and the historian have one aim with the physiologist and the
naturalist, the unprejudiced pursuit of that truth,
of which the cold objectivity inspires investigators
with the most ardent enthusiasm.

That Professor Isidoro del Lungo's book has an
undeniable value will be recognised and appreciated
by all who know something of this subject.   Unlike
many other works of a similar kind, it is no mere
compilation of dates and facts, gleaned here and
there, to which a modicum of taste and patience
has given the form of a book or essay.   A whole

library has been written about the women of the
Italian Renaissance, and this feminine—or rather
feminist—bibliography can boast of a long list of
titles and monographs. To these publications we
might apply a saying borrowed from a little play
by Ferdinando Martini, *Il peggio passo è quello dell'*
uscio, one of the cleverest curtain-raisers written
since Alfred de Musset laid down his pen—" *Ci*
sono delle donne, ma la donna non c'è." "Here are a
great many women, but a real, true woman is not
found amongst them," may be said of all those
books on the women of ancient times, and of the
Renaissance, because they mention only those who
became famous through their high position or their
deeds—exceptions to the rule, distinguished by
their virtues, their holiness or their heroism, from
the average women of their times, who were contented with merely leading quiet and modest lives.

Professor Del Lungo is a historian of great distinction; he has attained to high honour as member
of the Accademia della Crusca,[1] and the Accademia
dei Lincei [2] in Rome ; he is a member of the Royal
Historical Society of Tuscany, vice-president of the
Dante Society, and Senator of the Kingdom of Italy.
His history of the times of Dante is the result of

[1] A learned Royal Academy in Florence, literary and philo-
logical,—something like the Académie Française. The Accademia della Crusca is compiling the national dictionary of the
Italian tongue by order of the Government.

[2] The Italian Royal Society.

profound studies undertaken solely for the purpose of proving the authenticity of the *Cronica Fiorentina* of Dino Compagni, the fourteenth-century historian of the White Party. In the course of these studies, carried out entirely at first hand, Professor Del Lungo found himself brought into continual and direct contact with documents relating to the life of ancient Florence, documents wherein he discovered records and traces of many obscure women, who thus unconsciously revealed to him the secret of their forgotten existence. Students and scholars are able to call up phantoms from the shades without the aid of mediums or table-rapping, and, notwithstanding his gravity, the illustrious academician lent an attentive ear to those faint and faraway voices from beyond the grave, and felt himself impelled in these pages to record the transient impressions, to stay the fleeting apparitions, of the women who rose from the folds of those old parchments.

The value of the present volume lies entirely in the glimpses it affords into past lives, over which, from time to time, the author casts a glow of reality, of human, even pathetic interest, reflected from the more general and loftier matter with which he has surrounded this new material hewn from the hard rock of ascertained historical fact. It cannot be denied that there is a certain discrepancy between his magniloquent periods, and

the entirely modern curiosity evinced in the research
after various particulars and details of actual life,
details which the author has found in his documents, and presented to the reader with much fine
description and phrasing. For Del Lungo still
writes in the old classic style, a style eminently
synthetic, and therefore hardly likely to appeal to
modern English taste. His sentences recall the
gorgeous and florid oratory of the Cinquecento,
and his full and sonorous periods resemble those
which taxed the strongest lungs among academic
speakers. By this I do not intend to find any fault
either with his style or with his taste; both are
considered admirable in Italy, but no living Italian
writer would have the courage to imitate either.

Isidoro Del Lungo is the legitimate heir and representative of a glorious tradition, knowingly and
voluntarily pursued,—not from any desire to be
singular or from any craze for imitation, but simply
because it was congenial to his cast of thought,
most nearly expressed a mind educated in the strict-
est school of Italian classics. The individual style
of each writer depends upon his special method
of observation. Del Lungo cannot allude to any
particular detail without feeling obliged to enter
into an explanation of the general circumstances to
which that detail refers. He cannot, for instance,
speak of a leaf without mentioning the plant to
which that leaf belongs, and without further in-

forming his readers that the plant bears sweet-smelling, crimson roses, which are the glory of a famous garden. He is incapable of considering the leaf as a separate and distinct object, but must always see it attached to its parent plant, with a background of flower-beds and box-hedges shaded by ancient oaks, and affording a distant view of a beautiful palace. His is the old classical manner of observation, synthetic and harmonious, whereby each separate detail is enlightened by the whole and maintains its true value in the general scheme. Such is the art of Boccaccio in his finest prose works, and, in especial, of all the greatest authors of the Cinquecento.

It may be said, in short, that Isidoro Del Lungo is a classic writer who flourished in the nineteenth century, for his best productions, including the book which now appears for the first time in English, belong to the century which has recently closed. In his very classicism, however, we find undeniable evidences of a modernism of research and observation due to his historical method, which go far to make us overlook his frequent wordiness, and the many explanatory digressions which are liable to weary an English reader.

This work, now called *Women of Florence*, grew out of a number of detached speeches, first delivered as mere academic orations, and afterwards expanded into lectures, eagerly heard and read by those women of the present day who had inspired and suggested the studies on the women of the past.

As a speaker, Del Lungo's career has undergone a curious evolution. At first a lecturer who was entirely literary both in tone and character, more immediate contact with the public convinced him of the necessity of giving more lightness both to the matter and the form of his work, and of submitting more or less to modern influences and methods. Despite this he remained faithful to the fundamental rules of his art, which, though nowise changed, derived fresh vigour from the new elements owed to his sincerity both as historian and scholar.

In the present version, or rather adaptation, which has been prepared for English readers by a translator intimately acquainted with Italian style and language, the author's peculiar characteristics do not appear so prominently, having been modified as far as was possible without altering his individual character. Many passages, originally printed as notes at the end of each chapter, have here been transferred to the text. The clearness and interest of the argument have by this means been greatly enhanced, for the most original and realistic passages amongst the author's discoveries were usually relegated to the notes, only incidental allusions to them being made in the text. The reason for this lies partly in the fact that the different chapters were originally lectures, intended only to be read aloud, partly in the rigidity of the author's methods which do not permit him to invest such realistic details with too undue importance as compared with the rest of the matter. Another difficulty with which the translator has had to contend is presented by the constantly recurring allusions and quotations in which the author—thoroughly imbued as he is with the classical spirit—exercises alike his discrimination and his memory, and with which he assumes the reader to be equally familiar. Italian classicism, which even the Italians themselves now regard as pedantry, was a perfect mosaic composed of the phrases, proverbs, and sayings of other writers, of which the true connoisseur was expected to know the origin ; the more learned the writer, the more carefully chosen and the more apt must be his quotations and hidden allusions.

The new criticism has, however, changed all this, and such a *galimatias*, even though taken from works by the best authors, finds no admirers in England, where an author is expected to speak his own mind in his own words. Dante worshippers and students, however, the subject of whose study is in itself somewhat academic and rhetorical, do not disdain these expedients, at least in Italy, and echoes of Dante are to be traced in the best modern Italian prose, even in that of Giosué Carducci and

Gabriele D'Annunzio, just as it is obvious that
Biblical imagery and archaisms are employed by
certain English writers who wish to give an antique
flavour to their work. All this, however, has
perforce to be omitted even from an otherwise
faithful translation, because a translation is, after
all, only a sort of exchange from the currency of
one country into that of another, wherein nothing
is worth retaining save what is intrinsically valuable. Moreover, Italian thoughts and sentiments
have here to be stripped of the redundancy of their
native tongue, and clothed anew in a positive, clear,
and precise language, which abhors all dissimula-
tion and play upon words. Del Lungo probably
gains by this process ; certainly his book has become
clearer, simpler, less verbose, and thus more read-
able, attractive, modern, and, if possible, more
realistic to its new public.

In respect of the subject-matter of the book,
Del Lungo has here made use of many elements,
both traditional and literary, in addition to the new
human elements which he himself brought to light
in his researches, and it has been his chief aim to
make all these elements agree and harmonise together. He is too scholarly and too classical to
allow himself freely to decide between traditions,
to deny them, or to affirm them false when judged
by inexorable reality. His honesty as historian and
investigator forbids him to conceal any fact that he

may find in documents, but his art as an author counsels him to modify certain too realistic asperities, and to present them to the reader with comparisons and considerations that serve to tone down their predominating crudities. He is an idealiser of women, even of the women of long passed centuries, and he does not wish to dim their beauty and moral purity by insisting too much on certain details of vice and frivolity unfortunately encountered in every age. This picture of feminine life in the various periods is poetically idealised, because he bases much of what he says upon the authority of literary documents, and gives great prominence to those noble figures of women who in every age stand forth distinguished for their good qualities. From time to time, however, even in the midst of this ideal picture, we catch a glimpse of some fugitive and grotesque element which gives us an insight into a world and a way of life so realistic as to afford a startling contrast to the classic simplicity represented by certain other types of women. Here, as in the great illuminated choral books, in a corner of the decoration, amid the curves and arabesques, the grinning figure of a gnome or demon seems to mock the devout and serious saints depicted in the gorgeous initial letters and capitals.

It would certainly be as great a mistake to ignore the literary element in a history of life and manners as it would be to exaggerate the importance of a

series of data compiled from documents, unless the
series is very long and has been compiled with great
judgment. The same thing maybe said of statistics,
which pretend to furnish an average based upon a
limited number of cases. But when these researches
amongst documents hitherto despised by official
history have been scientifically and methodically
carried out, and account taken of a large range of
phenomena, it seems to me that there will be a
serious downfall of literary ideals, and that, in
good and bad alike, it would be an error to attri-
bute the weight and importance of historical fact
to what is usually only a product of the imagination.   To convince ourselves of this we need only
consider how unreal is the type of the modern
Italian woman delineated in the novels of Antonio
Fogazzaro, or the poems of Gabriele D'Annunzio,
or of the Englishwoman as she is found in the plays
of Pinero or the pages of "Society novelists."

All this, however, and even the author's bondage
to classicism, detracts nothing from the value of
this study upon the women of Florence. We
must remember that we have to deal not only
with a conscientious historian and artist, but also
with one of the most reliable of modern Italian
writers. Literary honesty is so rare a quality nowadays as to merit notice even by English readers.
If it were still the custom in the Accademia della
Crusca to take an academic pseudonym, the most

b

suitable for Isidoro Del Lungo would assuredly be
" The Austere " !　No other writer possesses in so
great a degree the sense for ancient times, the cult
of what our forefathers called *pietas*—domestic
feeling,—such intensity of love and respect for
the glorious past of his native land, a past whose
secrets he seems to know and understand.　Certain
outbursts of sentimentality, certain old-fashioned
notions of reserve held by our forefathers and far
removed from modern audacity, find in him a
sympathetic echo.　And this is not strange, for he
has spent his life in the constant society of those
proud merchants and partisans whom he has recalled
to life in the eloquent pages of his *Dino Compagni*,
the worthy historian of an age strong and firm in
its passions, its convictions and its faith, an age
which knew Farinata degli Uberti, whose vigorous
features have been immortalized for us by Andrea
del Castagno, the most expressive of our primitive
painters.

The female figures which Del Lungo depicts in
his pages, with few but bold strokes and with true
Tuscan sobriety of colour, have something of the
character of antique art as it is preserved in the
frescoes of the old masters.　It would be a mistake
to cast but a careless glance at the long array of
women here brought forward, and not pause even
to consider for what good purpose the author has
mentioned them.　Foremost in the list come the

A. del Castagno.

Alinari.

FARINATA DEGLI UBERTI.
(Florence: Convent of Sant' Apollonia.)

women glorified in poetry, women who have inspired men, from Beatrice Portinari to Vittoria Colonna; then come saints, from Piccarda Donati to Umiliana de' Cerchi and Caterina de' Ricci; then legendary heroines, from Dianora de' Bardi to Ginevra degli Amieri. But beside these more or less well-known representatives of feminine ideals, there are others whose portraits from life are here drawn for the first time, and by no faltering hand. Here are Nella Donati, Eletta Canigiani, Petrarch's mother; Dora del Bene, wife of a Florentine governor in Valdinievole; Albiera degli Albizzi, Simonetta Cattaneo, Giovanna Tornabuoni, Antonia Pulci, Lucrezia Tornabuoni nei Medici, Alessandra Scala, Clarice Orsini, Alessandra de' Bardi, Marietta Strozzi, Annalena Malatesta, Alessandra Macinghi negli Strozzi, Margherita Borgherini, and Isabella Sacchetti Guicciardini. Nor are these all, for in the midst of this company of gracious ladies we catch fleeting glimpses of many other faces to which no name can with certainty be attached, but which emerge from the obscurity of the past by virtue of some audacious act, some remembered saying, some one of the many characteristics sketched by those old chroniclers who have left such incisive word-pictures of their time. Del Lungo has, moreover, restored to their place of honour certain books of domestic records which none had troubled

themselves to read since the eighteenth-century
scholar, Domenico Maria Manni, brought them to
light. The chronicles of Donato Velluti, of Mor-
elli, and of Bonaccorso Pitti bear such precise and
vivid witness to the manners and customs of those
times that they provide reading both amusing and
instructive even for the present day; they are
human documents which reveal and explain the
hidden twists and turnings in those minds of olden
days better than all the learned dissertations ever
penned by historians and philosophers.

A knowledge and comprehension of the mysteries of the human body has only been acquired
by the aid of the microscope and the examination
of infinitesimal details; in the same way, a true
insight into the events of history, their cause and
effect, is only obtained by leaving aside empty
generalities and studying the small every-day happenings which sometimes develop into sudden re-
volutions, insurrections, and change of states or
rulers. The real but hidden cause of a political
crisis often lies in some social matter unnoticed
at the moment in which it took place. The beliefs,
opinions and customs of an epoch must be studied
before we pass judgment upon many events which
would seem the product of mere chance. It is my
firm conviction that were history to be rewritten
with due heed to woman's share in it, many small
causes heretofore disregarded, would be found fully

to explain great and unlooked-for results.   In this way the present book is an important indication of what history would be were less importance attached to treaties of peace, to wars and princely alliances, and if the infinitesimal but equally important factors in public weal or woe were taken into consideration.   For my part, I believe that at the bottom of every revolution, of every revolt, every overthrow of a kingdom or upheaval of the classes, every attempted change in governments, we should find the martyrdom, the vengeance, the power or passion, or the inexorable will of a woman. It must not be forgotten that the first chapter of the history of humanity was written by a woman.

GUIDO BIAGI.

FLORENCE,
THE LAURENTIAN LIBRARY,
June 1907.

INTRODUCTORY

ONE of the most beautiful pages in the *Confessions of Saint Augustine* is that wherein he praises his dead mother, so beloved and so saintly, and describes how, by the eloquence of her example, she won over her husband to the service of God, earning thereby the most reverent love and admiration. Elsewhere in the book this mother is depicted as weeping over her son's departure, or over his misdeeds, and it is in a great measure to the maternal tears that he himself attributes his own conversion and the first setting of his feet upon that right way which led to holiness and a great name, honoured through all succeeding centuries. It is by the double power of good example and affection that woman rules the family, and this is the part she has to play in the story of human life.

But in assigning to woman this gentler share in the world's history, it is not intended to deny in her those intellectual faculties which enable her not only to co-operate, but even to compete with man in all that bears witness to the divine portion of our nature. Indeed, far from lessening or weakening this faculty, the very frailness of her constitution intensifies it, giving her greater quickness and penetration. Old Franco Sacchetti says that " the understanding of women is keener and more quick than that of men," and in his "Ode to Pellegrina Amoretti of Oneglia," who was crowned with honour as doctor of Civil and Canonical Law at the University of Pavia in 1777, Parini writes :—

> " And well I know that thy sex,
> 'Midst the offices dear unto us and humble cares,
> Can raise itself, and by learned writings
> Win for itself immortality."

But in the admirable ordering of things whereby the ends of Providence are fulfilled, those mental faculties, which in man are employed in the pursuit of truth or the useful application of hypothetic principles, are in woman merged in sentiment, which in her unconsciously takes the place of science and art. Thus it is man's place to labour and provide for the more serious and material needs of domestic life, woman's place to console, to sweeten, to reward his labours. This is the eternal law, immutable in spite of all the ancient or modern Utopias ever dreamed of. Certainly there have been brilliant exceptions to this rule, such as Caterina Benincasa, Vittoria Colonna, Selvaggia Borghini, Maria Gaetana Agnesi, Clotilde Tambroni, Maria Giuseppa

Guacci, Caterina Franceschi Ferrucci, to mention only a few of the names which occur in the history of Italy, but the greater the intellectual power of these women the greater also was their refinement, modesty and womanly piety.

That her true place in the family and civil community, the exercise of this her gentle jurisdiction, was secured to woman by the establishment of Christianity has never been disputed, even by those who regret—often for good and liberal-minded reasons — the virtues of that ancient society from amidst the ruins of which came forth the straight road of the Gospel; and the very intellects which see in Christianity a regression or servitude dare not deny that this is one of its many services in the cause of human liberty. Wherever Christian civilisation has been opposed or overthrown, there woman has remained a slave; whenever in the modern world art and literature have been led astray by the immortal splendour of the classics, and in one form or another have reverted to paganism, woman has inevitably descended a step in her social position. In these days of ours there exists a certain art, a certain literature, which has nothing Christian about it, and upon whose banner the poet of *Evangeline* would assuredly have inscribed some such words as "Down! down!." The essential characteristic of these is their lack of respect for woman.

Through the affections, therefore, and virtues, gradually formed by that restraining civilisation which now for nineteen centuries has governed human destinies, woman wields a sovereignty of her own in the world far superior to that which she could achieve by means of her talents or studies, or by becoming a partaker in the thoughts, the projects, and the works of man. From being a delusion and a snare, the beauty of her outward form becomes the sign and mirror of her inward virtues; from a danger it becomes a blessing and a joy. Such, then, is the true destiny of woman; it is a destiny worthy of her, and in it lies also her own, her real history. Yet, to relate her history, we must gather together records and documents, and who can say whence they may so be gathered?

For it is not in outward facts, nor great names, nor noisy deeds, nor genealogies of crowned heads, nor in tragic loves, or ambitions, or striking heroism, or crime, that we find proofs of the constant and secret working whereby woman most effectually asserts herself. Certainly she has played her part in the outward and visible history of the world; but in that history which is told and written, which is buried in archives and revivified in books, woman's part is always small when set beside that of her companion, man. In the matter of actual deeds she contributes but little to the tale of battles and treaties, of successions and alliances, of violence, fraud, suspicions and hatreds, and at this she may surely rejoice. But if the inward history of human affairs could be described as fully as the outward facts, if the story of the family could be told together with the story of the nation, if human thoughts and feelings could with certainty be divined from human deeds, then the chief figure in this history of sentiments and morals would certainly be that of Woman the Inspirer.

It is not only poets who can be moved by inspiration. The eyes of Beatrice are not bent upon Virgil alone; they do not shine solely to draw Dante upward from sphere to sphere through the immensity of Paradise. Every sign of affection and care bestowed upon us is an inspiration for good, a consolation in work, an incentive towards higher things. The halo that surrounds woman in mediæval Italian poetry does not derive all its light from love and passion and pardon; much of it is simply the bright reflection of that womanly ideal, that "Eternal Feminine," which shows itself in so many different aspects. Doubts have recently been raised as to whether Beatrice ever actually existed. It is questioned whether it was really of the daughter of good Folco Portinari that Dante was thinking when he described the melancholy love-story of his youth, if it was indeed this particular lady whom he depicted as a divine figure in his Poem; or whether the symbolical Beatrice of the Divine Comedy had no earthly prototype, whether there was ever a real and living woman like her who is shown us in that sweetest of love-stories, the *Vita Nuova*.

But is it not more profitable to remember that all the great men of the past concentrated the flower of their affections upon some Beatrice of their own, whether maid or wife, a close neighbour or only seen from afar, a familiar friend of the household or one whose voice was only heard by chance as she talked with others, whether invoked as a lifelong companion or only worshipped from a distance? Whoever she may have been, she lived, she was real, and in her centred all their memories and repentances of youth, the love sanctioned by the family, the emotions of the fireside, the cradle, and the grave. To question all this would seem strange only to those who judge by modern standards that life in which heart and imagination are so largely mingled with the things of this world, that age of which the last symbols were the thoughtful statues of Michaelangelo.

Inspiration works in secret ways, because its ways are those of the heart. Woman alone has the power to inspire, but she must be gentle and tender, and it is the man and not the poet to whom she turns. When Vittoria Colonna died, Michaelangelo wrote those words, which, issuing

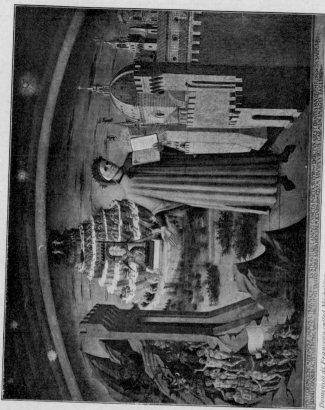

DANTE AND HIS BOOK.

(Florence: Church of Santa Maria dei Fiori.)

Domenico di Francesco called Michelino

Alinari.

from such a mind, are made sublime by their very simplicity: " She bore me great affection, and I had none the less for her. Death deprived me of a great friend." The artist and the poetess, of whom alone Ariosto sang, here seem to descend from their heights, to become the simple equals of those many others who in this world love and suffer, labour and die. Countless are the verses and the amorous poems, especially of that century, which might be cast aside as worthless, yet these curious specimens of art, more often of artifice, are human documents the value of which is increased, not conferred, by the personality of the subject. But not all the symbolism and the rhetoric of all these Petrarchists are worth that one little sentence of Michaelangelo's, "a great friend," nor can the severe simplicity of these words by any possibility be construed as foreshadowing the existence of those pedants who nowadays go about theorising upon what they call the emancipation of woman. And all the convulsions and the ravings and the arrogant trivialities of certain modern verses which call themselves love poems are not together worth those pages of simple Tuscan prose wherein the great Italian sculptor, Giovanni Duprè, tells one of those stories never intended to be placed amongst the world's records — a story whose humble heroine, the inspirer of the artist him-self, was a poor woman of San Piero, that very quarter of old Florence where stood the dwellings of the Portinari, the Alighieri, and the Donati.

Of the influence and work of woman in the family, the city and the nation—a work and influence as hidden as they are constant and wide-spreading, and the very nature of which forbids other record than the remembrance of grateful hearts—Florence possesses proof in a certain book, and, it may also be said, in one of her finest and most famous palaces. Upon the first page of the book the good man who compiled this tale of devotion wrote, " *To the Women of Italy. I pray them that they read this volume with their hearts.*" But that palace should surely contain a remembrance of Alessandra Macinghi Strozzi, who by her letters kept alive the love of their native city in the hearts of her sons, exiles, or wanderers seeking fortune in distant lands. Left a widow when still quite young, Alessandra watched over her children's interests with all the diligence and capability of a man, and by her care in small matters laid the foundations of the immense fortune which afterwards was theirs. She married them to Florentine maidens, and succeeded in procuring their recall from exile to be the comfort of her later life, dying a happy woman with children and grandchildren around her. Eighteen years afterwards, in 1489, her eldest son, become one of the greatest merchants and foremost citizens of his time, laid the first stone of the Palace of the Strozzi. Who can say whether the stately building would ever have arisen had it not been for the good old lady who was sleeping in peace beneath the arches of Santa Maria Novella! Her letters to her sons, written in that pure and forcible language of the Trecento, which the unlearned persons of the fifteenth century knew how to keep unspoiled, form a volume that is valuable for its very candour and originality. If Niccolò Tommaseo rejoiced over the "Diary of a Mother," wherein is recorded day by day all that happened to her little son, considering it a wonderful instance of psychological observation, how much more delight would he have taken, though for other reasons, in this unique collection of a mother's letters! For it was Tommaseo who wrote in his memoirs that the sources whence he had obtained inspiration were his mother, Virgil, Dante, and the people of Tuscany. And these letters, moreover, were not written by a mother who was especially learned or intellectual, or even a keen observer, but simply a good mother and an industrious housekeeper. Not only were they not written for publication, but that such would be their fate never occurred either to their author herself or any of her contemporaries. They are documents of no particular style, but full of thought and feeling; they possess no fine literary form and are even adorned with faults in grammar and spelling; they have no pretensions to be epistolary compositions, but are simple, homely letters, in which, through the mouth of a lady of Republican Florence, we can hear as plainly as though echoing through the streets and squares of to-day, the words, the interests, the hopes and fears of the Florentine people of four hundred years ago.

No day of our human life is without its memories of the past. Some there are to whom "sufficient unto the day is the evil thereof," and who cast these memories behind them. But better natures jealously cherish them as the daily bread demanded by the soul no less than the body, preserving them as the greatest treasure for those who shall follow after.

To revive in memory the times that are past, to learn the lessons taught us by the experience of our forefathers, and to keep alive the traditions of the great dead, are the best lessons that history can teach us.

CONTENTS

ILLUSTRATIONS

COLOURED PLATES

HALF-TONE PLATES

The binding design on this volume is after a Cinquecento original. The title design has been adapted by J. Rigby from MS., Dom. A. XVII. f. 49, in the British Museum. Date 1425–1430.

WOMEN OF FLORENCE

CHAPTER I

RISE OF THE COMMUNE OF FLORENCE

IT has often occurred to me that an interesting and
perhaps somewhat novel study might be found in
a review of the life of old Florence as illustrated
in the persons of her women—her history, in so
far as it depends upon her women citizens, their
influence upon, or the manner in which they were
influenced by, the great events of her passing ages.
These women of Florence may be studied from
the three several standpoints of historical reality,
legend or tradition, and poetical idealisation, while
from among the housewives of the time of Cacciaguida, the matrons of the earlier Medicean days,
or the gay and valiant ladies of the later Republican years, we may choose many types and figures
vividly illustrative of the actual life of their times.
Before proceeding to this study, however, one fact
must be clearly grasped.

A

From the first days of the Commune until the overthrow of the Republican orders in 1530, Florentine women, unlike their sisters in other cities of Italy, did not contribute with heroic deeds and virile energy to the cause of liberty. Neither in history nor in legend does Florence possess a Cinzica de' Sismondi, preserver of Pisa from the midnight assault of the Saracens. She has no Stamura, who with fire and sword intrepidly attacked the Imperial army besieging her native Ancona ; no Caterina Segurana, to whom Nice has erected a statue at that Peiroliera Gate which she defended against the Turks and the French ; neither does she own a Madonna Cia degli Ubaldini, that mighty woman of the Romagna, " leader in war and captain of soldiers," as she was called, who held Cesena against the bloody hordes of Cardinal Albornoz, resolutely resisting both the assaults of the enemy and the counsels of surrender made to her by her valiant men. Neither, it may be added, did Florence own a daughter like Caterina Sforza Riario, who, within the fortress of Forlì, disregarded alike her plighted word and even the lives of her children in order to avenge the murder of her husband, and who, we may remember without surprise, afterwards became mother of such a son as Giovanni delle Bande Nere, the greatest soldier of his age. Neither were they women of Florence, but of the land and time which saw the Sicilian Vespers, who helped to defend their city against the Angevin oppressor, and about whom the populace composed that song, of which Giovanni Villani has unfortunately preserved only a part, describing how " piteous it was to see the women of Messina, all dishevelled and bearing burdens of stone and lime " for the defences of the city. Heroic, too, though accompanied by all the display of the sixteenth century, was the act of the women of Siena, both gentle and simple, who, divided into companies distinguished by devices of violet, rose or white, worked with their own hands to build up the fortifications of that last stronghold of Tuscan democracy, well deserving the eulogy which Blaise de Montluc, Marshal of France, bestowed upon them as homage to their bravery.

Florence, indeed, has no heroines, or she has forgotten them. But what of that? Woman can neither change her nature nor the mission to the fulfilment of which she was created. With few exceptions, her story is a story without names but of every day and every hour, a story of tears shed, of grief comforted, of smiles and consolations bestowed upon others—fighters in the battle of life. To follow the thread of such a story is not easy, but neither is the pursuit of it more difficult than are other researches, moral or physical, into the mystery of human life. And since there have come down to us many pages of this story from ancient

times, when the individual was nothing accounted
in the rush of public events ; and since, in the beneficent opposition which barbaric violence offered
to the tyranny of the State, one of the symbols of
personal liberty and the avenging of the human
conscience was precisely woman—it would be il-
logical if her true story were lost during those
centuries of civilisation and Christian liberty which
are so much nearer to our own times, and therefore the more easily investigated.   That story
would, none the less, be short indeed, even if it
did not prove almost wholly lacking, in the glorious
annals of the Italian republics, were the search for
it to be confined to the history of the women of
their princely or feudal houses.   Men of high intelligence have not dealt thus with women and
their story.   One Italian writer, Niccolò Tommaseo, said that "to look upon woman as the
poets, historians and moralists, of different lands
and different ages, have from time to time depicted
her, is to find that this picture contains little less
than the ideal of the century."   Another writer,
Guasti, expresses the hope that a collection of the
letters of a Florentine lady of the Quattrocento
will prove the fact that "the private history of a
people is contained in the letters of its women."
And, finally, has not Goethe summed up the ideal
possibility of woman in one immortal abstraction—
"the Eternal Feminine," the eternal ideal woman

honoured by Carducci in that Queen who wore the crown of her people's undying love.[1]

Of the Florentine woman of the eleventh and twelfth centuries, at the commencement of the Italian Commune, we possess a picture authentic and vivid enough for any desire in the admirable description familiar to all readers of the *Paradiso*. Amidst the splendours of the Heaven of Mars, Dante depicts for us the old Florentine Commune, showing himself as a pious and deeply moved listener to the words of the knight and crusader, Cacciaguida degli Elisei. In this recital the poet gives the first place not to civic recollections, titles, or honours, or the desires and laments of public life, but to household memories, the gentle affections of the family, the holiness of the cradle and the grave; and over all this imagery, which makes of Canto xv. of the *Paradiso* a perfect domestic idyll, woman sheds the light of her sweet and gentle rule. Nor is woman here idealised by love or intellect, for Beatrice stands aside, a simple listener, with a gracious smile, to the dialogue between Dante and his ancestor. The woman of whom they speak is the woman of the hearth and the home, the life-comrade who shares joy and sorrow alike

[1] In a poem addressed to Queen Margherita of Italy, by Giosue Carducci.

with the man who is her love and pride, who
guards his possessions, brings up his children,
upholds him in success and renders him worthy
of it, encourages him in adversity and in peril,
sustains him in defeat, restrains him in victory,
and gives him a peaceful and quiet home in order
that he may be a worthy citizen of his native place.
She is guardian of the two qualities which Dante
regarded as the most important in social life,
namely, thrift and modesty.

> " Florence, within the ancient boundary,
> Abode in quiet, temperate and chaste."
> —*Paradiso*, xv.

Nor does she seek to display ornaments

> " That caught the eye more than the person did."
> —*Paradiso*, xv.

She is the joy and consolation of the house
wherein she was born, and when, in due time, she
exchanges this for that of a husband, both she
and he, the beloved and the loving, are satisfied with a dowry of reasonable amount, so that
"neither time nor dowry affright the father," as
Dante says. The austerity of the city's customs
spare her the frivolous cares and tricks which
make up an artificial beauty; she "leaves her
mirror with unpainted face," and, content with
her distaff and her spindle, weaves with her own
hands the simple garments worn by her husband.

Her undivided love asks for nothing more than a life spent uninterruptedly with him, and that they may at last rest together in the dear land of their birth—an aspiration which, as "the certainty of sepulture," wrings from his exile's heart the Poet's bitter cry of, "Oh, fortunate ones!" There in the home the young wife tends her babe, whilst the aged grandmother turns her spinning-wheel as she tells the elder children gathered round her legends of the early time of Italian greatness and Latin power—

> "Told o'er among her family the tales
> Of Trojans and of Fiesole and Rome."

For this woman of the Italian Commune divines and feels that it is the rightful inheritor and restorer of that glorious past, and that with the august name of Rome, which the children learn from the maternal lips to call the mother of their own city, there will grow up within their tender minds a conception of patriotism and fatherland never to be effaced. Such is Dante's picture of the ideal woman of those ancient times.

The life of this woman of the Italian Commune, no less than that of the various feminine figures which we shall presently discover in the history of Florence, must to a great extent be regarded as typical of that led by Italian women under the free communes. This is true because, so far as woman's gentle figure is concerned, diversities of province and difference of circumstances were usually subordinated to the points of resemblance and the general continuity of certain historical conditions, which, until the present day, contained within themselves the germ of national unity. For while Florence is, perhaps, richer than any other Italian city in respect of civic records, and documents of private or domestic history, it is also that one in which, on account of the language, events and things have been described with the greatest fullness. Universally celebrated as they are, the works of its historians, novelists, essayists, poets and dramatists, may with truth be said to belong to the nation rather than to the city alone.

To that Florentine woman of the eleventh and twelfth centuries, whose sweet image—associated with the memory of the sacred mother that bore him amidst invocations to the Virgin—moved Cacciaguida to such eloquence, Dante gave no especial name, because, to his mind, she was an abstraction—a universal, comprehensive and symbolical figure, uniting in herself all the individual personalities which formed the whole. Yet was that gracious vision, illumined only by the faint, quickly fading light of the domestic lamp, short-lived indeed. In little more than a century from the time when she was an historical reality the Florentine exile mourned for her as for something already long passed away. She was old, centuries old even then, because in her, as the Divine Poet depicted her, we find, unchanged throughout the course of stormy ages, the matron whom ancient times so greatly praised, who tended her house and spun her wool,—*domum servavit, lanam fecit.* To her charge was entrusted this part of the Latin tradition, that she might preserve it uncontaminated by Imperial orgies and excesses, amid the bloody conflicts of barbarism, in the silent desolation which followed the mighty fall, and finally through the commingling of races which befell the nameless and scattered people. That people clung fiercely to its traditions, however, while a family of it remained together, and of the family woman was the vigilant and wary guardian, and, where need arose, its strong protector. It may be said, therefore, that the woman of the twelfth century had not so much developed through the succeeding age, as that she had completed her task, and had yielded and adapted herself to the conditions which shaped themselves so differently around her, conditions alike of life, politics, custom and thought.

In the new civilisation, of which the Commune, an institution slowly elaborated, was at once the result and the summary, too many different elements, hitherto more or less latent and confined,

were developed by the breath of liberty for domestic
life wholly to escape change, whether in itself or in
its relations to the larger life of the community.
And it is not surprising that such a change was
displeasing to Cacciaguida. He remembered the
good old times of his youth, when the citizens still
dwelt in "little Florence divided into quarters,
with four gates," of which the Porta del Duomo,
or Cathedral Gate, as Villani relates, was the
"earliest fold and cradle of Florence rebuilt"—
rebuilt, as no Florentine doubts, by Charlemagne
and the Romans—"whither all the noble citizens
of Florence repaired upon a Sunday and paced
together around the Cathedral" (San Giovanni).
"Here were celebrated all marriages and peacemakings, and every festival and solemnity of the
Commune."

Cacciaguida lived during what may be termed
the unconscious and imperfect age of the Commune, when it was moved by neither the power
nor the storms of later days ;—the pacific age of
the Consuls, during which the community was
assuming form and shape, and remaining aloof
from the conflicts between Church and Empire.
These it could well leave to be fought out by
the Marquises of Tuscany and the Countesses
Beatrice and Matilda, whose nominal supremacy
weighed so lightly upon the independent city,
that not even the great and popular heroine, the

Countess Matilda, could ever make it effective. Rare dealings with the outside world of commerce or politics, the occasional passing of some Imperial ruler—almost invariably rendered harmless by the spontaneous homage offered to him, and by the fact that Tuscany usually lay outside the strategic itinerary followed by those Caesars and their adherents,—the sojourn of some fugitive Pope, or a petty feud with the country people, were the episodes of that quiet life led by the men whose thrift and simplicity were remembered by Cacciaguida. Then knights wore plain leathern belts with bone buckles, not ornamented with silver and pearls; citizens went habited in rough tunics of skin or dressed leather, not in mantles or robes of scarlet, all lined with grey minever; the houses were strictly measured to accommodate the number of inhabitants, and there was no luxury, no delicacy and no corruption.

The Emperor's sacred majesty was entertained and feasted as though he were one of the family. Conrad of Germany, to quote again from Villani, "delighted greatly in the city of Florence and did much for its prosperity, and many Florentine citizens were made knights by his hand and took service with him." Two centuries later came Otto IV., of whom our chronicler relates the following story, which is of special interest in this place : "When the Emperor Otto IV. came to Florence and beheld the fair women of the city gathered together in Santa Reparata to greet him, it chanced that one maiden—by name Gualdrada, and daughter of Messere Bellincion Berti de' Ravignani—was she who pleased the Emperor best. And her father told the Emperor that he had the right to kiss her, but the maiden replied that no man living should kiss her unless he were her husband. For which saying the Emperor greatly commended her; and the Count Guido, being smitten with love for her on account of her beauty, and being thereto counselled by the Emperor Otto, took her for his wife, caring neither that she was of a meaner family than he, nor for the amount of her dowry. Wherefore all the Counts Guidi are born of this Count and this lady." Unfortunately for the accuracy of this story, actual dates prove that Gualdrada and Guido had already been married nineteen years when Otto visited Florence in 1209; but this in no way detracts from the moral value of the pretty tradition. Dante speaks of this lady as "the good Gualdrada," and "good" here is equivalent to "wise and worthy"; and by Cacciaguida's praise of her father's simple customs we recognise him to be such as he is described in Villani's ingenuous chronicles. In such a community, small in numbers and jealous of the purity of its blood, Cacciaguida lived, and from such surroundings

he issued forth well worthy to buckle on the sword
for Christ, and, having received knighthood at the
hands of the Emperor, to die a hero's death in
Palestine.

Very different, alas, were the surroundings from
which the Poet ascended upon his spiritual journey,
leaving earthly misery for the land of the Blessed,
raising himself

> " From time unto eternity . . .
> From Florence to a people just and sane."
>   —*Paradiso*, xxxi.

It was a woman's tragedy which was pointed out
by Cacciaguida as the mark of division between
the two ages.   Buondelmonte paid with his blood
for having disloyally yielded to the persuasions of
a lady of the Donati and the beauty of her daughter,
thereby breaking his promise to his betrothed of the
Amidei family, and his murder marked the last
years of peace in Florence—

> " A victim in her latest hour of peace."
>   —*Paradiso*, xvi.

Although this drama may be legendary in some
of its details, its substantial historic basis nevertheless gives us an admirable picture of Florentine life
at the beginning of the thirteenth century.   The
community of " the Fold of St. John " was disturbed, for a feud had broken out between the
Uberti, of Germanic (or, as some say, of Cataline)

blood, and the Latin sovereignty of the Consuls. Imperial and ecclesiastical influences had already penetrated insidiously amongst the people and had inclined them to divisions, and this latent mine was fired by the beauty of a girl, the interested zeal of a mother, and the frivolity and disloyalty of a youth. None of these causes would have had the power to work such disasters in the chaste and sober Florence of the good old times, when the bell of the old Badia, as it marked the passing hours, marked also the passing of peaceful days amongst citizens who dwelt in mutual affection and courtesy. The story may well be related in Dino Compagni's own words :

" And the cause of all these happenings in Florence was that a noble youth of the city, by name Buondalmonte de' Buondalmonti, had promised to wed a daughter of Messer Oderigo Giantruffetti " (degli Amidei). " As he was passing one day before the house of the Donati, a gentlewoman named Madonna Aldruda, wife of Messer Forteguerra Donati, who had two very beautiful daughters, was standing upon the balcony of her palace. Beholding him pass by, she called him in, and showed him one of these daughters and said unto him, ' Whom hast thou taken for thy wife ? I was keeping this one for thee.' When he looked upon the maiden, she pleased him greatly and he replied, ' I cannot do otherwise now.' To which

Madonna Aldruda made answer, 'Yea, but thou canst, for I will pay the penalty for thee.' And Buondalmonte returned, 'And I do desire her.' So he took her for his wife, forsaking that other one whom he had chosen, and to whom he had plighted his faith." The father of the deserted girl lamenting with his friends, they deliberated how best to avenge her, and whether the culprit should be only wounded or killed outright. It was Mosca de' Lamberti who pronounced the fatal words, counselling the deed which brought about the tragedy. On Easter morning, 1215, as he was riding to his wedding with the Donati, Buondalmonte was slain upon the Ponte Vecchio, at the foot of that statue of Mars within which, according to the belief of the wise old Florentines, the devil was waiting to take his revenge upon the Christian city—

> "Which for the Baptist
> Changed its first patron, wherefore he, for this,
> Forever with his art will make it sad."
>
> —*Inferno*, xiii.

Another writer describes how the blood-stained corpse was carried through the city amidst cries and weeping, while the unhappy bride, who was at once the cause and the victim of the tragedy, sat with bowed head and flowing tears upon the bier itself. Certain it is that this woman, unfortunate in every respect, brings before us in her own

person the many and varied and unknown troubles
which, during the long years of civil wars, weighed
heavily upon the women of Florence, rendering
them, in the words of Manzoni—

" . . . Unhappy ones
Whom grief consumed ; brides widowed by the sword ;
Maidens betrothed in vain ; mothers, who saw
Their children pale in death . . ."

Villani tells of a "fierce and noble lion," kept
by the Commune on the Piazza di San Giovanni,
which, having escaped from its cage one day, went
in the direction of Or San Michele, and seized a boy
whom it held "between its paws." The mother,
whose only child this was, and he born after the
murder of her husband, "rushed at the lion with
great cries, as one demented, and tore the child
from between its paws, and the lion harmed neither
the child nor the woman, but only stood still and
looked at them." The lion could give children
back to their mothers, but the Commune, of which
it was the proud symbol, destroyed them without
pity. Other mothers in the streets of Florence
followed the example of her whose boy was afterwards called Orlanduccio of the Lion, but it was
from men that they besought pity, and men who
were moved by the fury of partisanship ! Bitterly
deceived was a certain woman belonging to the
White Guelphs of the time of Dante, who, bathed

in tears and with dishevelled hair, flung herself on her knees in the street in front of Messer Andrea da Cerreto, the judge, begging him for God's sake to save her two sons. " To whom, making answer that even now was he upon his way to the Palace for that purpose, did Messer Andrea lie, for he went thither indeed, but it was to the end that he might cause them be put to death." How few are there who to-day cross the majestic courtyard, or mount the stairway of the Bargello, and give a thought to all the blood which for more than six centuries flowed over those stones, blood which only the bitter tears shed in mourning for it were able to wash away.

Enveloped thus in the dark clouds of civil hatred, the women of Florence passed through the thirteenth century, the companions of sturdy merchants and artificers who fought as eagerly as they worked, and founded the Guelph democracy even while they pursued such other occupations as subduing the nobles, attacking neighbouring communes, resisting the Empire, and exacting respect from the Roman Curia itself. In spite of internal wars, art and the crafts flourished, and with them commerce and industries; with wealth came also new ideas and new customs, and the love of the beautiful, both in art and in literature, gradually began to exercise its softening influence.

In the year 1250 the city of Florence was in the period of its history called " of the first people," or " the old people," and Villani records how " in the time of this same people, and before and for long afterward, the citizens of Florence lived soberly and upon coarse food, spending but little money, and in their customs and manners rough and rude. They dressed both themselves and their wives in coarse cloth, many going barelegged without hosen, and they all wore caps upon their heads and boots on their feet.   The women had shoes without ornaments, and the greater number of them wore a narrow petticoat of the rough scarlet cloth of Ypres or Cam, belted about in the ancient fashion, and a mantle lined with vaire, having to it a hood which they drew over their heads, and the women of the lower orders wore the coarse green cloth of Cambrai, fashioned in a similar manner.   And 100 lire was the customary dowry given with a wife, and 200 or 300 was considered magnificent in those days ; and the maidens were usually twenty years of age or more when they were married." One of those " magnificent dowries " of 200 lire was that which Gemma, daughter of Manetto Donati, brought with her on her marriage to Dante Alighieri.   When we find the added remark, however, that although the Florentines of those days wore " garments like unto these and were rude in their customs, they were faithful and loyal to each other and to the Commune "—which " loyalty to each other," namely, civic concord, existed no more after 1215—we see that much of this description belongs by rights to an earlier period, from which the chronicler himself admits that he has taken it. His description, indeed, belongs to a period of transition when, upon the one hand, the " uncovered skin " and the boots recall the contemporaries of Cacciaguida who " went contented with uncovered skin," whilst on the other hand the names of those French and English stuffs of which the Florentine petticoats were made, the scarlet of Ypres or Cam, or the cloth of Cambrai, show that the times were past when

> " None as yet
> For sake of France was in her bed deserted."
> —*Paradiso*, xv.

Past, too, were the times when girls were married at a maturer age and for love unforced, marriages which, during the thirteenth century, formed in themselves weapons and instruments of defence against civic animosities. It came to be considered late if a girl married at twenty, or even at eighteen; fifteen was the " age of beauty," and while daughters were often married in haste in order to strengthen party ties or doubly to confirm a reconciliation between adversaries, the Commune itself not infrequently bore an active part in these arrangements.   An alliance was determined upon whilst the bridal pair were still in their childhood, and a girl of twelve or thirteen was considered old enough to be led to the altar and made a wife.   One of the old commentators of Dante says " they married them in their cradles." Guido Cavalcanti, the most graceful of the poets of those times, was married in this manner, for when he was but eight or nine years old his father, a Guelph, wedded him to a little Ghibelline maiden of five or six, Bice, daughter of the great-souled Farinata degli Uberti, who long survived her husband's early death (in 1300).   It was, perhaps, in this manner that the marriage was arranged between the youthful Beatrice Portinari and Messer Simone de' Bardi.

Inevitably as such marriages of policy lead to tragedies, it remains a notable fact that a lamentation for all the youth sacrificed to family tyranny forms the subject of the only example of credibly authentic feminine poetry which has been handed down to us from the thirteenth century.   This poetry is Florentine—three sonnets written by a lady who chose to conceal her name—the Vatican Codex which has preserved them calls her the Accomplished Damsel of Florence—and who, having greeted the Spring in the Provençal phraseology of the thirteenth-century rhymers, as the season when the world puts forth flower

and leaf, at once turns her verse into a lament
that :—

> " Delivered I am to fear and only grief,
>   Whiles every other maid in joyance dwells.
>   For, as my father is with me displeased,
>   In durance sore he maketh me to bide,
>   Having nor will nor wish so to be eased,
>   Who fain would give me an unwilling bride :
>   So of all pleasure is my life disseized,
>   And e'en of flower and leaf delight denied."

The outline of such a drama may well follow
here in all its sad realism.

In the year 1239 a lady of the Buondelmonti,
a Guelph family, "very excellent and wise and
beautiful," was married to Messer Neri, a brother
of Farinata degli Uberti, which means that relationship was established between the two families,
each head of its own party. A few years later
some of the Uberti were killed by the Buondelmonti in an ambuscade, and immediately the
whole city was up in arms and in an uproar.
Messer Neri degli Uberti sent his wife back to
her father's house, saying, " I desire not to have
children of a race of traitors." The poor woman
who loved him, obeyed and left him. The
marriage was annulled, but worse was to follow.
Concealing her story, her father made for her a
new contract with a Count of the Sienese Marshes
The sacrifice was carried out, but when the victim

found herself alone with her new husband she said to him : " Gentle Sir, I pray thee of thy courtesy that thou come not nigh unto me, nor do unto me any violence. For thou must know that thou hast been deceived, seeing I am not, nor ever can be, wife unto thee, who am already wife to the wisest and best knight in all the province of Italy, to wit, Messer Neri degli Uberti of Florence." The Count, being a gentleman in very truth, respected her, consoled her and restored to her her liberty, and the noble woman returned to Florence, but only to assume the habit of a nun in the convent of Monticelli, and to disappear from the world so completely that to-day none remembers even her name.

The convent gave shelter to many of these unhappy ones, who, as the " Accomplished Damsel " sings in another verse, preferred to leave the world and serve God in seclusion rather than face life at the side of an unknown and perhaps feared and hated husband. But even the convents were not always safe refuges for their innocence, their misfortunes and the liberty of their souls. As Dante said, God alone knew their secret sorrows—

" God knows what afterward my life became ; "
—*Paradiso*, iii.

or, to quote the words which he put into the

mouth of the celestial figure of Piccarda, who was mourning for the peaceful cloister to which she had fled in her girlhood, and

> "——the shadow of the sacred wimple.
> But when she, too, was to the world returned
> Against her wishes and against good usage,
> Of the heart's veil she never was divested."
> —*Paradiso*, iii.

The ancient commentators relate of Piccarda that she was " a woman of great beauty, the sister of Messer Corso Donati, and a nun. Now Messer Corso had occasion to make an alliance in Florence, and as he had none whom he could give or force into marriage, he was counselled to take Piccarda out of her convent and form the alliance through her. And by force he took her out of the convent and married her." It was under these auspices that Piccarda entered the family of the Della Tosa, who, although Guelph, and in closest relationship with the Church and the Florentine bishopric, appear to have been in the habit of violating the convents, probably because they easily escaped punishment. For when the exiled White Guelphs attempted to return by force of arms in 1304, one of the Della Tosa, or Tosinghi, as they were also called, broke into the convent of San Domenico to seize his two wealthy nieces. The mention of these deeds done by so powerful a family— Dante places them amongst those who grew fat at the expense of the Florentine Church—recalls a curious story of the thirteenth century concerning a supper, "The Supper of the Cursed Women of the Tosinghi," which the reverend chapter of the Basilica of San Lorenzo always gave upon the first day of May. Who the guests were is not known, but that they were very numerous is seen from the list of provisions provided. Probably it was a supper given in charity to the poor or religious, but the reason of this malediction, and wherefore a supper prepared at the expense of a chapter of canons should be named after the women of this family, remain mysteries. Dante only mentions one of them, Monna Cianghella della Tosa, whom he cites as a type of woman notorious for all those things the absence of which distinguished the Roman Cornelia.

The burden of all these disorders weighed very heavily upon the women. They suffered already from civil inferiority, being subject to laws which enforced not only subordination of their legal personality, but submission to the will of the procurator set over them by law, without whose permission not only could they neither make or break a contract, but could, in fact, take no legal step whatever. Thus two women, Monna Fiore and Monna Puccia, having fallen out and beaten each other black and blue, were reconciled. But in order to confirm this, and

to free Monna Fiore, the aggressor, from a fine
of 275 *piccioli*[1] inflicted by the Podestà, it was
necessary first that one notary should give them
a written permission, and, next, that this document should be authorised and made valid by
another notary.   Legal disabilities of the sort
needed only to be added to exiles, violence, mortal
hatreds and family disputes, to bring about civil
conditions utterly destructive of those domestic
ties which constitute real life for a woman.   Blood-
feuds, continued for ten, twenty and thirty years,
and handed down as inexorable obligations from
father to son, were the cause of bitter tears to the
wives and sisters, the daughters and betrothed of
the men involved.   Many sensitive souls, drawn
into this vortex in their earliest childhood, conceived a horror of the world which was inspired
in the first place by their own families.   By canon-
ising the women who withdrew from outside life
into the convent—Piccarda herself figures in the
Florentine Calendar amongst the Blessed as Sister
Costanza—the Church may be said not only to
have crowned the gentler virtues in that fierce age,
but also to have recompensed ineffable sorrows.
Many women, though nominally remaining in the
world, found consolation in a life of austerity and
prayer.   Umiliana de' Cerchi, wife and mother at

[1] *i.e.* in modern currency, about 95 centimes.

sixteen, and widow of a brutal husband at twenty, distrustful of her children's future in such cruel surroundings, returned to her father's house and devoted herself to charity.   Deprived of her dowry and hating the new marriage with which she was threatened, she shut herself up in the tower of her palace, which thus became both her oratory and her prison.   Although she tried to resist all tender human feelings, and replied to the good mothers who reproached her for neglecting house and children for the sake of prayer, that, "At the time of prayer your children must be as wolves unto you and your chamber as the mountains of Montalpruno," she nevertheless implored the Virgin with tears and cries to save the life of her little daughter, when, worn out with the hardships of penance, the child fell one day at her feet as though dead. Thus her life gradually faded away.   From the tops of the towers the balisters and traps rained down stones upon the fighters in the civil war which raged in the streets below, and the houses were fired one after another.   But Umiliana looked upon all these horrors as the triumph of the devil, who, she believed, had appeared to her, saying, "Arise, my daughter, and gaze upon the city which is being destroyed and burned."   She died in 1246, when only twenty-six years old.

This story of one woman of those days may serve

B. UMILIANA DE' CERCHI.

*From the old Print by Clouet (1682) after an original by Giotto (?) in the
Private Chapel of the Cerchi.*

as a true picture of the straits to which many of them were driven. More than a century later, in the person of a Sienese maiden, Florence and the whole of Italy could behold an example of human affections sanctified, and not extinguished, by religious fervour. In her, love of neighbour, of family, of country, and of Church burnt as a bright torch to lighten the storms of the world ; love and righteous anger were united with virile energy and womanly modesty, and St. Catherine of Siena lives in the memories of men as that "woman of consolation and of tears, child and heroine—Clorinda and Herminia together of the eternal poem of Italy," which her faithful biographer has called her.

With the thirteenth century passed away, never to return, the terrible conflicts which in an hour plunged the entire city in desolation, proscriptions which deprived it of half its inhabitants, and those homecomings in which the exiled presented themselves with fire and sword at the gates of their native city. The penalty of exile was still inflicted, it is true, and the condemnation of the father fell heavily upon the children even in the cradle, but the women were exempt and could remain in the deserted houses, guarding them and praying in the churches for the return of their banished men. A final look at one or two scenes of that thirteenth century, the mighty age which contained within its troubled breast the germs of modern civilisation, will not then be amiss.

The last act of the Guelphs before quitting the city at their first expulsion in 1249 was to attend, fully armed, at the burial of their standard-bearer, Messer Rustico Marignolli. Having interred him in San Lorenzo, they and their families departed and spread themselves throughout the Valdarno. The Ghibellines then destroyed the abandoned houses, and attempted to throw down a tower which took the name of "Guardamorto," or Keeper of the Dead, from an old cemetery which surrounded San Giovanni. This they desired to do in order that it might involve in its ruin the Baptistery and Church, Guelph buildings both, and the source of life to the banished party, as they were its resting-place in death. The second Guelph expulsion followed the battle of Mont-aperti : "Then there came to Florence the news of the dolorous defeat, and when the miserable fugitives returned, the lament of men and women was so great that it arose even unto Heaven, because there was no house in Florence, whether great or small, which had not some man either killed or prisoner. Then without any leave-taking the Guelphs departed from Florence with their weeping families, and betook themselves unto Lucca." [1]

[1] Villani.

Such an exodus was nothing less than an emptying of one city into another, and from their haven here the refugees were forced to listen in impotent rage to the news of the destruction of their homes, their memorials, and the future of their children. For when the victors re-entered the city with their German troops they half demolished it, both inside and out, casting forth the tombs and even the bones of the Guelphs from the churches. Yet, through some forgetfulness rather than any reverence, the tombstone of the standard-bearer Marignolli still remains in San Lorenzo. And if Florence was not entirely wiped out at that time, it was only owing to the courage and determination of one man, Farinata degli Uberti. Then, with the turning of fortune's wheel, came the Guelph revenge, less dreadful and more gradual, but more penetrating, more continuous, for it lasted as long as did the Republic, where the name of Ghibelline was hated long after the party had itself ceased to exist. The possessions of the Ghibelline families were confiscated, distributed amongst others, and dispersed as one destroys the lair of some wild beast. The Uberti were condemned to perpetual exile, and in their prayers the Guelphs implored God to exterminate them utterly ; even the statues of saints of the hated blood were removed from the altars ; it was forbidden to intermarry with the Counts Guidi and other country families, and the children of such unions were declared bastards. In short, there fell upon them that ban of excommunication from all social intercourse which accompanied the anathema with which the Church expelled them from her fold. Most of the Ghibellines gave way before this storm of persecution and joined the Guelph party, hoping thus to secure their recall, or leave at least to remain in the city. The descendants of Farinata were almost the only ones who remained faithful to the side of their ancestors, and throughout all the lands of Italy they proudly bore their sentence and their determination, fearlessly paying beneath the Guelph axe the debt, as they themselves called it, which their fathers had left them, and bearing themselves as did their great ancestor, whom Dante found among the tombs of Dis with his heretic Ghibellines and his Emperor Frederick.

But not upon the men alone fell these sufferings. Just as in Dante's poem we see beside that strong figure the shadow of a weeping father searching for his son, so beside those fugitives we can conjure up the forms of the poor women who followed them, ever tormented with the longing for their lost homes and country. And the strength of the women's feelings is proved by the description of one of those illusory peacemakings — when, for a few days, even the Uberti returned to Florence—wherein

we may read how, among the people who came
out to meet them, were women whose fathers had
been Ghibellines, and who ran to kiss the arms
of the Uberti upon the shields of the returned
exiles.

To these years of Guelph triumphs, and of the
peace which followed, belong those festivals of the
Kalends of May described by the old chroniclers
and by Boccaccio, when bands of flower-crowned
revellers went about with allegorical figures of
Love, and dancing and feasting filled the entire
day. "In the year 1282, in the month of June,
for the Feast of St. John, when the city of Florence
was in a state of felicity and repose, and was tranquil and peaceful, which was very useful for the
merchants and artificers, and most especially for
the Guelphs who ruled the city, there was formed
in the district of Santa Felicità, upon the further
side of the Arno, a company or troop of a thousand men or more, of whom the heads and origi-
nators were those of the house of de' Rossi ; and
they were all clothed in white, and had over them
one who was called the Lord of Love. And in
this company they did engage in nothing save in
games and in pleasure, and in dances amongst
women and knights, and others amongst the
people, going about in the city with trumpets
and divers instruments, with rejoicing and merriment, and feasting together at dinners and suppers.

And this festival endured for nigh upon two months, and was the most noble and the most renowned that ever was in the city of Florence or in all Tuscany; and there came unto it from all parts and countries many pleasant jesters and players, and they were all received and entertained honourably." [1] It was at this period, also, that Tuscan poetry flung off the restrictions of the Sicilian and Provençal schools, and took the name of the "sweet new style" which is typified by that enchanted barque wherein Dante imagines himself and his friends Guido Cavalcanti and Lapo Gianni, together with the ladies of their affections, gently rocked upon the waves of a peaceful sea.

But very soon the storm broke out anew. The evil consequences of all the discords fell upon those who had stirred them up, and the victorious Guelphs, beginning to quarrel among themselves, presently made the conquered city and their own houses the scenes of fresh disorders. They began to think that the triumph of the Guelph artisans was not secure without the oppression, or even annihilation, of the *Grandi*, or nobles, and the terrible Orders of Justice renewed in the streets of the Guelph Florence those sad spectacles which had been seen during the overthrow of the Ghibellines. Only a few years afterwards the White Guelphs and the Black Guelphs, Pope Boni-

[1] Villani.

face VIII. and Charles de Valois, were the sinister actors in a tragedy which found its worthy historian in Dino Compagni and its poet in Dante.

A few lines may now trace the picture of the city when, in November 1301, it fell into the hands of the French peacemaker. Through six days of pillage and desolation the hand of every man was against his neighbour, whether friend or foe; on all sides men sought to save themselves or their goods by concealment or flight. Here and there a palace was burning, whilst shops and houses were being ransacked, and torturings, woundings and murders were rife on every hand. Soldiers roamed about the country, stealing, burning and killing whatever they found. There was no respect for the honour of women, and the least sad cases were those in which forced marriages were imposed upon wives and daughters abandoned to the mercy of the enemy because their men were fled. A member of one of these unhappy families has left a sad record of those days : " They (the enemy) came during the night to our house in the Mercato Vecchio and stole everything that they could find, but on the evening before we had taken away the most precious things. We men were not there, for we had escaped the evening before. In that same night there came also another troop to our house and

C

stole all that the others had left. And when they had finished stealing, the Tosinghi and the Medici offered themselves unto our women. And I would not have it left unknown that in that night the children, both male and female, were left naked, lying upon the straw, for all their things and their garments had been carried away. Worse deeds were not done even by the Saracens in Acre."

This division of the Guelph party into Whites and Blacks concerned the women more, perhaps, than any other matter of the like kind. Nor is this surprising, seeing that the feud now lay between families closely allied by party interests, marriage and neighbourhood, and had therefore to do with relationships more intimate than any between Guelph and Ghibelline—a feud, indeed, of a kind in which woman could not stand aside. "The city was divided into two camps, and there was neither man nor woman, great nor small, priest nor friar, who did not belong to one side or the other." The novelist Franco Sacchetti, who lived towards the end of the fourteenth century, when touching upon the part taken by the women in these conflicts, and praising as a contrast their goodness in former times, wrote in one of his tales: "What can we say now of the subtlety of feminine malice? Their intelligence is more keen and more quick than that of men, and they more often do and speak that which is evil.   In other times they would have restrained their husbands, but in these days they encourage them to fight for their factions.   And for this reason have they brought much evil into the world."

Descriptions have come down to us, also, of curious episodes and small conflicts which took place behind closed doors.   One of these domestic faction-fights occurred in the house of Messer Vieri de' Cerchi upon the morning of April 23rd, 1300, only a few days before the Guelph disagreements found an issue in sanguinary violence.   On that particular day a sumptuous banquet had been prepared, and Madonna Caterina, a Bardi and wife of Messer Vieri, while showing her guests to their seats, chanced to place one of the Donati beside a Pistojese gentlewoman of the Cancellieri family.   Her husband, with more zeal than prudence, warned her, "Do not thus, for they are not of one mind ; place whom thou wilt between them." "Messere," said the Donati lady, who had overheard the warning, "ye do me a great wrong in saying that I or my family are partisans or enemies of any one, and now will I depart out of this house."   The Cerchi lady answered sharply, "Depart then, if thou wilt."   Thereupon the husband, much grieved by the quarrel, made his excuses and detained the gentlewoman by gently

taking hold of her; but the remedy was worse
than the disease, for she immediately reproached
him for his discourtesy in laying hands upon her.
Although he was a knight of much good sense,
Messer Vieri then lost all patience and exclaimed,
"Truly women are the very devil!"[1]   Whether
the angry Donati lady stayed or left is not known.
The dispute was continued amongst the men, and
only a few hours afterwards they were all going
about with their weapons in their hands, "because
they were such near neighbours that one was ever
at the house of another."

A threshold even more jealously guarded than
that of Messer Vieri de' Cerchi was, we may
suppose, that of San Pier Maggiore, an exceedingly old church of Benedictine nuns, which fell
into ruins over a century ago.   It was to this
church that the Florentine bishops, when they
made their solemn entry into the city, betook
themselves first of all, and here, with ceremonies
of which we possess the most detailed description,
and with nuptial rites and pomp, they espoused
the Reverend Mother Abbess, who, representing
in her person the Florentine Church, feasted and
entertained her new spouse for twenty-four hours.
To this convent of San Pier Maggiore, then,
upon a January day of 1299, came Lisa, daughter
of Ser Guidolino of Calestano, a Lombard free-

---

[1] *Chronicles* of Marchionne Stefani.

POPE BONIFACE VIII.
(Florence: The Duomo.)

lance who was an active partisan of the Black
Guelphs.   To her demand to be received as a nun,
the abbess, Sister Margherita, replied that their
number was complete, and that she could not,
therefore, receive Lisa without infringing the rules
of their constitution.   Thereupon the would-be
novice exhibited a letter from the Most Holy
Father Pope Boniface VIII., enjoining upon the
Mother Abbess to receive the new nun without
further difficulties.   But the abbess exclaimed,
"What sayest thou, Pope?   What Holy Father?
Boniface is not Pope, but the devil upon earth
troubling the Christians!   But the Lord God
will give so much power unto the Colonnas of
Rome that they will do unto him and his kindred
that which they did unto those same Colonnas
against all right and justice."   And the door of
the convent was banged violently behind the
furious and Dantesque abbess, who, for that
matter, lacked neither a biting tongue nor the
gift of prophecy, for the dreadful things which
the Colonnas did to the Pontiff in Anagni were
foretold by her four years before they happened,
whereas Dante's prophecy was only made after
the event.   Unmoved in her determination, Lisa
immediately appealed to the Episcopal Curia, but
it only imposed "perpetuum silentium" upon her
and her procurator, to the immense relief not
only of the Florentine bigots, who were just

sending out foot-soldiers at their own expense
to fight in the Papal war against "the perfidious
Colonnas," but also of the Commune, to which
a lawsuit with the convent of San Pier Maggiore
would have been no such small thing as might
be nowadays, but a very serious annoyance not
lightly to be added to the many others under
which the surly and unwilling citizens laboured
in those unfortunate years. It would seem that
soon after the event recorded above Sister Margherita relinquished her post as abbess, which she
had held since 1293, because at the Episcopal
espousals, again enacted in the May of 1301,
we find her name as being present at the ceremony, but not as the bride. It is interesting to
note that when she was elected, two of the seven
electing nuns, by name Sister Petronilla and Sister
Giovanna, refused to vote for any one until they
had obtained the advice of their own parents and
kindred. The scrutators who took the votes
declared this action to be wrong and against all
rights and custom, and the Bishop Andrea dei
Mozzi confirmed the election of Sister Margherita.
The refusal of the two nuns, evidently dictated
by party feelings, reveals the influence of these
even upon women vowed to abandon all worldly
interests.

The customs of the Florentine women of these
years were such as to call forth sharp words of

blame from Dante, who, by the mouth of a Donati spirit, threatens that the sins of Florence will draw down well-deserved punishment from Heaven, and that before the babes they now hold in their arms shall have grown to manhood, God will have caused them to weep over the misfortunes of their families and their city. The dates make it clear that Dante was alluding either to the defeat of the Guelphs at Montecatini in 1315, or to the Imperial vengeance which the poet and the other Whites hoped and prayed would be inflicted by Henry VII. upon the Black Guelphs.

It is noteworthy, in connection with our subject, that for Dante, as for all other great interpreters of human ideals, a disaster in war or a civil overthrow finds its most tragic expression in the mourning and weeping of women. Thus Homer shows us the weeping Trojan matrons, led by Hecuba, stretching out imploring hands to Minerva; the lamentations of wife and mother, and the fatal Helen, on the death of Hector, were answered by the groans of the entire people, and in the fall of the city the pitying soul of Virgil heard, even amid the clashing of arms and the roaring of the flames, the despairing shrieks of the women. The imagery of the Florentine Homer of the Middle Ages is less plastic but perhaps more forcible, and satire mingles its harsh note with the epic verse :—

> " But if the shameless women were assured
> Of what swift Heaven prepares for them, already
> Wide open would they have their mouths to howl ;
> For if my foresight here deceive me not,
> They shall be sad ere he have bearded cheeks
> Who now is hushed to sleep with lullaby."
>
> —*Purgatorio*, xxiv.

But the spirits to whom Dante confided his grief and anger at his unjust banishment did not foresee that exaltation of Guelphism into which the Blacks had led the Commune, and from which the more honest and temperate of the Guelphs, like Dante himself, had withdrawn even at the risk of being forced to quit their native place. That Guelph exaltation was henceforth to remain the basis of the political scheme upon which the democratic Commune then, no less than for the following seventy years of the Trecento, formed its constitution.

No useful purpose would be served by a discussion, in this place, of all the many and varied reasons that explain why the history of Florence in the Trecento, during the latter part of which period oligarchy prevailed, does not show that constant change of governments and factions, of defeats and banishments, of conquered and conquerors, that continual uncertainty of the

civil State which during the previous age rendered
the family so untrustworthy and stormy a harbour of refuge for woman. The alternate exodus
of Guelphs and Ghibellines between the years
1248 and 1267, the ostracism of Giano della Bella
—exiled together with his daughter in 1295—
the destruction and vandalism which ruined half
the city beneath the Ghibelline pickaxes, and the
proscriptions issued by the Black Guelphs against
their own adherents—condemned to become
" Ghibellines by force "—were all events which
impelled the men of the Trecento to adopt
the democratic traditions of the artisans, and so
to form the internal life of their Commune as
to yield constantly increasing opportunities to
the common people—an extension vainly opposed
by the Greater Guilds, and final cause of the
rise to power of the government of the Ciompi.
Those fierce contrasts inspired them also with
the traditions of the French Guelphs—traditions
that, within the very century, brought upon the
free city the corrupt and miserable tyranny of
the Duke of Athens, and after incurably infect-
ing the Republic with a flattering and dangerous
partiality, subjected her finally to those yet worse
troubles suffered by Florence in 1530, after the
siege, when the season for remedy was passed.
From the same causes, again, issued the only form
of Florentine government which endured for any

length of time—that of the Priori and the Gonfalonier of Justice, whose popular standard, first upraised by Giano della Bella, passed from one brave hand to another until, almost two centuries and a half later, it floated as the country's flag over the last battles for liberty.

While, compared with the preceding age in her history, therefore, the Trecento was to Florence a century of establishment and stability, the times were still pregnant with danger for the city in which the balance of parties and of the state remained all too often the sport of external influences. "There will be no new people," men said then, yet there were not lacking either great commotions or great dangers, nor yet wholesale overthrows. The city was besieged by the Emperor Henry VII.; it was threatened by Uguccione della Faggiuola and more seriously by Castruccio; it was drained of its best blood in the battles of Montecatini and Altopascio; the Imperial descents upon it of Ludwig the Bavarian and of Charles IV. were a severe strain alike upon the temper and the purses of its merchants, who were gaily plundered by almost all the sovereigns of Europe. The kings of France and of Naples took possession of the place as though they were at home, and one of their adventurers, the Duke of Athens, tried to settle himself there as lord and duke. The Scaligeri and the Visconti, the

Popes of Avignon and the Companies of Free-Lances, despoiled it by arms or by avarice, while epidemics, one more terrible than all others, turned its streets into deserts. Guelph tyranny was a hindrance to the prosperity of arts and the crafts, and provoked the excesses of the demagogy; but against all these shocks, through all these storms, the State stood so firm that the change to an oligarchy was accomplished without any alteration either in the form of the magistracy or, substantially, in the politics of the Commune.

Thus, during this glorious period, was Florence enabled to develop into ampler forms, and to the highest degree, the civilisation of which it had laid the laborious foundations in the darkness of earlier ages. Industry and commerce nourished it, fostered it, and spread it throughout the world; its ministers were the arts of pictured beauty exalted to such high perfection by Arnolfo, Giotto and Orcagna, masters and workmen of the Commune—the gracious combination henceforth called Tuscan art. To the scattered elements of the Latin tongue, which was gradually becoming the language of the people in all the various regions of Italy, Florence gave a definite form and made of it the language of the nation, the instrument of a literature which, through another great Floren-

tine triumvirate, came to be called the literature
of Italy.

This life, the more spiritual and civilised in
proportion as it was less agitated and insecure,
naturally yielded to the women of Florence a
new freedom no less than more material benefits.
In their history drama gives place to the every-
day events, sad or gay, of civic and family life:
beauty and tenderness again find safe homes as
in the good old times of their ancestors—homes
such as have long been denied them, yet now
the richer because adorned with new treasures of
wealth and of art. Yet more satisfying to their
sex, perhaps, do not the merchants of Calimala
and Por Santa Maria save for them the best of
that cloth brought from beyond the Alps, which,
transformed in appearance and tripled in value,
is destined to return across mountains and over
sea as produce of their Tuscan city.

They, truly, would not have been women had
they not delighted in, and joyfully surrounded
themselves with, all those proofs of wealth and
luxury which bore such pleasant witness to the
power and prosperity of the Commune. In vain
the monks and the preachers protested and admonished, threatened interdictions, and imposed
disciplines to correct and restrain worldly splendours and the excess of pomp and luxury. Even
Dante, whom nothing escaped, echoes the cry of

the times in this regard.   But they were so lovely
in the bright spring middays or the rosy autumn
sunsets, those dresses of varied colours, those
ornaments of silver and gold, surmounting fair
heads or encircling white necks, their brilliance
vying with the flashing of the bright black eyes!
Those gorgeous brocades seemed made on purpose to set off these supple figures only waiting
for the embrace of the dancers' arms!   And
what would have been the value of the pearls
and precious stones if they had not been used
to adorn bosoms throbbing with the joy of youth
and love?

But now, in 1324, the Commune, rigid upholder
of its own rights, drew up sumptuary laws of the utmost severity against the excessive luxury of dress
indulged in by the women of Florence, whose unwilling spirits were compelled to temporary obedience, no matter with what reluctance.   Scarcely
two years later, however, when the Duke of Cala-
bria came to Florence, called thither to exercise
the usual Angevin lordship over the Guelph republic, the women seized the occasion to surround
the French Duchess, Marie de Valois, and obtain
from her that there should be restored to them
"their unpleasing and dishonest ornament" (thus
grumbles Giovanni Villani) "of thick plaits of
yellow and white silk, which they wore in lieu of
tresses of hair around their faces—an ornament

dishonest and unnatural. And thus did the disordered appetites of the women overcome the reason and good sense of the men." A Ducal court, with its following of courtiers and Frenchmen, needed but a few years of sojourn in Florence to effect the inevitable. Therefore once again, in April 1330, the Florentines " took away all the ornaments from their women," and it may be truly said, to quote words well suited to the case, that they undressed them "from head to foot." For these were the new laws. "Seeing how that the women of Florence are greatly given over to the wearing of ornaments, of crowns and wreaths of gold and of silver, and of pearls and precious stones, and nets of pearls and other unseemly head-gear of great price; and similarly, seeing how that they wear garments cut out of divers cloths and robes trimmed with silk and of many fashions, with fringes and pearls, and often with buttons of silver gilded, four or six rows of them, sewn together in pairs, and with buckles of pearls and precious stones upon their breasts, with various signs and letters; and similarly, as they do make feasts of too great luxury, for marriages and upon other occasions, with excessive and unnecessary victuals; hereby is made provision and order concerning these matters; that no woman shall wear either crown or wreath, neither of gold nor of silver, nor pearls or pre-

cious stones, nor silk ; neither anything like unto
a crown or a wreath, not even of painted paper ;
she shall wear neither net nor plaits of any kind,
except those which are quite simple ; neither
any garment which is adorned or painted with
patterns, unless woven in the stuff; neither anything twisted or crossed, save a simple device of
two colours ; and she shall wear no fringes either
of gold or silver or silk, and no precious stones,
not excepting enamels or glass ; neither shall she
be permitted to wear more than two rings upon
her fingers, nor any belt or girdle of more than
twelve links of silver ; and henceforth none shall
dress herself in samite, and those who possess it
shall put such marks upon it that it cannot be
used by any other person ; and all habits of cloth
trimmed with silk shall be forbidden and taken
away. And no woman shall wear the train of her
dress more than two *braccia* [1] in length behind, or
cut out round the neck more than a *braccio* and
a quarter. And similarly, it is forbidden unto
boys and girls to wear petticoats and robes of
two colours, and all trimmings are forbidden,
even ermine, excepting unto knights and their
ladies. And unto men are forbidden every kind
of ornament, and belts of silver, and doublets of
silk or of cloth or of camlet. And at no feast

---

[1] A *braccio* was a measure which varied in different places ;
in Tuscany it was 58 centimètres = 23 inches.

shall there be more than three dishes, and at
marriages there shall not be laid more than
twenty platters,[1] and the bride shall not bring
more than six women with her.   And at the
feasts for new-made knights there shall not be
more than an hundred platters of three different
dishes ; and the new knights shall not dress themselves in such a manner that they can give their
robes unto the jesters."

For the enforcement of the above laws certain
officials, strangers to the city, were appointed, who
were to keep watch on men, women and children,
and to inflict heavy fines for disobedience.   And
rules and tariffs were imposed upon the various
trades and upon the sale of their merchandise,
and even the interests and management of the
family were interfered with.   And all this was
done without giving a thought to the losses
suffered, particularly by the silk merchants and
jewellers, trades combined in the same Guild,
"who for their profit did daily devise new and
varied ornaments."   The chronicle concludes
thus : "All the which prohibitions were greatly
commended and praised by all the Italians.   And
if the women had made use of excessive ornaments, they were thereby compelled to wear
only that which was seemly, for which they all

---

[1] *i.e.*, the company must not exceed forty persons, two persons
to a platter—the custom of the time.

lamented greatly, but on account of the strict orders they did refrain from their excesses. And since they might not have cloth trimmed with patterns, they desired to have it as curiously wrought in two colours as was possible, for which reason they sent their garments to be made even so far as Flanders and Brabant, not considering the cost. But it was a great advantage unto the citizens that they were no longer obliged to spend such large sums of money upon their women in feastings and weddings as they had done formerly. And these rules were very highly commended, because they were useful and wise; and almost all the cities in Tuscany, and many others in Italy, sent unto Florence for a copy of these rules, and so did enforce them in their own cities."

The persons who were the most uncomfortable under the new order of things were those "foreign officers" deputed by the Commune to enforce the observance of the new laws, and to uphold them against the bad temper and cunning of the Florentine women, who were all in league together for the defence of their dress. Of all the grotesque figures in which the merry tales of the people had caricatured the poor *podestàs* and captains, knights and judges, notaries and serjeants, whom the Guelph cities of Lombardy and the Marches sent as officials to Florence, and

concerning whom there was a proverbial saying,
"If there is any one to whom thou wishest evil,
send him to Florence as officer," there is, perhaps,
none more sharply drawn or more amusing than
a certain "justice of rights" of his own day described by Franco Sacchetti. We may be sure
that the vexations which this poor man suffered
were no new thing, for we have records of the
sumptuary laws of Florence from 1306, and
evidences of them from 1290. This justice
then, with his notary, did his very best to carry
out certain new rules, as usual "concerning
the ornaments of the women." His efforts
met with such results, however, that the citizens
made just complaints to the Signoria that "the
new officer doth his office so well that the
women have never been so extravagant in their
dress as they are at present." This is the answer
of that poor officer, Messer Amerigo, to the reproaches of the Lords Priori :—

"My Lords, all the days of my life have I
studied to learn the rules of the law, and now,
when I did believe myself to know somewhat, I
do find that I know nothing. For when, obeying
the orders which ye gave me, I went out to seek
for the forbidden ornaments of your women, they
met me with arguments the like of which are not
to be found in any book of laws; and some of
these will I repeat unto you. There cometh a

woman with the peak of her hood fringed out and twisted around her head. My notary saith, 'Tell me your name, for you have a peak with fringes.' Then the good woman taketh this peak, which is fastened round her hood with a pin, and, holding it in her hand, she declareth that it is a wreath. Then going further, he findeth one wearing many buttons in front of her dress, and he saith unto her, 'Ye are not allowed to wear these buttons.' But she answereth, 'Yea, Messer, but I may, for these are not buttons, but studs, and if ye do not believe me, look, they have no loops, and moreover there are no button-holes.' Then the notary goeth unto another who is wearing ermine and saith, 'Now what can she say to this? Ye are wearing ermine.' And he prepares to write down her name. But the woman answers, 'Do not write me down, for this is not ermine, it is the fur of a suckling.' Saith the notary, 'What is this suckling?' And the woman replies, 'It is an animal.'" The magnificent Lords Priori, who knew their women better than did Messer Amerigo of Pesaro, said amongst themselves, "We do but knock our heads against a wall; we shall do better if we leave these matters for those which are of greater moment. Whosoever will, may take this trouble upon himself!" At last one amongst them, assuredly the most learned of all that honourable company, gave this cold comfort: "I would have ye know that the Romans themselves could avail nothing against their women, though they overcame the whole world. For the women, in order to annul the laws made concerning their ornaments, went to the Campidoglio and there overcame the Romans, obtaining that which they desired." And then he cited Titus Livius, and they debated the matter. And they told Messer Amerigo to act as best he might, and to proceed with his duties, not troubling himself about the wreaths and studs and sucklings; and thus he did in future, says the novelist, concluding with the remark that "man proposes and woman disposes," a very old proverb as all know; and that without ever having studied jurisprudence the Florentine women understood very well how to have their will and wear their fashions in spite of all the laws and doctors of laws!

We of to-day, however, should only consider as a violation of individual liberty and of domestic privacy such severe sumptuary laws as those of which the records, so valuable for the history both of costume and of language, remain to us; laws which limited the extent of the wedding outfits, or, as they called it, the "donora" which the bride brought her husband, fixed the amount of the Longobardic *morgincap*, or morning gift, which the bridegroom gave the bride on the morning

Tuscan School

Alinari

THE MARRIAGE OF BOCCACCIO ADIMARI AND LISA RICASOLI.

(*Florence : The Accademia.*)

after the wedding, regulating it by the size of her dowry, and also controlled the luxury and profusion of the feasts and banquets. Yet these laws were inspired by a lofty democratic spirit, inasmuch as it was intended thereby to make the citizens' festivals as public as possible instead of their being held in private. " A common feeling called for common pleasures. The displays of the wealthy had always to be somewhat popular in nature, and being given as a public benefit and spectacle they had to be for the entertainment of all. The wide loggias open to the view of every one were then the drawing-rooms of the palaces. In this way a couple of weddings provided amusement for the entire city; the rich paid for the entertainments of the poor and they all enjoyed themselves together. The young men held jousts and tiltings, the women danced, and they amused themselves in the open air and in the public squares, and not by candle-light in stuffy rooms." Thus wrote, in 1836, that admirable Florentine historian, Gino Capponi.

It is hardly to be expected that the Florentine history of that century should offer any information about women other than moral rules and observations, certainly not the history of political events, for reasons which we have seen. Nor can we glean any material from the history of culture and learning, for this was so rigidly confined within certain limits that a learned man was called a "clerk," and it was a great mercy if woman was allowed to retain any kind of place and rights among the laity!

The "Accomplished Damsel," if, as it would appear, she was a real woman and not only a myth, is an exception, and there are exceptions to every rule. We have no evidence of the culture of women in Florence in the thirteenth and fourteenth centuries, save some translations from the Latin made at their instance, such as that of Ovid's "Heroides" (which they called the "Book of Women") undertaken at the request of Madonna Lisa Peruzzi by Ser Filippo Ceffi, a notary; or, more frequently, renderings of sacred or ascetic literature into the vulgar tongue by members of religious orders. Indeed, the preceptor and poet of the Florentine women of that day, Francesco da Barberino (of whom I shall have occasion to speak again later), makes it clear that there was no good quality in woman that he did not place higher than culture. He even doubted (after due consideration of the dangers of such knowledge) whether it were good or bad that a woman should be able to read and write, even though she were of high rank, thinking this necessary to those women alone who were destined for a monastic life. But beside the history of politics and culture there are other records, which we may interrogate with greater advantage—artless pages, written without any idea of publication and hitherto almost ignored by any but linguistic students. These records are the domestic Chronicles or Memoirs, one of which, dealing with the middle of the fourteenth century, furnishes us with some interesting feminine portraits.

The words of Messer Donato Velluti, which I quote here from his autograph manuscript, give a vivid presentment of the women he knew, either in his own house or in those of his friends, and who were nearly all of them " dear and good," an affectionate description which occurs so frequently in his ingenuous pages that I cannot always repeat it, even for the sake of counterbalancing the not invariably favourable judgments pronounced upon women, whether of the fourteenth or nineteenth century. Here, then, are the portraits of different types of women of Messer Donato's acquaintance. And since we have just spoken of fashions and dress, the first to be mentioned shall be a good lady to whom it proved a great advantage to have her head well covered :—

"Monna Diana was an exceeding good woman, and bore me much love, and she often kept me with her at Bogoli when I was a boy. She wore a great many things upon her head, so many that being one day at the old palace of the De' Rossi, opposite to Santa Filicità, where is now the inn, and a great stone falling from the top of the palace upon her head, she only felt it as though it had been dust fallen down through the scratching of the fowls; wherefore she called out, 'Chuck, chuck,' and she suffered no further harm on account of the many cloths which she wore upon her head."

These women possessed nerves and a power of endurance in no way inferior to that of their husbands, and they could look death bravely in the face, as the following passage shows: "Then came the pestilence of 1348. And Gherarduccio and his daughter and the sisters being already dead, Cino" (the last surviving of three brothers) "and his wife were in the country at their farm of Poggio, and there they both fell sick. And finding themselves sick, they determined to come into the city. And the wife's brothers being present, they caused Cino to make his will. After which they departed. And the woman was carried in a litter, and I visited her on her arrival; and her husband came upon a horse and a man rode pillion behind him. After this visit I went also into the Borgo San Jacopo to the burying of Bernardo Marsili, who had died whilst he was one of the Priori"—twenty-two years later the writer himself died in the Palace whilst he was one of the Priori—"and as I was returning and had reached the end of the street, there came two running together, and one said, ' Monna Lisa is dead,' and the other said, ' Cino died at the elm-tree of San Gaggio, upon horseback, as he was coming in from the country.' So I caused them to be buried."

Here is a picture of two women who had grown old living at home with their brothers : " Cilia and Gherardina never married. For a great while they remained maids in the world, hoping to have husbands, but when they lost all hope they became Sisters of San Spirito.[1] They earned much money, more, indeed, than sufficed for their support, by winding wool, and their brothers did never have need to keep a servant. They were exceeding kind of heart and great talkers. They died in that same pestilence of 1348, being both forty years of age, or more."

Very different was a certain Madonna Cilia, who returned as a widow to her brother's house, and who was so constantly involved in disputes and difficulties that "she spent large sums upon lawsuits, in which she took great pleasure, as she was a bad and crafty woman. And so much money did she spend in this way that, not desiring to sell her possessions, she was obliged to live and dress herself exceeding poorly, and she wandered about Florence all day long,—and now she lives by begging."

[1] " Pinzochere," devotees or lay sisters living still in the world.

Here, however, are two more attractive figures;
one is that of a little housewife, "Monna Lisetta,
small of stature, but a wise and good woman,
who stayed at home with her children after her
husband's death, leading a virtuous life and bringing up these children," who, however, all died
young, together with their mother, in the plague
of 1363. The second portrait is that of a beautiful
young wife, one of those faces which we not only
admire but ponder over when we see them depicted
in the paintings or frescoes of the old masters.
She was "Monna Ginevra Covoni, taller and more
beautiful than any of her sisters; one of the most
virtuous, wise, and industrious women whom ever
I did see, and who by her kindness, her pleasant
ways, and her goodness made herself beloved by
all." Finally we have the chronicler's own mother
and wife: "Monna Giovanna, my mother, was
a wise and beautiful woman, with a rosy and
fresh-coloured face, and very tall in her person,
honest and very virtuous. And much care and
labour did she endure in bringing up me and
my brothers, considering that we may be said to
have had no other discipline, and more especially none from our father, because he was almost
always absent. For which reason she was worthy
of all praise, and praised indeed she was for her
life and her virtue, seeing how that she was a
beautiful woman and her husband so much away.

In the freshness of my complexion I greatly re-
sembled her. She was an excellent manager,
and she had need to be, seeing how little our
father possessed, and that he was divided from
his brothers and had a large family. And the
cause of her death was this: whilst our father
was in Tunis we had received a farm in payment
of a debt. And in the summer time my mother
went to stay there; and when she was mounted
upon horseback to return hither, the horse took
fright and ran away and threw her off, so that,
falling upon the ground, she broke her leg. She
remained up there at the farm several days, and
did not cause herself to be bled; then she was
carried back to Florence in a litter, and her leg
was set. And being thus in bed upon St. Martin's
day, and there being many women with her, all
gossiping and chattering together, she suddenly
cried out, 'Ah, me!' and passed from this life.
May God keep her soul, for of a surety it is with
Him, she being a dear, good woman, and having
confessed only the day before." Then comes the
writer's wife, Monna Bice Covoni, "who was
small and of no beauty, but wise, good, pleasing,
loving, and of good manners, full of all virtues
and perfect, making herself liked and beloved by
all persons. And greatly did I value her, for she
loved me and desired me with her whole heart.
She was most excellent of soul, and I do think

that our Lord Jesus Christ received her in His arms, seeing that she was full of good works, almsgiving, and praying and visiting the churches. She lived with me in peace, and brought me much happiness, honour, and possessions. She had a great sickness in the pestilence of 1348, but she survived, though not one in an hundred did so. It was by God's mercy and for my salvation, for I am certainly of opinion that if she had died I should not have escaped the many accidents that did come upon me, although I nothing suffered from that pestilence. She died in July 1357, so that she had lived with me seventeen years. God keep her soul."

Such were the women, seen in the light of actual facts, who were the life companions of the Florentines during those early centuries which formed the strictly democratic period of the Commune, until that time towards the end of the Trecento when, the rage of the Ciompi having abated, there came to the front those dangerous popular heroes, the Medici. Such were the women of ancient Florence; upright and gracious figures, to whom is due no less a part of the glory of that age than was the share which they bore in the labours and the sorrows, the virile resolutions, the enlightened conceptions and the passionate mistakes of a strong people, a democracy truly worthy of the name, because it wrought without any ostentation, but with courage and the pure love of great things.

Reality is only one aspect of history, and not always the easiest to investigate or retrace. And even when the reality can be discerned with sufficient clearness there ever remains sufficient room for legend and the idealism of art, the one the transformer, the other the imitator of that truth which reality attests. But wide though the field be wherein the women of Florence may be considered in their relation, more or less intimate, more or less direct, to the ideals of poetry and art during the early centuries of modern culture, the dominion of legend here is no wider than it is in all other lines of thought and fact amongst the Italians. It has often been remarked that Italy is extremely poor in legendary stories at the very period when she might have been supposed to produce them, and the reason for this has been set forth by a German critic whose words I cannot do better than repeat :—

"Modern Italy issued from the ruins of an epoch of the greatest culture known to ancient times, the traces of which had never entirely disappeared. It did not come to birth from a period of barbarism, and has therefore not accumulated those traditions which originate in obscure and mythical ages."

These historical conditions directed the people's natural appetite for the marvellous towards *tramontane* sources, inducing that poetry of romance in which alone was Italy destined to father great and exquisite creations of art. They also constitute an explanation—and this the only possible one—of the strange phenomenon apparent in the fact that remote and exotic elements seem an indispensable element in any subject that Italian literature was to enshrine among its "legends." We can scarcely expect, therefore, that the nimbus of legend should surround the head of a Florentine woman—and one, at that, not of even the first centuries of the Commune, but of the period of its full maturity.

The novel became popular in the fifteenth century, but the subject belonged properly to the fourteenth, if we consider the action and circumstances. And such a subject has come down to us fairly intact, especially in its metrical form, in the story of "Ippolito and Lionora," one of the numerous versions of the eternal tale of thwarted love, from Pyramus and Thisbe down to that of the lovers of Verona immortalised by William Shakespeare and Vincenzio Bellini. But the Florentine legend lacks the final catastrophe, the love-story ending happily; it lacks almost the form itself of the legend, the bare simplicity of which has been amplified and enriched into the shape of a

tale. Ippolito de' Buondelmonti loved Lionora,
or Dianora, de' Bardi, and she loved him in return, notwithstanding the enmity dividing their
families, both of which belonged to the Guelph
party. Despairing of obtaining his heart's desire,
the young man wasted away and fell sick, and
when his weeping mother questioned him upon the
matter he revealed the secret cause of his misery.
Impelled by maternal love and finding no other
way out of the difficulty, the poor lady implored
an aunt of Lionora, who was Abbess of the Convent of Monticelli, to find a means of bringing
the lovers together. The aunt was successful, and
the youth and the maiden were secretly married,
it being decided that, for greater safety, their
meetings should hereafter take place in Lionora's own house. But one night, when Ippolito
was about to enter secretly, he was seized by
the officers of the Podestà. In order to save the
honour of his beloved he declared himself to be
a thief, and persisted in the untruth in spite of
the shame and grief of his own family. Apparently the women kept silence for fear that,
if the truth were known, the two families and
their adherents would break out into open conflict, of which the first victim would be Ippolito
himself. The noble youth was condemned to an
ignominious death, and as his last request prayed
that upon his way to execution he might be led

past the house of the Bardi, alleging as the reason
that, in order at least to save his soul, he might
crave their pardon for the hatred which, as an
enemy, he had borne them; but in reality he
only urged this request that he might see Lionora
once again before he died. His desire was granted,
and the dismal procession set out, accompanied
by the sound of trumpets and with the standard
of Justice carried at its head. Lionora came to
the window, and the eyes of husband and wife
met once more. Then suddenly, as though she
were out of her mind, she descended the stairs,
and, rushing forth from the house, she seized
the horse of the Podestà's officer by the bridle,
crying, "So long as there is life in my body thou
shalt not lead Ippolito to death, for he hath not
deserved it!" And she flung herself into the
condemned man's arms. The officer was at a
loss what to do next, and the people began to
murmur. Then the Signoria summoned the two
young creatures to appear before it: "Ippolito,
bound and with the rope round his neck, and
Lionora weeping and dishevelled, followed by a
great crowd of people." The young wife advanced and demanded justice, "that is, that ye
should give me back mine husband; otherwise
I shall appeal unto God and unto the world,
calling for vengeance upon such injustice, and
praying God that with His righteous eyes He

will look down upon your most iniquitous sentence and wicked judgment." Being made aware of the actual facts, the Signoria called the two fathers, " who understood the matter in the right way, and here in the presence of the Signoria and the people confirmed the relationship. And whereas for two hundred years the Buondelmonti and the Bardi had been enemies to the death, they now through this relationship became such great friends that all deemed them to be of one blood." Thus, after all, did legend provide a heroine for Florence—a heroine from the realms of love.

A love-story, too, is that of the girl who was buried alive, to which the date of 1393 is assigned by its rude Quattrocento verses. Ginevra degli Amieri (or Almieri, to use the popular corruption) was beloved by Antonio dei Rondinelli, but her father married her instead to Francesco degli Agolanti. She fell ill and became unconscious, and being thought dead was carried to her tomb at Santa Reparata. But as she lay in the vault her senses returned to her and she became aware of her terrible plight. Commending herself to the Virgin, and guided by a feeble ray of moonlight which crept through a small aperture in the vault, she climbed some steps and succeeded in moving away the newly placed stone. Thus Ginevra emerged from the tomb, and, gliding

E

under the shadow of the Campanile, she passed
through the narrow street which is said to have
been called " della Morte " in memory of her,
and made her way to her husband's house. At
her knock Francesco himself appeared at the
window.

" Who is there ?   Who knocketh ?   'Tis thy Ginevra ;
Hearest thou me not ? "

The frightened husband made the sign of the
Cross, promised to have prayers and masses said
for the poor wandering soul, and withdrew.
Ginevra proceeded to her father's house in the
Mercato Vecchio, and, knocking there, her
mother looked out.

" ' Open, open, for I am your child.'
' Go thou in peace, blest spirit mild ! '
And she closed the window again in haste."

The unhappy girl wandered away, weeping with
misery, and met with the same reception at the
house of an uncle. Then she remembered her
faithful lover and went to his house, and he,
although also believing her white figure to be
a spirit,

" Would see if her spirit could bring him harm,"

and immediately went down to the door, drew
her inside, called his mother and the other women

of the house, consoled her, tended her, and saved
her.   Her desire now was to be dead to the
husband who had buried her, and to contract a
new marriage with the man who had brought
her back to life; she took her case before the
Episcopal Curia and won it.   Here, indeed, did
Love triumph over Death.

Very, very old is a tale—not of love this, but
of patriotism—which goes back even to the times
of Totila, unless, indeed, it is to be considered a
posthumous invention of the people!   The barbarian king, having entered Florence by treachery,
installed himself in the very centre of the little
Roman city, in the palace of the Campidoglio.
Desiring to remove from his path " the greatest
and most powerful officers of the city, he one
day caused many of them to be summoned to
attend his council.   And as they arrived at the
Campidoglio and passed one by one through a
passage leading into the chamber, he caused
them to be slain in such wise that not one might
hear another; and the bodies he cast into the
aqueducts."   But a fruit-woman of the market,
whose stall was by the church of San Pietro
near at hand, became suspicious and warned the
citizens to "have a care, because, as in the
fable of Æsop, although many entered, not one
had been seen to come out again."   This warning saved many lives and gained for the church

the name of San Pier Bonconsiglio.[1]   It did not, however, prevent the destruction of the city at the hands of the barbarian.   In course of time the fruit-seller and Totila changed their identity; he became the Duke of Athens, the most abhorred phantom of tyranny that ever lingered in the memory of Florentine people, she the Cabbage-woman of Florence, while for the council of officers in the palace of the Campi-doglio has been substituted a masked ball at the ducal residence, with trapdoor exits for the guests.   Moreover, the great bell of the Cathe-dral, the last ringing of which, at a late hour every winter's night, gave the signal for " lights out "—according to the good old usage of our grandfathers, who went to bed early in order that they might rise at daybreak—is known to the people as the Bell of the Cabbage-woman, and recalls to their memories how, through the action of this good Florentine, the Duke's mur-derous entertainment ended in his ignominious expulsion from the city, a popular story for which no historian has been able to discover a founda-tion of fact!   In spite of this the Cabbage-woman

[1] St. Peter of Good Counsel.   Borghini, however, sees no connection between the name and the fruit-woman, but believes that the church was so named because in early times the City Council used to meet there, as on certain occasions the Romans used to assemble in the Temple of the Capitoline Jupiter.

A PORTRAIT OF SIMONETTA CATTANEO.

Variously attributed to Pollajuolo and to Piero Di Cosimo.
(Chantilly.)

cf. Page 168.

THE CAMPIDOGLIO, FROM AN UNFINISHED DRAWING BY
B. RUSTICHI.

cf., Page 68.

of Florence, the heroic wife of "Stenterello,"
still shares the honours of the Florentine popular
theatre with Ginevra degli Almieri, who is always
released from her tomb, or otherwise assisted, by
the aforesaid Stenterello.   When the populace
has adopted for its own certain favourite characters, it clothes them with its own ideas and sympathies, modifies and transforms them, and varies
their personalities, but it never kills.   Popular
heroes and villains never die !

Another traditional love of the Florentines, also
belonging to the democratic age of the Commune,
is Monna Tessa, the virtuous servant of Messer
Folco Portinari, who is supposed to have suggested and largely assisted in the foundation of
the hospital of Santa Maria Nuova.   The people
daily see the marble effigy of the charitable old
woman at the entrance of the great building which
succours them in sickness and misery, and it would
be quite useless, if not a piece of pedantic cruelty,
to try and convince them that the tradition of
Monna Tessa, attested by a seventeenth-century
inscription below the figure, is just as doubtful
as it is certain that that same marble relief is of
a date at least a hundred years later than that
at which Tessa is supposed to have lived, or that
this marble, formerly in a chapel of the church,
represents either some benefactress of the sacred
place or one of the nuns belonging to it.   It is

probable, too, that the tradition arose from, or
was at least supported by, an inscription of the
Trecento cut in rough Gothic lettering upon an
altar table—also situate in the same chapel until
the year 1647—wherein prayers were asked for
the soul of one Monna Tessa, wife of Turo, a
saddler, who had caused that altar to be erected.
Moreover, it would be a difficult matter to attri-
bute so much power and such great results to
the work of a woman in a position of servitude,
in times, too, when a servant was little more
than a slave. Slaves, indeed, these women were
called, and many of them were even brought
from the East and kept as such in Florentine
families. Happily, the populace leaves these and
other similar considerations to the erudite, and
fondly cherishes the image of its dear Monna
Tessa—the poor serving woman. To it this
humble soul, born in its own ranks, intimate
with all its sufferings, and who lived in the same
world amidst the same sorrows, is an angel of
consolation in these sorrows, a comforter and a
helper in pain. Surely there is no woman, however learned, who would aspire to the glory
of disproving the authenticity of Monna Tessa!
Far sooner would some clever painter of that
truth which, outside all accidents of person or
time, is the everlasting stamp and seal of human
nature, depict her in the house of the Portinari,

wholly engaged in her domestic duties, sweeten-
ing with deeds of charity her life of patience
and resignation, and inclining the hearts of the
wealthy Messer Folco and his wife, Madonna
Cilia de' Caponsacchi, to succour the poor and
needy. Nor would such an one fail to add to
her picture the figure of the young daughter
of the house, the predestined Beatrice—a little
child lulled to sleep upon the knees of the poor
and faithful servant.

The grandest monument of the Florentine democracy, the Cathedral of Santa Maria del Fiore,
contains, among many tombs of the thirteenth
and fourteenth centuries, others yet older, for the
foundations of the naves of Arnolfo and Talenti,
the lofty tower of Giotto and the walls whereon
uprose the mighty dome of Brunelleschi, were
laid upon the site of the ancient cemetery of
Santa Reparata. And surely the souls of those
sleepers must have exulted in the change that
obliterated their tombs, and enclosed their bones
within the foundations of the majestic temple
which their children were building to the glory
of God.

An old "Obituary" preserved in the Cathedral
archives has handed down to us the list of those
who were buried both in the ancient cemetery
and within the precincts of the new church, and

in those parchment pages, yellow with age, we may read the names of those who slept there, united in the peace of death.   Here are Uberti and Buondelmonti, Lamberti and Adimari, Cavalcanti (here, too, is Guido the poet) and Donati, Abati and Brunelleschi; we find the names of men who fought at Montaperti (amongst them is the great-souled Farinata), of many executed by the Black Guelphs, or slain in civic strife.   Here, too, are names of artists, especially those who worked for the church, and of their wives, beginning with Arnolfo himself and Madonna Perfetta his mother, truly an enviable mother to possess such a son and such a tomb!   And numerous unknown names are there, which, just because they are unknown, excite our imagination and direct our thoughts back to the history of an age which still lives in the admirable monuments which immortalise the minds and hearts of its people.   Many of these are women's names which sound strange to our ears, being even of Longobardic origin—Bellantese, Bellamprato, Bellatedesca, Berricevuta, Ringraziata, Dolcedonna, Altadonna, Donnetta, Buona, Moltobuona, Dibene, Piubbella, Rimbellita, Belcolore, Macchiettina, Vezzosa, Ruvinosa, Leggiera.[1]   Others again are of historical interest,

[1] Obviously enough, most of these names have a meaning, probably in allusion to some distinction or quality of the women who bore them, or derived from the description of some remote ancestress. (*Trans.*)

either on account of the families they represent
or for their own sake. Such is the "Tessa" or
"Contessa" which occurs so frequently in honour
of the famous Countess Matelda. How many unknown stories do these names represent, how many
heroines of forgotten tragedies of love or devotion
sleep for ever beneath that sacred ground!

> "Never didst thou spy
> In art or nature aught so passing sweet,
> As were the limbs, that in their beauteous frame
> Enclosed me, and are scattered now in dust."
> —*Purgatorio*, xxxi. 49–51.

These are the words wherein the divine shade of
Beatrice recalls the time when she was a mortal
upon earth ; but they are words which might well
be inscribed upon the tombs of these unknown
women, they too, perchance, as loved and lovely
in their day as many whose personalities and
memories have survived.

It is in the name of Beatrice that the reality of
history and the fair fancies of legend are united
with the noble ideal which the love of the beautiful has formed of the highest manifestation of
beauty among all created things, namely, woman
herself. From none other of all the graves of
ancient Florence, whence we have called forth the
shades of the glorious days of the Commune, does
a Florentine woman arise encircled with such an

aureole of splendour as surrounds the figure of Dante's Lady.   And if the tomb of Beatrice Portinari still existed, as does that of Folco in Ravenna, should we not regard it with no less reverence than that with which we view the last resting-place of her exiled lover.

CHAPTER II

FROM DANTE TO BOCCACCIO

A STUDY of the women of Florence during the early centuries of the Commune could not be held complete did we omit to glance at them as they survive for us in the pages of the great chroniclers of the time. Having considered them from the standpoints of historical fact and of tradition, therefore, it is now necessary to pass to their ideal representatives as portrayed in Florentine literature from Dante to Boccaccio, portraits from which we may learn how those from whom they were drawn inspired and affected the hearts and minds of the foremost exponents of thought in the still adolescent, but already virile Italian tongue. And this consideration—to control a theme which would otherwise prove too boundless for our purpose—shall be limited to a study of what may be called the Florentine personality of woman.

In that young world of Italy—whose enthusiastic re-awakening to life was traditionally symbolised by its rejection of the imminent fear of

the destruction of the world current in the tenth
century — feminine beauty exerted a powerful
and beneficent influence, and this for many and
various reasons.   Nowhere was that influence so
strongly felt, nor with such great results, as in
the ancient city of Florence, at the time when
the angels of Cimabue—already human figures
and no longer mere Byzantine outlines—had
suddenly yielded place to the passionate and
eloquent paintings of his disciple Giotto.   One
such call to awakening must have sufficed Florence, but already a second summons thrilled her
ears.   Surely though the world contains few
scenes more apparently suited than the hills of
Fiesole and Maiano to echo *pastorette* and *ten-
zoni* [1]—the graceful artifices of those Byzantines
of speech, the Provençal poets—the ancient city
had heard the true, strong voice of a man.   And
what a man was he who drowned for her those
feeble sounds with songs of deep and genuine
feeling !   For a youth of the Alighieri,

"the inventor of the sweet new lay,"

counting himself but as

"the scribe of love, that, when he breathes,
Take up my pen, and, as he dictates, write,"
                    —*Purgatorio*, xxiv. 49.

---

[1] Pastorals and amorous dialogues between a knight and his
lady or a poet and a shepherdess—the favourite forms of early
poetry.

was writing things of deep meaning and not mere empty sounds, "sweet songs of love" to which sweet notes of music were made by the poet's friend, the Florentine musician Casella.

A great lover of Florence, Tommaseo, called her "fair atom of the earthly dust," and no part of all the city better deserves the name than does the short space of street which lies between the house of the Portinari in the Corso and the old Badia—the scene of that love-story which had its idyll and elegy in the *Vita Nuova* and its poem in one of the greatest conceptions of the human intellect. Gladly would we re-people that little cradle of great events with the fair figures of those "sixty of the most beautiful women of the city," whom the youthful poet tells us that he enumerated and put into an epistle in the form of the *serventese*.[1] For the loss of this we are but badly recompensed by the *Serventese of Beautiful Women*, written by Antonio Pucci in 1335, of which the commencement alone,

> "The graceful *serventese*, full of love,
> Through all the flower-city seeking goes
> To find the ladies who are worthiest
> Of so much honour,"

---

[1] The *serventese* was a kind of poem sung by the troubadours or *trouvères* and imitated in Italy. It dealt less with love than with matters of politics or religion. The name is derived from the Provençal *sirventes*, properly meaning a poem composed by a minstrel in the service of his master.

is an exception to his usual rugged style, and by a later similar fragment attributed to Boccaccio.

This homage of Dante to the beauty of the women of his own city was lost in the noise and tumult of party conflict, yet he was not then the lean and dolorous thinker of the *Divina Commedia*, but a man young and in love, whom death had not yet robbed of his beloved nor exile of his country. Of this out-pouring of romantic homage we know nothing except what he himself tells us, and then only that there were sixty fair women, and that in counting and numbering them " it chanced most marvellously that he could not suffer the name of his own lady to bear any save that of nine," the mystical number.

The clash of swords and the cries " To arms ! To arms ! Kill ! Kill !" rudely dispersed those dances of knights and ladies celebrating the return of Spring on the Calends of May, or the greatest of civic festivities on the day of St. John. Dispersed, too, were those allegorical companies robed in white and headed by " a leader called the Lord of Love," who imitated the magnificence of feudal times by keeping open house and public distribution of largesse to the people.

The poet, in his twentieth year, could fill his days with dreams of love, picturing himself in an enchanted vessel upon a sunny sea, with his friends, Guido Cavalcanti and Lapo Cianni, and

the three ladies of their respective affections; but
first awakened to the bitter reality of life by the
death of his beloved, he presently had to bear the
burden of public misfortunes, civil deceptions,
and of his own mistakes and wanderings. Then

> " The sweet love-rhymes which he was used
>   To seek within his inmost thoughts,"
>   *—Rime.*

gave place in his stricken and repentant soul to
the scorn which purified, the grief which inspired,
and the meditation which transformed into the
purely ideal all those exterior objects of which the
dignity rendered them worthy. As the *Convivio*
expressly witnesses, the prevailing scholastic philosophy gave a fresh impulse to the progress of that
austere intelligence towards the ideal, so that
his contemplative eyes, losing sight not only of
the woman who

> " Had left his sight and was become
>   A beauty spiritual and great,"
>   *—Rime.*

but also of the whole reality and range of life,
beheld now only the one infinite, supernatural
ideal, itself the one true thing. But even in that
limitless space the eyes of Beatrice shone eternally

> " From that day, when on this earth I first
>   Beheld her charms, up to that view of them."
>   *—Paradiso,* xxx. 29.

The love-lit eyes which at the Springtime rejoicings in her father's house, at wedding feasts, in
the street, or when praying to the Virgin in
church, were ever turned towards the poet, now
illumined that inward vision. And here I need
only recall the reality of the *Vita Nuova*, a reality
which no other book ever set forth in so spiritual
a manner. If the eyes of Beatrice as a mortal
confounded and " overcame " him, they were her
eyes when she was " risen to be a spirit and increased in beauty and virtue," which drew him by
some miraculous power from heaven to heaven,
until he beheld the supreme vision of the Eternal.

> " Beatrice upward gaz'd, and I on her."
> —*Paradiso*, ii. 22.

Of all the lauds which have been heaped upon
women, there never was higher praise than this.

Although the reality of Beatrice is confirmed
beyond all doubt by the important line,

> " Observe me well.   I am, in sooth, I am
> Beatrice,"
> —*Purgatorio*, xxx. 73.

there exists, nevertheless, no authentic description
of her face and form.   I am not referring to the
Divina Commedia, where she appears only as a
spirit and a symbol, but to the *Vita Nuova*, in
which she is seen as a woman who inspires love
and dies.   It may be said that the Beatrice of the

Vita Nuova, although a living woman, is made so angelic that her mortal lineaments are lost in the aureole which encircles her, as one

> " descended
> From Heaven to earth, a miracle to show " ;
> —*Rime*.

and it is rather in the *Divina Commedia*, when the celestial lady has descended "from the seats of the blessed to succour him who so greatly loved her," that she sometimes assumes the aspect and demeanour of real human life. Thus she reveals herself as still moved by human feelings when she cannot speak to Virgil of Dante's peril without tears, reproaches the latter for his worldly infidelities and humbles him even to the point of weeping, confides him to the care of Matelda that he may undergo the mystic immersion which is to make him pure, or smiles upon his fears as a helpless creature incapable of bearing the burden of the divine knowledge which oppresses his feeble senses. Human she is also in her gently laughing reminder

> " . . . . Of her
> Whose cough emboldened, as the story holds,
> To first offence the doubting Guenevere."
> —*Paradiso*, xvi. 15.

It has been sought to determine at which point in the narrative of the *Vita Nuova* Beatrice changed

F

her name from Portinari to Bardi, because it has
been said that "her marriage with another man
must have deeply distressed the soul of the young
and loving poet." I do not believe this. In my
opinion the love of Dante, the awe which took
entire possession of him "even at the sound of
Beatrice's name," was simply the love of the
mediæval poet for the lady of his imagination.
To me this fact seems so certain that it can with-
stand the test of the most passionate and inflamed
passages to be found in all that psychological
confession. The suggestion made by Todeschini
on this subject is, however, extremely probable—
namely, that Beatrice was married to Messer
Simone de' Bardi at a very early age, and I am
certainly inclined to look upon this alliance between the Portinari, many of whom were Ghibellines, with the Bardi family, who belonged to
the Guelphs and the Grandi, as one of those reconciliations between families of opposite parties
brought about by Cardinal Latino at the peace
of 1280.

There is, similarly, little room to doubt that
the marriage of Dante Alighieri with Gemma,
daughter of Manetto Donati, blood relative to
the famous Messer Corso, the great agitator of
the Guelph party, was essentially designed to
cement an alliance between "neighbours," using

that term in the historical sense of *quasi consorti* [1]
—its usual sense at this period. This, although
it cannot be actually proved by documentary evidence, is rendered only too probable by all that
biographers and scholars have written or discerned
concerning Dante's marriage and his unfortunate
wife, from Boccaccio's romance to the presump-
tuous eccentricities of modern critics. It is,
also, the more probable because, in the matter
of arranging marriages in his family for party
purposes, the terrible Messer Corso's methods
threw those of the most intriguing woman into
the shade, in addition to which his audacity and
his violence were such as to earn for his family
the ominous nickname of *Malefa' mi*.[2] To gain
his ends he hesitated neither to drag his beautiful sister out of her convent, nor to take for himself as third wife, when he was no longer young,
a daughter of the Ghibelline soldier of fortune,
Uguccione della Faggiuola, in succession to a
Guelph Cerchi and a Ghibelline Ubertini. His
first wife, the Cerchi, was supposed to have died
of poison administered by her husband himself,
a deed doubly horrible and sinister if committed

---

[1] *Consorte*, in its ancient sense, meant men of the same
interests, the same political party, often of the same blood.
The old use of the word "fellow" is possibly an equivalent ;
cf. "my fellow in adversity."

[2] "Doers of evil"; literally, "Evil dost thou unto me."

solely to open the way to further politically ad-
vantageous unions.

Yet one figure amidst that ominous family of
the *Malefa' mi* stands out with double sweetness
and piety, namely, the gentle figure of Nella, the
virtuous widow of the dissolute Forese Donati,
the companion of the youthful Dante during the
brief period when he, too, led a life of worldly
pleasure :—" My Nella," as Forese calls her in
the *Purgatorio*, " who still weeps and prays for
me, the only one to do good works of all the
barbarous people amongst whom I left her."

I cannot see why Dante's idealistic cult for
Beatrice should be any impediment to his affection for the mother of his children, or prevent
him from loving her in exile as well as at home,
any more than his amorous servitude to Monna
Vanna was a hindrance to Guido Cavalcanti, the
husband of Bice degli Uberti.   Neither do I believe, as do some interpreters of the *Vita Nuova*,
that the " gentle lady " who dwelt near the house
of the Alighieri, and who " looked forth from a
window very pitifully" upon Dante's grief for the
death of Beatrice, was Gemma Donati, to whom
he was probably already married.   Others suppose this gentle lady to have been the Matelda of
The Earthly Paradise, whom—to provide reasons
for this identification—the sober dress and natural,
homely manner of a simple Florentine are alleged

to suit better than the wreath of the famous Countess or the wimple of a little German nun. The gracious visions of a maiden culling flowers, or moving with little steps across the grass, or lowering her modest eyes at his call,[1] are things which the sight of this lady must have evoked from the poet's own youthful memories.

Florence could, however, in no way be connected with the youthful memories of that century's second great idealiser of woman, for the same wretched discord of factions and parties which prevented Dante from spending his later years, and dying, in the city, caused Petrarch to be born and brought up far from Florence. Whether or no, given other conditions of life and of preparation for it, his mind and talent might not have followed a very different course we cannot tell. But certain it is that, while the inward workings of his spirit, and the concentration within himself of all his perceptions and their concomitant sentiments, found manifold and indefatigable expression, Petrarch's genius responded seldom, and then but faintly, to the stimulus of outward facts and the realities. Whatever his own belief in so much of self-revelation as he has left to us, not only was Laura no Florentine, but she is simply a generalised likeness of woman.

[1] *Purgatorio*, xxviii. 49–69.

All the qualities attributed to her by the poet were evolved from his own imagination, from his own exquisite and somewhat morbid sensibility; hence Petrarch has been justly looked upon as the precursor and anticipator of the great modern poets who sing of the universal and infinite sadness of all things.

His mother, however, was a Florentine, Eletta Canigiani, and he first saw the light whilst his parents were living in exile at Arezzo. His mother took him to Incisa when he was only seven months old, and eventually, with him and a younger boy, followed her husband into Provence, where she died when she was only thirty-eight and Francesco barely fifteen years old. The lad composed thirty-eight Latin hexameters to the memory of his mother, and none who realise what was the sensitive, even hysterical, nature of the humanist can marvel at such metrical arithmetic being the expression of his filial affection.

" Hearken unto me, oh sainted mother, if virtue which hath been crowned in Heaven doth not disdain other honours. An elect soul art thou in name and in deed; a dweller in Paradise, and here below eternally held in remembrance for thine uprightness and great piety, the dignity of thy mind and the chastity of thy fair body from its earliest years even until death. All must venerate thee, and I weep for thee perpetually, for thou hast left me and my brother in our youth upon the cross-roads between good and evil, in the midst of the tumult of worldly things. But with thee have vanished and with thee are buried in the tomb all the happiness and the hope of our forsaken house and all our consolation, and to me it seemeth as though I were buried with thee beneath the same stone."

After he has wept upon her bier and bathed her cold body with his tears, he promises to write her a longer and better song of praise, and that his mother's name shall live in his verses together with his own, desiring that if his own be destined to perish, hers at any rate may survive. But all this grief in Latin, measured out into thirty-eight lines, is of far less value than is the glimpse of an anxious mother in one of his many sonnets to Laura :—

> " Never did pious mother to her loved son
> With such anxiety and heartfelt sighs,
> In doubtful state, such faithful counsel give."

And of still less value is it when compared with that tender and virile conception in the immortal *Song to the Italians*, wherein love of country and love of family are regarded as one and the same thing :—

" Is't this, the earth whereon my feet first trod,
  Where I was nourished with such gentle care ?
  Is't this, my country in whose faith I trust,
  Mother of all, most gracious and most fair,
  Within whose breast my parents sleep in God ? "

Because she gave Petrarch his " beloved parents
and his native tongue," Florence has been exalted
in worthy verse by Ugo Foscolo, the " Singer of
the Tombs." But it was surely due to his mother
that, notwithstanding the paternal exile, notwithstanding the restless wandering from place to
place, the speech heard on the banks of the Arno
remained that which gave chaste utterance to his
love ; that, thanks to his admirable mastery over
the refined and graceful subtleties, and one might
almost say the fragrance of the Tuscan tongue, he
remained capable of giving perfect expression to
the most elusive and delicate thoughts. The
Florentine exile who guided that precocious boyhood doubtless made it her constant care that
between the readings of Cicero and Livy, midst
the joyous diversions of the amorous language of
the troubadours and the sonorous eloquence of the
courtier of the Avignon Babylon, there should also
sound frequently in her son's ears the harmonious
echoes of her own familiar native tongue. That
the poet who was crowned upon the Capitol, who
was conversant with the classics and the heroes of
antiquity, should never have recognised how much

gratitude he owed to her for such a benefit, for
this almost second motherhood, even for the works
written in his own Italian tongue, is only the
usual fate of mothers, who, asking no reward for
their love, but repaid by their own sacrifice, bend
their white heads in resignation as though upon
the pillow of their own repose.

The land of Provence was a hospitable refuge
for many Florentine exiles, one of whom, Azzo
Arrighetti, became the ancestor of a family famous
in later times, Riquetti de Mirabeau. A pleasant
country is Provence, with a climate as soft as that
of Italy, accessible to Italian commerce and, during that century, under Papal influence. But the
Italian women who, like Eletta Canigiani, were
driven thither either by exile or by other chances
of fortune, perhaps as wives of the Florentine
merchants, notaries or craftsmen whose business
took them abroad, must indeed have found that
feudal society different in all its ways from their
own. We can but surmise what impression they
made in that land of barons and troubadours, of
tournaments and organised gaiety, in the midst
of great knightly traditions, beside those ladies
who still live in our imagination as gravely pro-
nouncing their verdicts in the Courts of Love,
or deciding their controversies according to one or
the other of the thirty-one articles which con-

stituted their book of laws. It would be interesting to know the intimate thoughts or the uttered opinions of those staid fellow-townsmen of that good Gualdrada who is said to have publicly refused the imperial kiss of Otto IV., when, at the festival in Avignon which drew a sonnet from Petrarch, they beheld the virtuous Laura receiving the kiss of the youthful prince, who was afterwards Charles IV., upon that brow and those eyes with the mere praise of which the poet was obliged to content himself. Or what did they think of the tale in the *Decameron*, wherein the gallant Pietro d'Aragona, attending the wedding of the young Florentine maiden who had fallen in love with him in Palermo, and whom he had persuaded into a sensible marriage in her own rank, in the presence of her parents and bridegroom "took her head between his two hands and kissed her brow"? What the Italian women thought of these royal and imperial embraces, a Florentine of two centuries later, and from Avignon itself, Giovanni Rucellai, wrote to his friends in Florence when, full of the memories of Madonna Laura, he told them how in that joyous land "kisses were as lawful as were looks with them." But, he added, they were those silent kisses the secret of which he was learning together with the French language, kisses which Luigi Pulci, in his poem, the *Morgana*, had already described as being "after the French fashion" and always leaving a rosy mark behind!

The Florentine writers of the Trecento included one who, having for some time sojourned in Provence, and being struck by the simplicity or uncouthness, as it might well seem, of the Florentine women of the democratic Commune when set beside the noble and educated ladies of feudal society, determined to come to their aid. The Utopia—for no other word is so applicable —of Messer Francesco da Barberino took the form of two of the most curious books produced by that literature, namely, the *Documenti d' Amore* and the *Costume e Reggimento di Donna*, written in a sententious, or rather distinctly gnomic or aphoristic style. Of these singularities, however, the Trecento can show other notable examples, not, indeed, long and solid works like these, but lyrical compositions, and especially songs such as those of Bindo Bonichi.

The *Costume e Reggimento di Donna* is, in particular, a complete guide for women, wherein, whatever her social class or condition, every child or widow, mother of a family or recluse, queen, countess, duchess or princess, down to the humble townswoman, nun, maiden, nurse, fruitseller, or even female barber, not forgetting pedlars and beggars, may find instruction and advice and an ideal model upon which to form her conduct. It is to be feared, however, that notwithstanding the diffusion of his books, good Messer Francesco found but few disciples amongst the merry gentlewomen, lovely maidens and learned dames, who greeted him in the houses and streets of Florence. The rules to be observed are comprised under no less than fifty-four heads, not counting a dozen preliminary " warnings," and special precepts for reigning houses. There are here enough laws, rules, instructions, admonitions and counsels to astonish not only the simpler classes, but even the gentlewomen of a free and liberal-minded community.

A recent historian of the Republic, Monsieur Perrens, has certainly exaggerated the vulgarity of the daily life of the women of Old Florence, weaving with French vivacity, out of episodes culled from Italian novelists, a series of pictures and incidents which read like a selection from, or rather like an inventory of, the romances of Emile Zola. It is, nevertheless, a matter for serious doubt whether many of the fair readers of Messer Francesco's *Reggimento e Costume* were capable of observing the precepts by which he expected to regulate the behaviour of a girl when she received her betrothal ring. That she should " stand with her eyes lowered and her limbs still " is no doubt correct and possible, but that she should also "seem to be alarmed" may lawfully be supposed an injunction less strictly observed. When her consent is asked, she should "wait until she had been asked once or twice," and at the third time of asking she should "give her answer in a sweet, low voice." The remark is added that the alarm, the hesitation and the faint voice, may be slightly moderated if the bride is no longer in her first youth! The precepts for nuptial celebrations further contain the recommendation to eat very little at the wedding feast, but in order that the stomach may not suffer from this abstinence, it is better for the bride to take a little preliminary refreshment in the privacy of her chamber. As a gloss to the precept that she had better wash her hands beforehand, in order that she may not seem to dirty the water in the basin presented to her at table, it must be remembered that a fork was an instrument scarcely known in those days, and that gentles and nobles alike used their fingers to convey solid food to the mouth.

All Barberino's precepts are illustrated by examples or stories, many of which are very charming; but almost all the personages described are other than Italian, being natives either of Provence, Normandy, England or Castile, knights, counts, barons or kings, and the "example" is often prefaced by some saying or conceit of the troubadours.

The whole work, furthermore, is, like the *Roman de la Rose*, dominated from beginning to end by an army of allegorical female figures, typifying this or that virtue, and each attended by her maid or page. Here are Honesty, Patience, Chastity, Hope, Caution, Courtesy, Religion ; also Voluptuousness, Repentance, Eternal Light, and others, all of whom are subordinated to the Madonna, who is Wisdom. The conversation between these symbolical ladies and the writer runs like a connecting thread through the whole book, which is also lavishly enriched with descriptions and moral sayings couched in warm and striking colours. The style, much besprinkled with proverbs, and written in hendecasyllables with the accent mostly upon the fourth and seventh, has probably not its like in any other work of old Italian poetry, and may almost be said to resemble the modern artificial reproductions of the mediæval blue and gold.

A rough idea of Messer Francesco de Barberino's verses may be gleaned from the following picture of a princely house on the day of a wedding :—

"The trumpets and all instruments do sound,
Sweet songs and merriment are heard around ;
Flowers and verdure, carpets, curtains fine,
All laid upon the ground,
And great silk hangings covering the walls ;
Silver and gold the tables furnish forth,
Gay covered beds, and bright and fair the halls ;
The kitchens full of every kind of dish,

The damsels quick to serve each lightest wish,
And youthful maidens busy everywhere.
On balcony and terrace covered in,
Are many knights and gallant gentlemen,
Women and maidens of great beauty, too.

.   .   .   .   .

Then come, in plenty, wines and sweetmeats rare,
And fruits abundantly of every sort.
And birds sing, both in cages and on roofs.

.   .   .   .   .

The perfumed gardens are thrown open wide.

.   .   .   .   .

The ladies have their Spanish dogs with them,
And parrots for their feeding fly about,
Falcons and hawks and other kinds of birds.

.   .   .   .   .

The palfreys, gaily decked, wait at the gate ;
The doors are open and the people leave
In manner just as seemly as they came.

.   .   .   .   .

In curious fountains plays the water clear,
Throws its fair streams and glistens far and near.

.   .   .   .   .

The women seated all around in talk
Discourse of love and all its many joys.

.   .   .   .   .

Spring laughs from all the fields in sunshine bright ;
There are no walls which do keep out the sight."

Two admirably effective lines describe the end
of a nocturnal festival at break of day :—

" Sounds the awakening call, appears the day,
Stilled is the noise, all fall asleep straightway."

Of the seasons at which, and for what things,
a woman should pray to God, he tells us :—

> . . . " And better far
> Are fervent prayers and few,
> Than to pray much
> And not pray from the heart.
> God looketh not to find
> Nothing but bended knees,
> But humble hearts are what He seeketh for.
> And it is written that brief prayers are those
> Which most to Heaven ascend.
> 'Tis folly, then, to tire with empty words.
> But look thou well that thou dost only say
> Prayers fervent and correct,
> Imploring things which lawful are and good.
> For some there are, who pray to God that He
> Will still keep fair the colour of their face,
> And make them lovelier than all other dames,
> And grant that yellow shall their hair remain ;
> Or they do ask for ornament and dress.
> Do not consume thyself for these vain things,
> And thus provoke against thee the Lord's wrath."

Again the poet describes the absent-minded-
ness of those in love :—

> " A woman sitteth to spin at the window,
> There passeth a lover and she turneth round,
> She stayeth her hand, and, tangled the thread,
> Spoiled is the thing which she had begun.
>   .   .   .   .   .   .
> Thus one who doth at the window sew
> When meaning the needle to prick in her dress
> Full often her own hand seweth instead."

Economy in the matter of ornaments seems to have been no more a feminine vice in the Trecento than it is to-day:—

> " And if a wreath she weareth,
> Well, if it be but one,
> Both beautiful and small.
> For, as thou dost know,
> 'Tis held to be correct
> To wear a bundle in place of a wreath.
> And the lovelier she is,
> The smaller should she wear it.
> For not the wreath itself,
> But pleasing, doth give pleasure ;
> And 'tis not ornaments make woman fair,
> But her own beauty gilds that she doth wear."

Girlish caprices, again, which would be called romantic now, have not apparently varied :—

> " And here we have a fault
> Especially to be found
> In these young maidens fair,
> Which, if I could, I gladly would undo.
> Many there are, who, to divert themselves,
> Or sometimes just for foolishness,
> Have a desire to see
> How much they are beloved.
> And sometimes for disdain
> Of some slight passing word
> They heard, and were displeased ;
> Sometimes because they would be left
> To do as pleaseth them ;—
> Feign that their sides do hurt,
> Or else their teeth,

G

Or else their heads,
Or else they nonsense talk.

.   .   .

And some begin this play
Intending soon to cease this foolish thing.
But having once begun,
Find that they must go on,
Lest, do they cease, others may say
' Behold !   She did but feign ! ' ' "

Upon other subjects the writer has found "many various customs and many opinions,"—as concerning the correct salutations and obeisances to be made by the bride.   He evades his difficulty by advising that she

" Inquire the customs in her own city,
And of the country whither she doth go,
And use them with discretion, as she can."

The reader must clearly bear in mind that the deliberate aim of this book, as also of the same writer's *Documenti d' Amore*, was to civilise the customs of the people by means of a theory, poetically set forth, of a refined and courtly mode of life. This understood, no further explanation need be sought as to the reason why a Florentine, living in Florence at a time when the influence of the Provençal and Sicilian poetry had already passed away, should naturally and without a preconceived design write in the Provençal and French style, mingle the Tuscan with other kindred tongues, and found the description of his ideal woman upon a type not represented in the actual life of the day. The poets who described the customs of the period, however, portrayed a type of woman composed of many conflicting elements—Provençal gallantry, pagan sensuality, mere vulgarity, ascetic austerity and hardness. It was from the extreme conflict of these elements, so peculiarly a characteristic of the Renaissance, that there was to emerge a unity—the new type which had something of each, and yet was unmistakably different from all.

Careful search might doubtless reveal to us many examples of such composite characters, but the life of the period inevitably tended to cause the loss and destruction of every kind of record. Private papers were the least likely to be preserved, and we are, therefore, the more fortunate in that one genuine collection has survived to reveal to us a very charming personality. These letters, written by a Florentine lady of the latter half of the Trecento, Dora del Bene, were addressed to her husband during his absence as the representative of his Commune, in Val di Nievole. She writes from the country, and gives him information concerning village affairs, domestic interests, and the health of her daughters. The sons are with their father, learning betimes, either in commerce or in Government employment, to accustom

themselves to a life of hard work in the service
of the family or the Commune, and acquiring a
knowledge of the world, into so many parts of
which they were to carry the name of Florence
and of Italy.

In this correspondence the writer's expressions
of respectful affection for her husband, who is
addressed in the superscription as " wise and discreet," "most beloved," "most reverend," and even
"venerable," are accompanied by certain polite
phrases, which prove that the women of Florence—
following the advice of an anonymous expounder of
Ovid—were not averse from letting their husbands
see that they were not merely " country women,
who knew how to do nothing save card wool," but
intelligent and courteous, "showing their good
qualities, and how pleasant and amiable they were,
so that their husbands could find no other women
who would so greatly please them or do their
will." Naturally, the letters of so austere and
robust a character as Dora del Bene do not contain
the same expansiveness and exaggeration as those
of our more sickly age. Thus she writes :—

" We are all well, praise God ; but it seemeth
unto us that we should be better if we were with
thee. Farewell ; I commend thy Dora unto thee.
A thousand greetings." Elsewhere she says :
" Thou writest to me that thou canst not sleep
at night for thinking upon Antonia. . . ." This

was a daughter whom they were thinking of marrying. " But it is not Antonia who robbeth thee of sleep. But when I can bear it no longer, I shall fall upon thee when thou art not expecting me, and the sole reason of my coming will be to scold thee."

It is plain that she is jesting and feigning jealousy, and that sort of jealousy which the above-mentioned expounder of Ovid says arises from " good love, when the woman loves her rightful lord," and is distinct from that other kind of jealousy which comes from " folly." The same expressions are found both in Italian and Provençal rhymers, and also in Dante's phrase of " foolish love "—one of the many which commentators have failed to recognise, borrowed from the common speech of his day, rather than as Dante's own invention. The letters of Dora del Bene are dated in various ways: " Written the XVIII day of April, at the hour of the Ave Maria." . . . " Written on the VIII day of May, after Vespers, under the loggia," with a loving reminder for the husband and father that it was " the hour which awakens desire," and the place where the family gathered together in the evening for cheerful repose after the fatigues of the day, which finally closed with prayer. The last of these letters, the one alluding to jealousy, is signed " Dora, thine enemy," the very counterpart of the language used by the versifiers towards their ladies and tyrants.

Although she may be less conspicuous and less immaculate, it seems to me that this picture of a woman of real life loses very little when compared with the model women portrayed by Messer Francesco da Barberino !

There was, however, one state of woman's life in Florence which possessed rules and precepts—not written with style or elegance, perhaps, but homely and popular. This was the married state, rules for which were set forth in those *Avvertimenti di Maritaggio*, of which there still exists more than one example in prose or verse, consisting of some twelve or fourteen rules, with which the mother provides the daughter as a safeguard in her new life. Not only the mothers, but also the casuistic theologians tormented these married couples with cautions and warnings, frequently translating into the vulgar tongue things which would have been better left in Latin. Other books of advice are, none the less, full of charm and homely good sense ; and from one of these a mother's farewell letter, before her daughter is led to the altar, may here be transcribed :—

"MY DEAREST DAUGHTER,—Much do I pray thee, and even command thee, that thou distress not thyself because I have given thee in marriage, and thou art obliged to leave me, for thus thou mightest anger thy new husband to whom I have married thee. But, sweet my daughter, if it had been right to keep thee with me until mine end, thou shouldst not have left me, so great love have we one for the other. But reason adviseth it, and the honour of our house demandeth it, and thy condition and thy years require that henceforth thou shouldst have a companion, so that thy father and I and our kindred may have joy of thee and of thy children, the which, we hope in God, thou wilt have. Now must I tear thee from my bosom ; now must thou leave the dominion of thy father and go unto that of thy husband and thy lord, to whom thou owest not only companionship, but service and obedience. And above all things, in order that thou mayest know how it beseemeth thee to render service and obedience, hearken unto my counsels, and receive them as though they were commandments; because, if thou dost observe them well, thou wilt have the love and favour of thine husband and of all other people.

" The first commandment is, that thou dost avoid all those things whereby he might be angered or reasonably provoked. And see that thou be not mirthful nor laugh when thou seest him out of temper ; and equally be not thyself provoked when thou seest him merry. And when he is troubled, or filled with anger or with grave thoughts, do not intrude thyself upon him; but withdraw thou apart until his brow shall have come clear again.

"The second commandment is, that thou seek to know what viands he most prefers at dinner and at supper, and see that these be prepared for him. And if it should happen that those dishes do not please thee, I would have thee, nevertheless, feign as though they did please thee; for it is seemly that a wife should conform unto the tastes of her husband.

"The third commandment is, that when thy husband is wearied through weakness, or fatigue, or any other cause, and that he is asleep, thou shalt have a care not to awaken him without a lawful reason. And if thou art obliged to call him, see that thou dost not arouse him suddenly, or in haste; but gently and softly shalt thou awaken him, so that he may not be angry with thee; for it is by such things that men are often moved to great indignation.

"The fourth commandment is, that thou be a faithful guardian of both his honour and thine own; and do not interfere with the chest or purse or any other place where he keepeth his money, in order that his suspicions may not fall upon thee; and if by accident, or for any other cause, it happeneth unto thee to touch them, do not take anything, but replace them discreetly. And

unto no person whatever, for no reason whatever,
shalt thou either give or lend of his goods without
his consent; for he is thy lord in such a manner
that neither for the love of God, nor for any other
reason, canst thou give of his goods unto the poor
without his command. Wherefore do thou have
the utmost care to guard his possessions. For a
man is praised for being bountiful, but a woman
is praised for being careful of her husband's
things.

"The fifth commandment is, that thou shalt
not show thyself too eager to know the beliefs
and the secrets of thy husband; and if it should
happen that he telleth them unto thee, then see
that thou dost not repeat them unto any person
whatever. And likewise have a care that thou
dost not repeat out of thine house the things said
familiarly in thine house, even though they be of
but small account. For it is evil beyond measure
that others should know the affairs of thy household, more especially from thine own mouth, and
a tattling woman is held to be mad and foolish
and her husband doth hold her in abhorrence.

"The sixth commandment is, that thou shalt
love and trust thy servants and thine household
as is seemly, and especially those who are in the
favour of thine husband; and do not censure
them or dismiss them for a small reason, since so
wouldst thou be ever in hatred with them, and it

might happen that they and others of the household should so detest thee and speak evil of thee that hardly shalt thou free thyself from the reproach, and it might easily happen that thy husband and other persons should come to hate thee likewise.

"The seventh commandment is, that thou shalt not do any great thing of thine own accord without the consent of thine husband, however good reason there may seem unto thee for doing it. And take heed that thou dost on no account say unto him, 'My advice was better than thine,' even though it truly was better, for by so doing thou couldst easily drive him into great anger against thee, and great hatred.

"The eighth commandment is, that thou shalt not ask anything of thine husband which is not seemly and which would be too difficult for him to perform; and especially shalt thou ask nothing which thou thinkest would displease him or which would be contrary unto his honour, in order that thou mayest not be the cause of his hurt, injury or destruction.

"The ninth commandment is, that thou shalt endeavour to keep thy person fresh and beautiful, well adorned and neat, but in a manner that is honest and seemly, and without any false or displeasing adornment. Because if thy husband did behold thee adorned in an unseemly manner and contrary to his desire, he might very easily hold thee in doubt and suspicion ; whereas if he seeth thee honestly adorned, he will hold thee yet more dear.

" The tenth commandment is, that thou be not too familiar with thine household, nor too much inclined towards them, especially those who wait upon thee, whether maid or manservant. Because too great an intimacy causeth wrong-doing, and familiarity doth breed contempt. Wherefore is it far better to show thyself somewhat haughty and reserved toward them, and it is not a good sign to behold a servant behaving proudly to her mistress, for, seeing this, people do commonly say, ' The servant doth play the lady, whereas the mistress doth play the fool.' [1]

" The eleventh commandment is, that thou shalt not be too great a gadabout, nor go too much forth out of thine house. For the woman who stayeth much at home and walketh but little abroad is the delight of her husband, as saith Solomon, and he had great knowledge of the matter. A man is obliged to attend to his business without doors that so he may provide for the things of the house ; and it is the woman's duty to attend to the affairs of the family and the household. And this thou couldst never do pro-

---

[1] " *La serva signoreggia, se la madonna folleggia,*" an old Italian proverb.

perly, my daughter, if thou wert a gadabout. Further, I do desire and command thee that thou take heed not to talk too much; for chiefly doth it beseem women to talk but little, and showeth honesty in them. And if a woman were in truth foolish, and only talked but little, she would be esteemed wise. And I do command thee that thou be modest and not seek to know too much; neither must thou believe in the soothsayers or in their doings and incantations, for it is very unseemly that women should desire to know as much as do men concerning the doings of men.

" The twelfth commandment, and the most important which I can give thee and the which I do most impress upon thy mind, is, that thou do nothing, either in deeds or words or appearance, whereby thy husband might become jealous. For jealousy is that which the soonest of all things would deprive thee of his love, and ever afterwards he would hold thee in suspicion and would himself be inflamed against thee, and thou wouldst be hated not only by him but by all his kindred and friends; and thou wouldst fall into such disgrace that never shouldst thou be clear from it, for this fault leaveth a stain which can by no means be assoiled. Let this commandment be unto thee greater than all the others; be thou assured that there is nothing which a husband holdeth more dear in his wife than the honesty

of her body; and so on the contrary. Be thou
solicitous of showing him all honour and reverence, whatsoever may happen. And when he re-
turneth home, do thou always give him a kindly
reception. And cheerfully do greater honour unto
his kindred than unto thine own, for so will he
do unto thine. And if it should chance, upon
the arrival of some other honourable person, that
thou art engaged upon some menial work of the
house, do thou instantly take up thy spindle and
distaff and conceal the menial work, whatsoever
it may have been, in order that thou appear not
country-bred. In the affairs of love depart not
from that which is honest, according to what I
told thee when we did speak alone together, in
order that too great desire out of due time shall
not rob thee of his affection. And thus love and
not anger will be the reason why he watcheth over
thee. So shall the ardour of his love be a witness
to thine honesty.

"And if thou dost all these things, thou wilt
be thine husband's crown of gold."

"Then did the gentle mother and wise lady bless
the loving daughter and meek maiden, and make
the sign of Holy Cross upon her, and commend
her unto God, praying her tenderly that she would
always observe her commandments, and that before
all things she would love her dearly."

Such admonitions were rules which came from

the heart and from out of the reality of life ; not, like the precepts of Barberino, from the land of Utopia.

Francesco da Barberino died at an advanced age in the year 1348. But the plague, which numbered this courtly poet of the Florentine women amongst so many other victims, was destined to inspire another and a far more powerful spirit. That passion of enjoyment which, as Matteo Villani testifies, intoxicated all those who had escaped the death and the terror, found its interpreter in Giovanni Boccaccio, the origin of whose art is betrayed by its exuberance of colouring, its redundant softness of outline, the vividness of its action, and but too surely by its debased moral sense. Little or nothing of the ideal is to be discerned in his women, in so far as idealism implies a resemblance, more or less marked, between the figure described and the type of the artist's dreams. But he gives an admirably clear and intimate representation of the actual life of the middle-class Florentines of his day.

I do not propose to discuss Boccaccio's imaginary story-tellers, who most assuredly never met together beneath the sacred roof of Santa Maria Novella, profaning its holiness with gay conversation, nor ever lingered upon any one of the neighbouring hills in company with frivolous youths, while men were hourly dying in the plain below. Those women, Pampinea and Elisa and Fiammetta,

DETAIL FROM THE MARRIAGE OF GRISELDA (FROM BOCCACCIO'S STORY.)

(*London : The National Gallery.*)

however they were called, do not differ greatly from the characters of his youthful romances, whether in prose or verse, and several even bear the same names. But whether nymphs or women, or a combination of both, Boccaccio's ladies— even when real women, as in Fiammetta's story— are invariably figures outside the actual and historical order of things. All appear in more or less classical attitudes of grief or love, of despair or jealousy, but never, in spite of this, does one rise to those regions where dwell the immortal creatures of our imagination, from Beatrice to the fair betrothed of Renzo, from Laura to Margaret, from Erminia and Fiordiligi to Thekla Wallenstein and Ermengarde. Boccaccio's only real contributions to the art of female portraiture are those contained in the short dramas of that book which, in distinction to Dante's work, may rightly be called the "Human Comedy." Of all these, one only, and this not certainly, shows evidence of being drawn according to a preconceived ideal, namely, she whom Petrarch distinguished as "differing very greatly from all the others," the virtuous and low-born Griselda who was considered worthy of being wedded and then sorely tried by her feudal lord, a moral and historical myth of eternal popularity in art and tradition alike. But the most lifelike figures are undoubtedly those which Messer Giovanni portrayed from life—Florentine women both gentle and simple, of town or country, merry or malicious, or sometimes even noble figures, whom he either drew from living models or evoked from tombs but recently closed. In contemplating these portraits from the life, transformed by no process of idealisation and the proportions of which are unaltered by any sympathetic partiality, we discern but too clearly that the Middle Ages are drawing towards their close. The age of mysticism and contemplation, of great conceptions formed in the midst of great afflictions, is passing away, and worldly reality offers her triumphant nakedness to the sinuous and elegant garments which humanism is preparing alike for its adornment and its disguise.

When we desire again to live over in thought the centuries long passed away, it is nevertheless to the Middle Ages that we turn, not perhaps intentionally, but naturally, and as though our minds were unconsciously drawn towards that period. The paganism of the Renaissance which we encounter on the way may gratify barren curiosity, flatter our vivacity, or re-animate fantastic ideas of the erudite, but the heart remains untouched, and the longing which impelled us to try and unite the present with the past remains unsatisfied. A page of Dante, however tortured and twisted by grammarians or rendered obscure by the seekers after allegory, will answer more of the spirit's needs and solace the heart more per-

fectly than could ever the *Mandragola* of Niccolò
Machiavelli, or the *Calandria* of Bernardo Dovizi,
Cardinal Bibbiena, galvanised into a semblance of
life though these be by the most ingenious con-
trivances of modern scenery. Many reasons contribute to this, but the first and foremost is that
the spirit lingers most willingly there where the
heart finds readiest response to its most noble
feelings. But since the civilisation into which we
are born has taught us to seek in all artistic representations of life the Christian conception of the
feminine ideal, it seems to me that the Renaissance
—the great results of which should not make us
forget its mistakes and shortcomings—either failed
sufficiently to recognise, or was not potent enough
to maintain at the height to which it had uplifted
him, the great synthetic poet of mediæval thought,
and could do even less for his contemporaries.

Italian literature is founded upon a Poem, pri-
marily inspired by a woman, the action of which
is alternately directed by three women, who prepare it upon earth, and guide it through the
eternal regions to end in Heaven itself. These
three women are Mary the merciful, Lucia the
watchful, and Beatrice, the praise-giver and witness
to the works and the mysteries of God. If man,
overwhelmed by the afflictions of this life, can
reach salvation by the arduous way of contemplation, these are the three " blessed women " who

H

watch over him in the courts of Heaven.   If Virgil
leaves the sacred places of wisdom to come to the
aid of Dante in peril, it is because Beatrice sends
him; visible signs, or sounds, or supernatural visions
fill all Purgatory with the name and virtues of
Mary; upon the summit of the sacred mount
where bides lost human happiness, he beholds in
Leah and in Rachel respective symbols of the
active and the contemplative life ; and before this,
dreaming himself transported by the imperial eagle,
he has been taken by Lucia from the flowery valley
to the threshold of Purgatory itself.   In the Earthly
Paradise he is initiated by Matelda into the mysterious transfiguration of the political and religious ordinances of society; Matelda leads him to
Beatrice; through the mystical ablutions in Lethe
and in Eunoë, Matelda, gracious figure that speaks
to every poet of gentle womanliness, enables him to
put off the old man, to be born anew, and so fitted
for that ascension to the heavens, with strength
for which the eyes of Beatrice again inspire him.
Finally, in the Rose of the Blessed these three
women, saviours and liberators of man, occupy
glorious seats in that bright assembly of Christian
humanity, where, at the feet of Mary the Divine,
sits Eve, perfect in beauty—two, through sin and
redemption, the beginning and the fulfilment of
the story of the Universe.

Such is woman's share in the fundamental conception of Dante's Poem. And rising with wearied hands from his finished book, the Poet, turning his eyes to where the daughter of Folco Portinari beckoned to him from the threshold of eternity, might well repeat those last exultant words of the *Vita Nuova*, "Of thee have I said that which was said never of any woman."

CHAPTER III

BEATRICE IN THE LIFE AND THE POETRY
OF THE THIRTEENTH CENTURY

JUST outside the city of Florence, between the second circle of walls and what was then a wooded slope rising gently towards the hills of Fiesole, but is to-day the highest and perhaps the pleasantest part of Florence—the city has now enveloped and destroyed even its third circle of walls — there stood the suburban church and convent of Sant' Egidio. Here, upon the 12th day of January 1288, the friars of the Order of the Penitence of Jesus Christ assembled round a notable citizen of Florence, who in their presence was dictating his will to his notary. By this act Folco di Ricovero di Folco dei Portinari—member of a family formerly Ghibelline and consular, but among those which, migrating from Fiesole, and enriched by commerce, finally passed over to the Guelph faction, ensured the perpetual continuance of the hospital that his splendid liberality had recently built close to that monastery.

VILLA PORTINARI : CAMERATA. TWO VIEWS
OF THE LOGGIA.

"Humbly do I commend my soul unto the living and true God," ran the words dictated by Folco to the notary Tedaldo Rustichelli, "and I do desire to be buried in the chapel of my hospital of Santa Maria Nuova. Unto God, unto the Lord Jesus Christ, and unto the blessed Virgin Mary, His Mother, do I offer the aforesaid hospital and chapel, or church, as an atonement for the sins of myself and my family, and for the service of the sick poor. My heirs shall support it and shall be the patrons thereof. Unto the religious and the poor do I bequeath . . ." a long list of brotherhoods, monasteries and hospitals, both in the city and the country. Then, only, he made provision for his family, naming them one by one—first his wife, Madonna Cilia dei Caponsacchi, another of those families

"... descended
Into the mart from Fiesole ";
—*Paradiso*, xvi. 121.

but a family which had remained Ghibelline and one of the Grandi. Having next secured to his natural sister, Nuta, continued residence and support in one of the houses of the Portinari, he paused to point out the houses belonging to the family, from possession of which—whether by succession or right—he excluded all females, in order that the property should remain in the Portinari family—the old family mansion in the parish of

San Procolo, which he and his kinsmen had restored ; a house in the parish of Santa Maria in Campo, close to the city walls ; the palace inhabited by himself, which had towers, and was situated in the parish of Santa Margherita ; and other houses and small dwellings. After this he named his children—four of them unmarried girls, Vanna, Fia, Margherita and Castoria, to each of whom he bequeathed a dowry of eight hundred *lire a fiorini*,[1] and two married, Madonna Bice into the Bardi family and Madonna Ravignana to a Falconieri. To Madonna Bice he left fifty *lire a fiorini;* Madonna Ravignana was already dead, so he bequeathed an equal amount to her son Nicola.   His own sons, Manetto, Ricovero, Pigello, Gherardo and Jacopo, Folco nominated as his heirs, but the three latter being still minors, he entrusted, together with the daughters of similarly tender age, to the guardianship of their two elder brothers, in conjunction with Messer Vieri di Torrigiano de' Cerchi, Messer Bindo de' Cerchi, and two of his own kindred.   The testator describes himself as " healthy in mind and body, thanks unto God " : very probably, he was still a comparatively young man, seeing that of his large family of eleven children two only had reached the age of manhood, while, at a time when early marriages were the custom, only two of his six

[1] The value of a *lira a fiorini* was at that time equal to francs 3.85 = 3s. 2d.

TWO SAINTS WITH THE WIFE AND DAUGHTER OF
FOLCO PORTINARI.

(Florence: The Uffizi Gallery.)

daughters were married.   Of these two Ravignana
appears to have borne a son : no mention is made
of any children of Beatrice.

A few months later, on June 23rd, Folco himself first opened his beloved hospital, with solemn
ceremony assigning to it lands, furniture and sacred
vessels and vestments, causing himself and his
descendants to be invested as perpetual patrons by
Andrea de' Mozzi, Bishop of Florence, and instal-
ling the first rector with the ringing of bells and the
chanting of the *Te Deum* in the new church.   A
year and a half later, on the last day of 1289, the
good Folco was lost to his children and his poor for
ever.   His tomb, bearing his coat-of-arms and an
inscription in Gothic lettering, remained in the
church for several centuries, watched over by a
picture of the Virgin, by Cimabue, which Folco
had himself placed over the altar.   To this, in
course of time, succeeded an " Annunciation " by
Andrea del Castagno, and eventually a painting by
Alessandro Allori representing the Virgin Mother
surrounded by saints.   Neither the chapel nor the
original hospital—afterwards called the Hospital
of San Matteo—are in existence at the present day,
and the traces of both the one and the other, as of
the bones of Folco and his wife and children, have
been lost to sight beneath the mass of notarial documents preserved in the *Archives of Contracts*.   The
only one of all the Portinari tombs which has sur-

vived is that of Folco himself, and well it deserved
to escape destruction. Reconstructed with reverent care in modern times, this has been placed
in the church of Sant' Egidio—the church of the
now existing hospital of Santa Maria Nuova. Yet,
while the scene of his charity thus once more
possesses the presence of its tutelary genius, but
few know of this tomb, or rather cenotaph, which
bears the following inscription : *Hic iacet Fulchus
de Portinariis qui fuit fundator et edificator [h]uius
ecclesie et ospitalis S. Marie Nove et decessit anno
MCCLXXXIX die XXXI decembris. Cuius anima
pro Dei misericordia requiescat in pace.* The tombs
of his son Manetto, who died on August 28th, 1334,
and of Accirito, the son of Manetto, who died on
June 17th, 1358, were also in San Matteo, but have
long since disappeared.

According to such evidence as we possess, Folco's
life was not a long one, but it was a life full of
goodness and charity, as his last will amply testifies.
There are also other proofs of his worth and activity
as a citizen. His name is found in both the registers of magistrates who, between the years 1280
and 1282, laid the solid foundation of Florentine
democracy ; first in that of the " Fourteen " good
men elected by Cardinal Latino to seal the peace
established between Guelphs and Ghibellines, and
again among the *Priori delle Arti*, or heads of guilds,
under whose guidance the craftsmen of Florence

THE TOMB OF FOLCO PORTINARI AS RE-ERECTED IN THE
CHURCH OF SANT' EGIDIO IN FLORENCE.

began their ascendancy in the State. Folco was a member of both these magistracies, being elected one of the Fourteen in March 1282, as he was again one of the Priori chosen in the following August at the first ordinary election of six Priori, one for each quarter and for each of the Greater Guilds. Folco represented the quarter of Porta San Piero and the Guild of the Merchants.

In these lists, as well as in the Priori registers of 1285 and 1287, when he was again a member, the name of Folco was one of those representing the element of nobility—which had adapted itself alike to the commerce and the magistracy of the city— while it stood also for the Ghibelline element. This latter had become gradually modified during the second half of the century—even before the Guelph triumph of 1267—until in the last thirty years it had divided into the two distinct parties of the genuine Ghibellines, who were averse to popular government, and the moderate Ghibellines, who both in government and commerce were willing to accept the useful aid of the people and of the Guelphs. Upon such a basis was formed the new division of the citizens. On the one hand were the people and such of the *Grandi* as "nevertheless were merchants"; on the other those *Grandi* who had remained uncompromisingly conservative, a division recognised and confirmed by the Orders of Justice in 1293. In the same way, on one side

were Ghibellines showing favour to Guelphs and Guelphs friendly to Ghibellines—whence sprang the Guelph and Ghibelline agreement to approve and accept a popular government—on the other the rigid Guelphs who had been dispersed by exile, or the radical Guelphs, called Black Guelphs in the year 1300. All those Guelphs and Ghibellines who had made friends under popular auspices were classed together as White Guelphs. Folco died too soon to be himself one of the White Guelphs, but his name survived in their party in the persons of his sons and kindred, and was found also amongst the victims of the violence and the triumphs of the Blacks. The youth Pigello was poisoned by a priest of the Blacks, and in the *Reform* of Messer Baldo d'Aguglione in 1311, amongst those rejected by the populace—which was exclusively composed of Black Guelphs — were the Portinari, among them Dante.

Enough has been said to show that the White Party really existed several years before it received its distinctive name ; the will of Folco Portinari is not without importance in the study of the rise of these two factions. With equal confidence in both, he entrusted the guardianship of his sons to his kindred the Portinari, and to the Cerchi—his companions in business and the future heads of the White Party. One of the trustees nominated was Messer Vieri di Torrigiano, who afterwards, in the

TWO SAINTS WITH TOMMASO PORTINARI AND
HIS SONS.
(Florence: The Uffizi Gallery.)

conflicts between the Cerchi and the Donati, succeeded, by virtue of his commercial power and his
authority as a prominent citizen, in curbing the
fierce ambition of Messer Corso Donati, until it
burst into open violence and triumphed with the
aid of Pope Boniface. Of his two elder daughters,
Folco married Ravignana to Bandino Falconieri,
afterwards one of the principal members of the
White Party and a great orator in the Councils of
the People. The other daughter, Beatrice, was
married to Messer Simone de' Bardi, by birth of
the *Grandi*, but also a powerful banker and money-
changer, strictly Guelph and eventually one of the
Black party. All these connections—between the
Ghibelline Portinari and these Guelph families—
between the Portinari belonging to the nobles and
the Falconieri belonging to the people—between
the Portinari, adherents of the Cerchi, and the
Bardi who were partisans of the Donati—appear to
have been political marriages designed to cement
civic reconciliations, or arranged by the Commune
itself, at its own expense, to obviate further divisions and wars so far as might be possible. Love,
naturally, was little concerned with these marriages,
in which, more often than not, the contracting
parties were mere children, whose contracts and
promises were made by others on their behalf.
Moreover, even when marriages were not arranged
for civic reasons, the bride was "given"; having

no power to dispose of her own heart and hand, her father gave her, her husband received her; frequently she was his father's choice rather than the woman sought and won by his own love.

The custom, the habit even, of those days was to make love in verse, though it must not be supposed that love was not also made in other ways. But, just as in the eighteenth century ladies had their "servants," and discriminated nicely between themselves as wives and themselves as ladies served by attendant cavaliers, so the women addressed by the ancient rhymers had nothing whatever to do with the women who were their life companions, and whom, perchance, they dearly loved. The "gentle lady" of the sonnet and of the ballad remained outside the household. At home, and in the bosom of their families, the men had plenty to occupy them without making amorous verses; they were merchants, cloth-weavers, money-changers, lawyers; they were also magistrates, members of a party, volunteers, or they went as ambassadors of their Commune, or as judges, to other cities of Italy. Besides all this, they were careful fathers of families, who placed the custody of house and property in the reliable hands of their true "ladies," their wives, who realised by their usually numerous progeny the hopes and plans cherished by the fathers who had united them as husband and wife.

Love-songs and poems, then, were the channel

through which these men gave utterance to all
the fond fancies and romantic ideals left unde-
veloped, or suppressed, by the severely practical
and laborious life which parental authority or
domestic and civic interests compelled them to
lead for the sake of their families. It might seem
that a fictitious woman, imaginatively conceived
under such conditions of life, must be an ethereal and poetic figure, the object or theme of
all the sighs, longings, romantic doubts and confidences, inevitably lacking in marriages wherein
the bridegroom had no choice. But this was not
the fact. As Dante, with clear phrases and unmistakable imagery, sets forth in the *Vita Nuova*, the
psychological conditions of the life of those times
precluded such a thing. Courtesy or warm hearts
prompted men to express their feelings in rhyme,
but their practical natures, concrete habit of mind
and dislike of anything abstract or indeterminate,
required that the woman to whom they addressed
their verses should be a living reality, with name,
surname and place of habitation. They also wished
to practise their Italian love-rhymes, "that style
invented for utterance of the language of love"
upon some living lady "to whom the understanding of Latin verses was not easy."

The poet's "lady," therefore, existed in all her
feminine reality, even to the detail of not understanding Latin. His thoughts and words were

addressed to a woman whose visible beauty he
could admire; he could really rejoice at her
smile, sigh at her absence, condole with her grief,
weep upon her tomb and piously cherish her
memory. But in all this homage paid and received
there was nothing that could arouse the jealousy of
either the lady's husband or the poet's wife, nothing
that could cast a shadow of scandal upon the name
given her to bear and to honour by an honest
gentleman. Conjugal peace, as nowadays, may
often have been disturbed, but not on account of
these pretty verses, and there is not a single piece
of evidence to prove that such poetical love-affairs
ever unsheathed a sword in vengeance, or brought
about civic discords among this proud and hot-
blooded people ; not a single codex of all the many
filled with amorous rhymes and sentiment can be
registered among the fatal documents which occasioned civil feuds.   But this impunity, if so it
may be called, did not prevent the bard from en-
veloping his adoration in a soft mystery, guarded
with secrecy lest aught of its gentle fragrance be
lost. Hence the custom of pretending love for some
other lady in order to conceal the true allegiance,
as where Dante, in the *Vita Nuova*, refuses to answer
all questions addressed to him by others ; in poems
enumerating—in Provençal fashion—the loveliest
ladies of the city, carefully links the name of each
only with that of her rightful lord ; and in sonnets

and ballads never designates the object of his devotion except by her baptismal name, or by some other which offers no clue to her identity.

Surnames, again, though useful in historical research and in critical controversy, are apt to be unmanageable in poetry; for this reason alone many of the ladies whose praise one may still read in verse of the period have been forced to leave their historical names behind them, and the poems honouring their charms to give no hint of their real personalities. And probably nobody would have inquired about them had not one of their number been encircled not only by the soft rays of an ideal—though fantastic—love, but also by the splendid aureole of one of the greatest conceptions of human genius. Surrounded by this glory, the image of her who was woman in the *Vita Nuova*, angel and symbol in the *Divina Commedia*, rises from her grave after six hundred years, and almost seems to speak again the very words—

> " Observe me well.   I am, in sooth, I am
> Beatrice "—

which her immortal lover put into her mouth on the green slope of the sacred hill, in reproach for having allowed other images or worldly realities to take her place in his thoughts.   We, I think, may imagine them spoken anew to those who, having since then laboriously sought the truth in all that concerns the past, recognise in that " Bice "—woman and angel—the daughter born into the family of the Portinari, and married into that of the Bardi.[1]

Boccaccio is well known to have been the first writer who identified the living woman with the symbolical figure, a practice promptly appropriated as their own invention by other writers. The shadowy visions of the *Vita Nuova*—the simple " apparition " of a girl " of very tender age," the first meeting with "that youngest of the angels "—the great novelist amplifies into the May Festival in the house of a neighbour of the Alighieri, " a man much honoured amongst the citizens in those times "—Folco Portinari. The genial but always analytical biographer, who sees and takes into account all the historical possibilities relating to his subject, finds in this May Day of 1274, when Beatrice made such an impression upon the youthful Alighieri, not their first meeting, but the moment at which she first inspired him with love.

In the *Vita Nuova* the story is told of how " before the eyes of Dante there appeared for the first time the glorious lady of his thoughts "—she whose name was Beatrice, even in the mouth of those who "knew not wherefore she was so called":

[1] " Bice," the usual diminutive of Beatrice, is commonly used of Beatrice Portinari in the legal documents still extant.

she knew not how well she deserved the name of glorious lady, nor what beatitude dwelt within her, nor for what great things she was destined. The child "wore a robe of a most noble colour, of crimson, simple and seemly, with a girdle and ornaments suitable to her tender age," and she was "almost at the beginning of her ninth year." Dante, in 1274, had almost reached the end of his ninth year. From this time onward Love "took possession of his soul," and frequently, even during his boyhood, impelled him to go in search of her; and when one day, exactly nine years later, "this admirable lady appeared unto him clothed in purest white, walking between two gentlewomen of more years than she," and as she passed through the street "saluted him very virtuously," he seemed exalted to the utmost height of bliss. From that moment, which—according to Dante's own chronology, based upon the mystic number nine—occurred in the year 1283, begins a second period of nine years, a period filled with all the thoughts, fancies and visions, all the raptures and distractions of love.

According to Boccaccio's story, "Dante, who had not yet accomplished his ninth year, because little boys were accustomed to follow their fathers, and especially to places of entertainment and feasting," went with his father one beautiful spring day to the May festival given by the Portinari family. "Here did he mingle with others of his age, of

I

whom there were many in the house of feasting,
both boys and girls ; and when the banquet for the
elder guests had been served, he began to play with
the others in childish fashion, that he might divert
himself according to his youthful age.   Amongst
the throng of children there was a daughter of the
aforesaid Folco, whose name was Bice—for he
calleth her always by her first name, which was
Beatrice—and whose age was perchance eight years.
She was exceeding graceful and beautiful in her
childish fashion, and in all that she did very
courteous and pleasing, with manners and speech
of a gravity and modesty beyond her tender years.
Moreover, her countenance was very delicate and
of an excellent shape, and besides its beauty it was
full of such simple grace that by many was she re-
puted to be an angel.   Such as I have described her,
therefore, and perchance even more beauteous, did
she appear upon that feast day unto the eyes of our
Dante."

In this strain Boccaccio continues his narrative
until the death of Beatrice, but in the *Vita Nuova*
all these events are described with a touch so light
as to seem almost afraid of the material with which
it has to do.   Persons and doings portrayed with
the most spiritual imagery, sometimes but faintly
indicated or veiled with a periphrasis, are so raised
above, and almost detached from real life, that the
continuity of the argument is often impossible to

follow.   In the *Treatise in Praise of Dante*, as Boccaccio elsewhere calls his work, events are, on the
contrary, clearly described, set forth in order as
they would occur in real life, and are further provided with moral comments pointing their good or
evil influence upon Dante's life.

"Passions and deeds"—in the figurative phrase
of the *Vita Nuova*—employed that first nine years of
love ; particulars of them Dante mentions only as
he, for instance, mentions the incident of Beatrice's
first appearance, and that other incidents were of
somewhat the same nature—quite allusively.   Boccaccio very positively speaks of these chance meetings as "childish accidents," but he, too, omits details.   The *Vita Nuova* immediately passes to the
year 1283, to the episode of the greeting and to
the sonnet describing the vision of the Lady asleep
within the arms of Love, who feeds her with the
Poet's heart.   The lines relating this earliest vision
are, of all Dante's verses, perhaps the nearest to
the old Provençal or troubadour manner ; they are
succeeded by other visions interspersed with other
rhymes descriptive of the episodes in Dante's love.
These episodes, however, are only connected by the
slenderest thread with outside reality, and even
where he mentions actual things, whether a street
of the city, a church, the death of Beatrice's friend,
or a wedding or the father's funeral, they are in no
case described more than incidentally.   The civic

episodes in Dante's life are only mentioned once, so
far as I can see, but of this I shall presently speak
more fully.   Boccaccio gives us much more information, although he does not waste time over
details, still less in describing mere formal episodes.
He tells us very precisely not only that "the flame
of Dante's love increased with his increasing years,
to so great an extent that no other thing afforded
him either pleasure or repose or consolation save
only beholding his lady," but also that, "forsaking
every other matter, with the utmost solicitude went
he ever whereas he believed that he might behold
her, deriving from her face and from her eyes all his
good and his whole consolation."   Here follows a
moral digression upon the inconveniences arising
from love, especially in the lives of those who are
studiously inclined; inconveniences, observes Boccaccio, counterbalanced in the case of Dante by the
fact that his love for Beatrice inspired him to write
verses.   He adds, however, that "fine speaking" is
not the end and aim of absolute excellence nor the
"summit of all learning," yet it was to nothing
more than "fine speaking" that Dante was inspired
by his love for a woman.   As a last question, he
doubts whether the Florentine's graceful outpour-
ings in praise of his beloved were sufficient compen-
sation for the injury which they may have caused
"to his sacred studies and his intelligence."   However high-sounding they may be, these are words of

incredible meanness, considering how large a part Beatrice, the identical Beatrice of the *Vita Nuova*, plays in that Poem the greatness of which Boccaccio —as he proved by his *Comento*—worthily felt and esteemed.

According to the sentence quoted above, " forsaking every other matter," we must either assume that Dante's youth from his eighteenth to his twenty-fifth year was wasted in an assiduous courtship of the lady for whom he longed, and for whom, like one of the vulgar effeminates of the *Decamerone*, he neglected everything in the world, even his duties ; or we must realise—since Boccaccio himself expressly declares that Dante's love was of the purest description, free from any trace of licentiousness—that the narrative of the amorous sentiments belonging to Dante's " new life " must be accepted as a positive and precise account of facts of which the given words are only a figurative description. Otherwise, and taken literally, these utterances can only be read as meaning that Dante passed the years between the incident of the greeting and the death of Beatrice—from 1283 to 1290—in visions and tears, in writing down by day all that he dreamt of by night, in soliloquies and languishings ; and that he withdrew himself entirely from the civil life of Florence, which in precisely those years reached the highest and most vigorous development ever

attained by a democratic government.   It is surely
impossible to imagine that the best years of Dante's
life were spent not in noble silence, not in the
solitude of fruitful meditation, but wasted in the
hysterical idleness of a passion which could only
have brought about its own vain ending.   All the
mediæval doctrines of the superiority of the contemplative life to the active life could not save from
ridicule the love-sick Dante, taken literally as represented in the *Vita Nuova*, or, for that matter, in
Boccaccio's own *Fiammetta*.

As has already been said, we can trace in the
pages of the *Vita Nuova* only one actual connection
between Dante's fanciful love-story and the real
events of his civic life.   This occurs in the passage
concerning a certain expedition made out of Florence, in company with a large number of other
persons, by the side of a river towards a place at no
great distance from the city—an expedition upon
which Dante went very unwillingly on account of
"absenting himself from his happiness," and which
took place in 1285, when he was about twenty years
of age.   "I was forced to depart from the aforesaid
city and to go towards those parts where there
sojourned a gentlewoman of Florence who likewise
had been compelled to leave the aforesaid city," but
in her case it was for a distant place from which she
would not return for a considerable time, whereas
Dante hints that he himself would return shortly.

From the words employed it is evident that the
expedition was one of duty or necessity, the term
andata signifying, at this period, a "going out" of
citizens upon some military or political errand in
the service of the Commune. The simple facts were
in all probability these : A certain gentlewoman of
Florence had been taken by her husband to some
other Italian city at a distance from her native place,
for the women were not invariably left behind, and
men who went with the permission of their own
communes, to act as Podestàs or captains in other
places, where they would have to stay for at least
six months or even a whole year, sometimes took
their wives with them. In the direction of the city
where this lady dwelt, therefore, though not so far,
marched the cavalcade of which Dante unwillingly
formed a member, and if the surmise that this
occurred in 1285 be correct, we have fairly certain
documentary proof that it was a real military
"cavalcade," and not merely one of the pleasure
excursions outside the city, "by the side of a clear
river," mentioned later in the book.

Concerning these military expeditions or "caval-
cades" we can obtain plenty of information from
old documents, and one of them suffices to explain
this incident of the *Vita Nuova*. "This is the
manner of collecting troops for the Commune of
Florence against the Pisans, which the Florentine
merchants have found to be the best and the most

useful and convenient for the city of Florence, and for the artificers and the Crafts and all the merchants of the aforesaid city of Florence." The manner was as follows : the shops were all closed, and the great bell of the Commune was pealed to summon together all the citizens and peasantry. Then lists were made out, each containing fifty names of men between the ages of fifteen and seventy, half of whom were to go out with the army into the field, whilst the others—upon payment of a sum of money—remained to guard the city.

About the middle of the month (June), the Podestà and two hundred horsemen of the citizens of Florence were to raise their standards, and move into the enemy's territory. The two hundred horsemen were each to be accompanied by a follower and second horse, both well armed. It is practically certain that the name of the twenty year old Alighieri was to be found in one of these lists of fifty, and it is but natural to conclude that the youngest and oldest of those inscribed were retained to guard the city, whilst the more vigorous ones, from twenty to fifty years of age, were chosen to go out against the enemy. That this particular expedition of the Florentines against the Pisans was subsequently abandoned at the instance of the Pope makes no difference as far as the Poet is concerned, nor yet that the vague chronology of the *Vita Nuova* renders it uncertain whether this incident really occurred in 1285. There were not lacking similar expeditions in other years, against one Commune or another, in which Dante would most certainly have taken part. Towards the end of this same year of 1285, in fact, fifty " good gentlemen of the city," each with his follower and two chargers, went on behalf of the Commune of Florence to assist the Sienese in a small war around Poggio Santa Cecilia, one of the strong frontier fortresses of the people of Arezzo. The citizens were summoned for such services from the different quarters of the city in turn, and were compelled to obey. Hence Dante's words, " I was forced to depart." This short war and siege ended in April with victory for the Guelphs.

Identification of the particular Guelph expedition upon which Dante was compelled to go, whether against Pisa or Arezzo, towards the lower course of the Arno, whether in the summer or the winter of 1285, or in another year, is here of altogether secondary importance. The interest of this passage—and it is of great interest—lies in the fact that, better than any other part of the *Vita Nuova*, it enables us to trace the connection between historical reality and the idyllic and mystical story of Dante's love. The Florentine expedition is winding its way along the banks of the Arno ; Dante is riding with his companions in arms, a youth amongst other youths, in all the pride of his twenty years and the consciousness that he is one of the Guelph magnates wielding, on behalf of the Commune, the sword of the Alighieri which had already done honourable service in the hand of an ancestor who died defending the Carroccio at Montaperti. Floating in the wind are the banners of his city, the scarlet Lily, the Cross of the People, and the word *Libertas* in letters of gold, which are the emblems of Florence. The reason for all this was, of course, the Guelph war —the league of Florence, Genoa and Lucca against that hated Ghibelline rival, Porto Pisano, and the soaring ambition of Ugolino della Gherardesca, the tale of whose horrible death was to be rendered immortal by that young volunteer who rode along wrapped in soft dreams of love. Other parts of Tuscany and other enemies may, however, have been the objective on this occasion. Arezzo and Siena were troubled by restless and discontented citizens. Arezzo's warlike bishop was a Ghibelline, but her exiled children and their adherents in the city were all Guelphs, and vainly aspired to a popular form of government similar to that established in Florence. Siena changed her policy from year to year ; just now she was Guelph with Florence, yet barely twenty-five years had passed since the battle of Montaperti, and four more would see Campaldino.

But in the *Vita* all these solemn and tragic

realities give place to the poetic dreams of a soul's romance. Actually and outwardly Dante is not alone, being "in the company of many others," but inwardly in his soul he is riding in absolute solitude, his thoughts of love the only companions he can tolerate. The paradox of the great African, "It is when I am doing nothing that I am doing the most; never do I feel myself less alone than when I am alone," may be well applied to the mediæval psychology of those dreaming "servants of Love." Dante says of himself that, "Although I was in the company of many according to the outward view, this going displeased me so greatly that my sighs were scarce able to disperse the anguish which my heart did feel, because that I was separating myself from mine happiness." It is difficult to realise that these were the words of one of those fiery men of the thirteenth century, riding out to war beneath the banner of his Commune. It is true that he was a poet, but he was a poet who sang that the Lily of his Florence must never be reversed in an enemy's hand, held that the arms of the great families de-rived their chief glory from having been borne in the martial undertakings of their country, and, in the ice-bound depths of Hell, fell furiously upon that traitor to his flag, Bocca degli Abati, not with hard words alone, but with hands and feet as well. Such was the true poet, and what the poet was, that also was the man. In the *Vita Nuova*, on the contrary, the man is but a rhymer, whose verse embroiders upon a ground of fact the unreal fantasies and graceful dreams of love, and who produces a book which is indeed based upon truth, but whose colouring, figures and action are entirely imaginary.

The picture of Dante dolorously sighing amongst the knights of the cavalcade is quite as imaginary as was the personage who, invisible to all the rest, joined the company and discoursed to the poet of love, inspiring him with a sonnet by the way. This personage was Love himself, who, attired as a poor pilgrim, was supposed to have wandered thither from the city where dwelt that lady of whom Dante had already made mention. His eyes were bent upon the ground in apparent fear, and he cast hasty glances at the shining waters of the Arno, which, according to Dante's habit of turning the real into an abstract image, is only mentioned as a "transparent and beautiful stream" flowing beside the road traversed by the poet. An instance of this mingling of reality and imagination is the fact that love is called an apparition, and that even the image of the pilgrim-god is presently changed, in this ninth chapter of the *Vita Nuova*, into a mere sentiment. This image of Love, however, is here represented as being somewhat shy towards the other members of the cavalcade, and when he vanishes Dante continues to ride accompanied by silence and sighs as before.

The *Vita Nuova* is a book whose colouring, figures and action are imaginary, but which is based upon a foundation of reality. Real are all the facts and circumstances of daily life to which the figures and deeds and all those love rhymes refer; real are the personages alluded to; real is it as far as Dante Alighieri and Beatrice are concerned, or the two gentlewomen of whom he made use for his defence, whether introduced for this reason alone or because they had been admired by the Poet in his youth. The obsequies of Beatrice's friend and father are real, as is also her brother's friendship with Dante, just as real as was Dante's friendship with him to whom the *Vita Nuova* is dedicated and who—though the name, as every other, is concealed—is unmistakably shown to have been Guido Cavalcanti. Real were those fair Florentines enumerated in the *Serventese* of the lovely women of the city, who in various ways took part in the psychological development of the story—real, even to the gentle lady who dwelt near the house of the Alighieri and aroused a transitory love in the heart of Beatrice's adorer, and the pilgrims who passed through Florence on their way to Rome. The inspiration of the Poem, first vaguely conceived as a celestial glorification of Beatrice, is equally real. Her personality, living and true and Florentine like the others, was first idealised into an abstract woman— after the manner of all poets—and then transfigured and upraised to the sublimity of a symbol by the work of him who, finally conscious of his work, knew that he had "said of her things said never yet of any woman."

Recalling a previous reflection upon Boccaccio's veracity, it may be asked to what extent his authority is to be accepted when he declares that Beatrice was of the Portinari family, and the daughter of Folco. It is, however, one thing to say that the *Treatise* of Messer Giovanni amplifies and colours, or even invents, details and circumstances, in order to render events more vivid, but another thing to say that when he asserts a fact, that fact must not be believed. The question in this case is one of fact—that a Florentine citizen, not later than the year 1363 or 1364, affirmed certain facts about a flourishing and well-known family—specifically that a woman of that family, the grandchildren of whose brother or sister must then have been actually living in Florence, and as easily recognisable by the old men of the city as was Ciacco by Dante, because they were all born before factions ruined the city—was the Beatrice of Dante's poem. Further, as explicitly declared in the *Comento* a few years later—Boccaccio affirmed this " according to the narrative of a trustworthy person, who was acquainted with her, and very closely allied to her by blood." Nowadays, we can only guess who was this Portinari by searching dry burial registers or poring over the leaves of genealogical tables, but the contemporaries of Messer Giovanni Boccaccio needed only to look about in order to determine her identity with some member of the Portinari family who was alive at the date in question. Failing a likely identification, the vaunted authority would have been proved null and void. "What nonsense do you tell us?" Florence would have cried to Messer Giovanni, who in the church of Santo Stefano di Badia—now destroyed —was expounding the writings of Dante by word of mouth. This expounding was according to the solemn provisions decreed in the Councils of the Commune, and caused great stirring of the citizens' memories, so that it would have been worse than folly for any man, this man in particular, wilfully and for no possible reason to propound not a rhetorical flower or an oratorical amplification, but a simple bald falsehood.

To pass from argument to fact, the following small addition to the biography of the great writer of Certaldo is of some interest in connection with our subject. Amongst the *fattori*[1] in the bank of the Bardi, there was from 1336 to 1338 a certain "Boccaccio Ghellini (Chellini) of Certaldo." Other *fattori* of the Bardi, with equal interests in the business, were several Portinari, descendants and partisans of Folco—an Andrea, a Ricovero di Folchetto, a Sangallo di Grifo, a Lorenzo di Stagio,

---

[1] *Fattori* were commercial agents of a firm or company.

and a Ubertino di Gherardo di Folco, who lived
in Paris to look after the Bardi affairs and died there
in 1339. This man was a nephew of Beatrice Portinari. As the son of this Boccaccio of the bank,
Giovanni Boccaccio would have ample chances of
forming intimate relations with both Bardi and
Portinari, and when he asserts that he obtained the
identification of Dante's Beatrice with Beatrice
Portinari from a near relative of the latter, we might
surely credit his word even without the concurrent
identification found in the terms of Folco Portinari's own will. But another witness of great
authority, earlier than Boccaccio and quite independent of him, has recently been added to the list
of those confirming the identity of Dante's Beatrice
with Folco's daughter. In the *Comento* of Pietro
Alighieri—according to the new reading in an
authentic codex which has returned to Italy
amongst the Ashburnham manuscripts—occurs
this passage : " It must first be said, however, that
a certain lady named Madonna Beatrice, greatly
esteemed for her manners and her beauty, did
actually dwell in Florence during the lifetime of
the author, being born of a family of certain
Florentine citizens who were called the Portinari.
Whilst she lived, this lady was admired and beloved
by the author Dante, who composed many songs in
her praise ; and after that she was dead, in order to
exalt her name, it is thought that she appeareth

many times in his poem in the allegory and character
of Theology." Thus, about 1360, wrote in Verona,
where he lived as a judge of excellent repute, the
son of Dante himself. This authentic and independent testimony is again in perfect accord with
the will of Folco Portinari, wherein in 1288 he
mentions " Madonna Bice, his daughter, and wife
to Messer Simone de' Bardi." [1]

There is but little information to be added concerning the married life of Madonna Beatrice, who,
according to the *Vita Nuova*, died in the June of
1290, in all the mysticism of the number nine—the
ninth decade of the century, the ninth day of the
month according to the Arabian calendar, and the
ninth month according to the Syrian calendar. Concerning Beatrice's husband, however, students have
discovered that in 1290, during the Guelph war
against Arezzo, he was councillor of the Commune with Messer Amerigo di Nerbona, captain of
the Taglia in the name of King Charles of Anjou ;
that in June 1301, after certain negotiations with
the Counts Guidi, he took part in an attempt of the
Blacks to overcome the Whites (as they succeeded
in doing), and was sentenced on this account. It is
also alleged that upon the victory of the Blacks in
October 1302, he became officer of taxes and con-

[1] Folco's will was published in 1759 by the Jesuit, Giuseppe
Richa, in a History of the Florentine churches.

K

tributions under the Commune. The two first facts are both true and consistent with the position of a knight and nobleman, but the last-named office was only assigned to one of the people, and could not, therefore, have been held by this Simone, who has been confused with his kinsman of the same name. The mercantile books of the Bardi—preserved in the private archives of the Ginori family in Florence —prove that the same names are constantly recurring among the members of this very numerous family. I have, however, traced the identity of Beatrice's husband beyond all doubt, as by the courtesy of the Marquis Carlo Ginori I was permitted to examine these documents which yet await a study worthy of their importance.

In one of those voluminous registers are found, in the same year 1310, the names of four brothers, Cino, Bartolo, Gualtieri, and Messer Lapo, the sons of Messer Jacopo ; Messer Nestagio di Bardi ; Messer *Simone* di Geri, and Puccino di *Simone*. Thus at the end of the thirteenth century and beginning of the fourteenth, there were two men named Simone in the Bardi family. Of these, Simone di Messer Jacopo, brother of Cino, Bartolo, Gualtieri and Lapo, who was the officer of Contributions in 1302, had been one of the Priori in 1287, and a councillor of the Commune in 1278 ; he died in 1310, and in the registers of that great mercantile company of the Bardi, his sons, "Puccini and brothers,"

are inscribed in his place. The other, Messer
Simone di Geri, knight, councillor in the Guelph
army with Amerigo di Nerbona, partisan of the
Donati faction—of the Black Guelphs—and their
representative with the Counts Guidi, was undoubtedly the Messer Simone de' Bardi mentioned
in Folco's will as the husband of Madonna Bice de'
Portinari, of whom records exist until the year
1315. One of the ancient commentaries on Dante's
Poem, moreover, contains the sentence, "Mona
Beatrice, who was daughter to Folco de' Portinari
of Florence, and wife to Messere Simone di Geri
de' Bardi of Florence."

There were two men named Simone, therefore;
a plain Simone, son of Messer Jacopo, and a
Messer Simone, son of Geri. The title of *Messere*
was by no means a title given merely out of com-
pliment, or which could be used or not at desire;
it was only given to judges—doctors of law, *i.e.*—
knights, or those who enjoyed some ecclesiastical
dignity. Thus, neither in his will nor in the
Prioristi,[1] nor elsewhere, is this title of *Messere*
applied to Folco Portinari; and neither Guido
Cavalcanti nor Dante himself ever had the right to
use it. It was a title reserved strictly for those
entitled to it for one of the above-mentioned
reasons, and it conferred on the holder a certain

[1] *Prioristi* are the lists of the Priori belonging to the different
families of the Florentine State.

position in the eyes of the people. An old chronicler, Donato Velluti, relates of a certain "Castellano Frescobaldi, who afterwards became Messer Castellano, how he went to be made a knight in Naples by the hand of King Ruberto" —the same who also made poets.

Simone di Messer Jacopo, he of the Contributions and the Priori, reared five children, but no record or document of any kind has yet been found to prove that Messer Simone di Geri had any off-spring. Madonna Beatrice still remains without direct descendants.

Folco's daughter clearly had no children, none at least alive, when her father's will was made in 1288, nor does she appear to have had any between this date and that of her death. Dante expressly relates in the *Vita Nuova* that his Beatrice died in the June of 1290, and although no documents prove that Beatrice Portinari died upon this date, none contradict it, seeing that the only document in which she is mentioned proves her to have been alive in 1288 and wife to Messer Simone. This lack of descendants accords well with the lady whose death, according to the chronology of the *Vita Nuova*, occurred only two and a half years after the date of the will. The death described in the *Vita Nuova* is certainly that of a Florentine lady who died in Florence upon a definite date, not a date chosen arbitrarily by the author. Exercising his

ingenuity thrice to find in this date the mystic
number nine, Dante thereby identifies with it the
" lady of his thoughts," and concludes with the
statement that " she herself was a nine ; that is to
say, a miracle, the root of which is the Trinity
itself." He analyses the year, month and day of
this date according to three calendars, finding it to
be the ninth of the month of the second Giumâdâ,
of the year of the Hegira 689 of the Mussulman
calendar, which corresponds with June 19th, 1290,
according to our reckoning. Had Beatrice been
merely " the lady of his thoughts," or one of the
many abstractions supported by the opponents of
the idea that she was a real woman, Dante surely
would not have invoked the Mahometan or Syrian
calendars in order to juggle the mystic numbers
from a date which refused them to any process of
Christian reckoning.

So far as documents are concerned, the date of
Beatrice's marriage is also uncertain. We do not
even know in which year the beautiful child of
the May festival in the quarter of Porta San Piero
passed over into the splendid houses of the Bardi
and took up her abode within those dark walls,
strongly fortified against citizen aggression, which
stood, and still stand, " near the bridge of Ruba-
conte " upon the further side of the Arno. Since,
however, these alliances were usually made at a
very early age, and for the sake of domestic or civil

interests, two families, rather than a youth and
a maiden, becoming united to satisfy ambition or
to heal feuds, it is more than likely that Beatrice
was already married when Dante again beheld her
in 1283. The *Rime* twice refers to her as "Monna
Bice," and the title Monna or Madonna, like that of
Messere, was only applied to persons of a recognised
civil standing, others being denoted by their name
alone. The Alighieri and Donati marriage was
probably of the same kind, and many recent dissertations upon the subject of Madonna Bice and
Madonna Gemma would have been of greater value
had they been based upon those known facts which
explain certain passages in the *Vita Nuova*, supposed to refer to the marriage either of Dante or of
Beatrice.

For such reasons, therefore, it is almost certain
that the respective marriages of the Poet and his
Lady were events entirely outside of, and indifferent
to, the psychological drama of the *Vita Nuova*, and
consequently it is useless to seek references or allusions to them in any episode of the book. Dante's
sympathetic neighbour, who also appears in the *Convivio* as a symbol of Philosophy, was a real living
Florentine, but she was certainly not Gemma, who
was probably by that time the mother of his children. In reading this book, a clear distinction must
be drawn between history and psychology. To the
psychological narrative, which is composed of facts

represented, according to the mediæval school of love, without any regard for reality, belong the visions and dreams, the hyperbolical descriptions of the effect produced by the sight of Beatrice upon the Poet or on others, the trances into which he falls and the various ladies who then appear to him, the questions of casuistry or love dogma scattered here and there throughout the tale, the grief of the citizens of Florence, and the epistle of condolence on Beatrice's death. The historical probability of these and other similar things may be very justly doubted, if we consider human nature in general, and human nature in the Florence of those times in particular, but it must not, therefore, be concluded that the *Vita Nuova* is entirely deficient in historical truth, and that Beatrice was a mere myth, as is sometimes supposed. Of events which actually happened it contains few, but those few cannot be overlooked without injury to the story. It is needless to enumerate them here, but such, for instance, as the death of Beatrice's friend, the departure from Florence of the gentlewoman whom Dante feigned to admire, the Guelph expedition, Dante's illness, during which he was nursed by his sister, his friendship with Guido Cavalcanti and with Beatrice's brother — probably Manetto — the positive statement that she was nine and eighteen years of age on the dates at which he saw her, the reckoning of her death according to the three calendars, and the death of her father, are all facts which bear unmistakable evidence of having been taken from life. The date of her father's death as given in the *Vita Nuova* corresponds with that of the death of Folco Portinari, namely, December 31, 1289, and Dante writes of his Lady's father that "as many persons believe and as is assuredly true, he was good in a very high degree." Certainly there is no tomb upon which these words might be more justly inscribed than upon that of the man whose goodness bequeathed to his fellow-citizens a work of charity as everlasting and inexhaustible as is the human pain and misery that it relieves.

It is not possible here to study the whole of the *Vita Nuova* under this twofold aspect. Such a study, moreover, would lead, on the one hand, to the complete divesting of the Poet's biography of everything in his youthful period which did not belong to actual fact, and, on the other, it would reduce to their true value all those traditional affirmations perpetually repeated since Boccaccio first gave utterance to them. One of these assertions is that the marriage of Dante with Gemma Donati—Beatrice's marriage is never mentioned—was arranged by his family to console him for the death of Beatrice. Herein is a confusion of two orders of things which are entirely separate and distinct from each other. It is, of course, quite possible that Dante's marriage may have preceded

the death of Beatrice, but there are various reasons
for believing the contrary—Boccaccio's declaration,
and certain unpleasing but definite records of
Dante's worldly life, namely the sonnets relating
to the *Dispute with Forese Donati*, and to those years
spent together in dissolute living to which he alludes when he meets the virtuous Nella's repentant
husband amongst the sinners making atonement
in the sixth circle.[1] If this moral lapse was one of
the misdeeds of which Beatrice accuses him in
cantos **xxx.** and **xxxi.** of the *Purgatorio*, as having
been committed after her death and in forgetfulness
of her, these sonnets must have been written subsequent to June 1290. This would confirm Boccaccio's statement that the marriage took place after
Beatrice's death, but the dissolute Dante of these
revelations hardly agrees with his description of the
weeping and desolate poet, provided by his relatives
with a wife as consolation.

Whenever Dante's marriage may have taken
place, there is nothing by which it can in any way be
connected with the death of Beatrice, or attributed
to any particular condition of mind. If we choose
to believe all that Boccaccio relates, however, we
may trace a close and detailed connection between
the two events. His *Trattatello*, or Treatise, describes how " the most beauteous Beatrice " died at
the close of her twenty-fourth year, and repeats

---

[1] *Purgatorio*, xxiii. 115–117.

all the laments, sighs and despair of the *Vita Nuova*
—with literal interpretations and numerous addi-
tions. Boccaccio here describes the consolation
offered by his kindred, to which, after long resistance, Dante finally listens :—

" Then, in order not only that they might draw
him out of his grief but might also make him joyful,
they proceeded to take counsel together to give
him a wife ; and thus, in like manner as the lady
whom he had lost had been the cause of his sadness,
so the lady he had newly gained should be the cause
of mirth. And when they had found a maiden who
would be suitable unto his condition, with all the
arguments which they deemed would persuade him
did they discover unto him their intentions. But
since without spending much time upon the narrative, I cannot touch particularly upon each thing,
I can only say that after long resistance their arguments prevailed. He was married."

Upon this follows, as unexpected, as it is a
furious, invective against the marriage of men of
learning, to whom, as we have already seen, this
rigid censor would even forbid love, while poor
Madonna Gemma—although not by name—is
accused of being a tiresome wife, an accusation
unwarranted by a single page of the scanty few
in which the *Life of Dante* alludes to her.

One piece of consolation, offered to Dante on the

death of Beatrice, was very different from that
described by the novelist-biographer. This consolation, addressed by one poet to another, one
lover to another, contains imagery gracefully interwoven with that of Dante's own love poems. The
Canzone a Dante per la Morte di Beatrice, came from
his friend, the poet Messer Cino of Pistoia, who
shared with Guido Cavalcanti and Beatrice's brother
the warmest sentiments of friendship which Dante's
heart could feel. Excusing himself for not having
sooner called upon Pity and Love to come and console Dante in his grief, he urges him to be brave,
and teaches him how to find comfort in hope and
in the thought of Beatrice herself.[1]

TO DANTE ALIGHIERI

CANZONE ON THE DEATH OF BEATRICE PORTINARI

Albeit my prayers have not so long delay'd,
  But craved for thee, ere this, that Pity and Love
  Which only bring our heavy life some rest ;
Yet is not now the time so much o'erstay'd
  But that these words of mine which tow'rds thee move
  Must find thee still with spirit dispossess'd,
  And say to thee : " In Heaven she now is bless'd
  Even as the blessed name men call'd her by ;
    While thou dost ever cry,

---

[1] In place of Senator Del Lungo's prose transcription of this
poem, I give the beautiful version by Dante Gabriel Rossetti,
published amongst his " Translations from Early Italian Poets."
(*Trans.*)

' Alas ! the blessing of mine eyes is flown ! ' "
    Behold, these words set down
   Are needed still, for still thou sorrowest.
Then hearken ; I would yield advisedly
Some comfort : stay these sighs : give ear to me.

We know for certain that in this blind world
   Each man's subsistence is of grief and pain,
    Still trail'd by fortune through all bitterness :
At last the flesh within a shroud is furl'd,
   And into Heaven's rejoicing doth attain
    The joyful soul made free of earthly stress.
   Then wherefore sighs thy heart in abjectness,
Which for her triumph should exult aloud ?
      For He the Lord our God
Hath call'd her, hearkening what her Angel said,
     To have Heaven perfected.
   Each saint for a new thing beholds her face,
And she the face of our Redemption sees,
Discoursing with immortal substances.

Why now do pangs of torment clutch thy heart
   Which with thy love should make thee overjoy'd,
    As him whose intellect hath pass'd the skies ?
Behold, the spirits of thy life depart
   Daily to Heaven with her, they so are buoy'd
    With their desire, and Love so bids them rise.
   O God ! and thou, a man whom God made wise,
To nurse a charge of care, and love the same !
     I tell thee in His Name
From sin of sighing grief to hold thy breath,
     Nor let thy heart to death,
   Nor harbour death's resemblance in thine eyes.
God hath her with Himself eternally,
Yet she inhabits every hour with thee.

Be comforted, Love cries, be comforted!
  Devotion pleads, Peace, for the love of God!
  O yield thyself to prayers so full of grace;
And make thee naked now of this dull weed
  Which 'neath thy foot were better to be trod;
  For man through grief despairs and ends his days.
  How ever should'st thou see the lovely face
If any desperate death should once be thine?
        From justice so condign
Withdraw thyself even now; that in the end
        Thy heart may not offend
  Against thy soul, which in the holy place,
In Heaven, still hopes to see her and to be
Within her arms.   Let this hope comfort thee.

Look thou into the pleasure wherein dwells
  Thy lovely lady who is in Heaven crown'd,
  Who is herself thy hope in Heaven, the while
To make thy memory hallow'd she avails;
  Being a soul within the deep Heaven bound,
  A face on thy heart painted, to beguile
  Thy heart of grief which else should turn it vile.
Even as she seem'd a wonder here below,
        On high she seemeth so,—
Yea, better known, is there more wondrous yet.
        And even as she was met
  First by the angels with sweet song and smile,
Thy spirit bears her back upon the wing,
Which often in those ways is journeying.

Of thee she entertains the blessed throngs,
  And says to them: "While yet my body thrave
  On earth, I gat much honour which he gave,

Commending me in his commended songs."
Also she asks alway of God our Lord
To give thee peace according to His word.

Dante did not forget the *Canzone* of Messer
Cino, and included it amongst the examples of his
Pistojese friend's writings quoted in his *Volgare
Eloquenza*. Neither must it be forgotten that this
faithful friend and companion laid another tribute
of Tuscan poetry upon Dante's own tomb, as by
that time he had already done upon the grave of
their beloved Emperor, the "great Henry." Of
the Emperor, with whom died also the hopes
of the exiles, Cino sang that in heaven he had
been reunited with his virtuous wife, Margaret
of Brabant, who was another victim of that fatal
Italian expedition. For Dante he prays God that
he may be sheltered in the lap of Beatrice, and he
inveighs against that "iniquitous sect" which enriched Ravenna with the treasure that Florence
lost.

A few years later, L'Ottimo, one of the earliest
and best commentators of the *Commedia*, placed
Cino's consolatory poem to Dante side by side with
the latter's verses in honour of Beatrice, " when she
was bodily amongst the mortals." The names of
the two poets and their ladies were, also, united
by the poet of love, Francesco Petrarch, in his
Triumphs. " Here are Dante and Beatrice, here
Selvaggia and Cino of Pistoia," thus in a manner

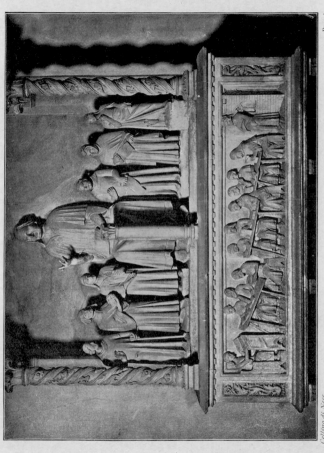

Cellino di Nese.   *Brogi.*

THE TOMB OF CINO SINIBALDI. THE BAS-RELIEF REPRESENTS HIM LECTURING
TO HIS PUPILS, AMONGST WHOM IS PETRARCH.

(Pistoia : The Cathedral.)

satisfying the wish and complaint of Cino, who
desired that in Dante's Paradise his Selvaggia
should be given a seat of glory by the side of
Beatrice.

These poetical lines of Messer Cino, and not the
domestic romancings of Boccaccio, were the consolations received by Dante on the death of " the
lady of his thoughts." And if they reached him
in the midst of those youthful wanderings from the
right way, they must surely have awakened within
him the consciousness that he was straying from all
those noble and gracious ideals which he had associated with that "lofty vision" from the other world.
As far as actual facts were concerned, however, the
poet-lover of Selvaggia Vergiolesi could have sent
those verses equally well even had he already become the husband of Margherita degli Ughi, and
father of several children, and the poet-lover of
Beatrice Portinari might have received them with
propriety even at the side of Madonna Gemma
Donati, and surrounded by the sons who were one
day to comment upon their father's poem. Thus
Guido Cavalcanti sent his last ballad from the
marshes of the frontier "direct unto his lady,"
and hidden from the knowledge of vulgar persons,
though he well knew that his wife and sons awaited
him at home, and that in their arms he would meet
death. And when Dante went forth into that exile

from which he never returned, and as "the first arrow from this bow" felt the pain of leaving behind him "everything most dearly beloved," his wife remained to watch over the desolate house, whilst he bore with him, amidst the hard realities of life, the ideals of his affection and his intellect, the superb mystery of his soul, the conception of his divine Poem.

In that conception Beatrice reigned supreme, but supreme among other and real women—holy Rachel and Leah, Lucy and Our Lady; human, like herself, Beatrice. The action of the Poem commences with the lament of the gentle and divine Lady, and the pity of Lucy, for the man lost amidst the tribulations of life in the world, and closes with the triumph of Mary, and the prayers addressed to her by men through the mouths of the saints. Between are the two figures of Matelda and Beatrice ; Beatrice is the foremost, but they are both ministers of the grace of God in the conversion of Dante—ministers of the sublime and comforting truths of the spirit amidst the miseries of want and crime, and the blows and disappointments of this life. In the presence of Beatrice who, lost to his sight for ten stormy years, has become the heavenly symbol of the height to which a human being can ascend through contemplation of the divine ; in the presence of Beatrice, " the glory of the human race," Dante, with repentant tears, accuses himself for his infidelity—infidelity to his poetic lady, to the woman, to the symbol. Symbol, woman and poetic lady, these three were inseparably united in Beatrice, but that for which the poet wept in his remorse was the woman, Beatrice Portinari—a name henceforth never to be erased, whether from the history of her century or from the eternal memory of mankind.

CHAPTER IV

THE RENAISSANCE AND THE LAST YEARS
OF FREEDOM

In the year 1473 the customary splendour with
which the Feast of St. John was celebrated was enhanced by the magnificence of the reception accorded to Eleonora of Aragon, daughter of the
King of Naples and bride of Ercole d'Este, Duke
of Ferrara and Modena, a reception which agreed
with the traditions of the artisan republic, and was
also favoured by the Medici. When the young
bride entered Florence on June 22, she found the
shops decorated with the utmost gorgeousness
which the wealth of the merchants enabled them to
display; she witnessed the procession of the "Companies " of boys dressed in white as young angels ;
she saw the stages set up in the Piazza del Signoria,
on which were to be represented scenes from the
Old and New Testaments, the offerings made to
the church of their Patron, Saint John, by the Signoria and the other magistrates of the Commune
and the Guilds, and the Companies of the People
with their banners. The Guelph party, and the

subordinate or dependent Signori and Communes, brought banners or flags of great value and beauty, and immense wax tapers painted with historical figures and wreathed with flowers. Then came the offering of olive-branches by the prisoners and the condemned—a custom to which Dante refused to submit,—and finally, on the afternoon of June 24, were seen the splendid horses, which had been previously presented and were now to run in the race for richly embroidered material to make the banner of St. John. The course for this race, starting from the " Prato," or meadow by the city gate, passed through the Via della Vigna, the Market and the Corso, and ended towards the Porta alla Croce.

The old men of Florence still remember this course, for it was used in quite recent times. But very different from anything which the oldest of them can remember must have been the pleasures prepared for Madonna Eleonora at that June fes tival of 1473. Among several palaces fronting the Arno, upon the green meadow on the outskirts of the city, whence the horses started for their race, stood the Palazzo Lenzi, now the Pisani Gallery; there in the open air heavy with the scent of flowers from the surrounding gardens and loggias, a dance was prepared. The old diaries are silent concerning this ball; the journalists of four hundred years ago left no records in their dry pages of the dresses donned for their admirers' benefit by those fair

women who survive for us in the pictures of Botticelli and the frescoes of Ghirlandajo.   Yet, a
Florentine ball at the time of the Renaissance deserved to be described by a poet.   Then dancers,
undazzled by the glare of modern artificial light,
were bathed in the soft glow of the afternoon sun
before it set behind the Pignone ; they were not
deafened by the thumpings of the band each time
the dance brought them near it, but moved to the
amorous strains of the lute and the viola, and the
graceful rhythm of *The Song of the Dance*.   Let me
here recall the description of such a festival left
by Angelo Poliziano, the recorder and gossip of
the elegant lords and ladies of those days, in whose
smooth Latin couplets we find accurate pictures of
the life of the time combined with the imagery of
art, truth with fancy, all that was Florentine and
Christian with classic paganism—the very atmosphere breathed by scholars and artists in Florence
under the most magnificent Lorenzo :—

"The rosy-faced Apollo has already led
forth the day which brings again the feast of
Saint John the Baptist, when to the city, once
a colony of Silla, are directed the white feet
of the King's daughter, who, having left the
city of the Sirens to become the bride of Ercole, desires to rest upon her long journey.
Her arrival is hailed with the utmost rejoicing
by children, by young and old alike, by mat-

rons and by brides radiant in their fresh beauty;
the whole city is aroused, and there is a sound
of joy in every place. There is a street which
the Florentines call Pantagia,[1] where stands a
splendid temple dedicated to all the celestial
beings. There rises the superb palace of the
Lenzi; close by smiles the green stretch of
meadows, and the fruitful earth is decked in
all the colours of the Spring. Whilst the
coursers are pawing the ground at the start-
ing-place, waiting for the signal to spring forward in the race, the regal maiden abandons
herself to the graceful delights of the dance,
and now behold all the fair ladies engaged in
the mazes and the measured steps of the ball!
Foremost amongst all the nymphs shines the
beautiful Albiera, and her beauty sheds around
it the trembling light of its own splendour.
Fanned by the wind, her hair floats over her
white shoulders while her black eyes send
forth rays of gentle light; among her companions she seems the morning star by whose
rosy brightness the lesser stars are eclipsed.
Young and old, all admire Albiera; of iron
must he be formed whose manhood is unmoved at sight of her virginal beauty! With
delight, with applause, with gestures, with
looks and voice, all praise Albiera."

[1] A Greek name for Borgognissanti.

Albiera di Maso degli Albizzi was a girl between fifteen and sixteen years of age, the betrothed of Gismondo della Stufa.   She fell ill immediately after this ball, and died in a few days.

" Alas, poor Albiera ! " cries her poet, " to be reft so young from parents and bridegroom! Who now will trust in human fortune when thy beauty is destroyed by cruel death, oh, Albiera !   Gone is thy face of lilies and roses ; gone are thy bright eyes whereat Love lighted his torch, and thy hair which made thee like unto Diana the huntress when it flowed loose over thy shoulders, and was as the adornment of Cytherea when twisted in a golden crown around thy head.   The Loves and the Graces had made thee lovely without thy knowledge ; every virtue was thine, modesty and seemliness of behaviour, good sense, discretion, loyalty, cheerfulness, fair manners, grace, sincerity : yet are now all become but a handful of ashes ! "

Elsewhere in the long elegy the poet, in mythological terms, describes the long illness of Albiera, whose beauty, he declares, attracted the envious notice of Nemesis, the mysterious goddess. Therefore, when the maiden had returned home from the ball at the hour when night is falling, and modern ladies are only just commencing their toilettes for the balls of to-day, the dread deity Fever, sent by

Nemesis to that unfortunate house, crept up to her bed as soon as she had lain down to rest. For ten anxious days her parents, her brothers, and her betrothed hung over the pale and disfigured face; she bade the last farewells to her dear ones and to life, which was fading from her ere it had well commenced, and then, amidst the despairing tears of her family, she died. Death restored peace to her countenance, which appeared as though she slept. Her fellow-citizens surrounded her inanimate body with mourning and sympathy ; the "nymph" who had fallen a victim to the goddesses Nemesis and Fever was given Christian burial, and the Ovidian couplets of Messer Angelo transform even this. He describes the funeral, the open bier covered with a black cloth and the dead girl lying on it, her hair cut close, and a wreath of flowers round her head. The priests surround her, chanting psalms ; the bells toll ; she is followed by the entire population dressed in mourning, and amongst them walks the bereaved bridegroom, at whom all point with compassionate finger. In the church of San Pier Maggiore the candles are lighted and the incense is burning ; the priest gives absolution and benediction, and the tomb of the Albizzi opens to receive the young bride. The poet does not say whether she was buried in the habit of a nun, as was the custom, but the fact that her hair was cut short renders this probable.

This elegy, and other minor dirges by Poliziano, were not the only tributes to the memory of Albiera from the Latin muse of Florentine humanism. Her death called forth more elegiacs and laments than did even that of the beautiful Simonetta, which took place only two years later. But art in another form contributed to the apotheosis of Simonetta Cattaneo, a Genoese who came to Florence in 1469, as the sixteen-year-old bride of Marco Vespucci, also but sixteen years old, and died of consumption in 1476. Unless some industrious investigator can succeed in discovering the marble bust which Poliziano mentions as having been made by order of her betrothed, there is nothing to recall the girlish features of Albiera, but there is, on the contrary, some difficulty in selecting the true one amongst the many supposed portraits of Simonetta. Some find her likeness in the picture in the Pitti Gallery, attributed to Sandro Botticelli, of a delicate blonde with a long neck and gentle, thoughtful face, dressed in modest, middle-class fashion ; but this is more probably the portrait of a lady who lived half a century earlier. Others point to a picture beneath which is inscribed the name of "Simonetta Ianuensis Vespuccia," preserved in the gallery at Chantilly, the supposed work of either Pollaiuolo or Piero di Cosimo. Again represented as a fair and delicate figure, she is this time full of gaiety and bright beauty : the long neck is bare, as also the bust and

Botticelli (?)   Alinari.

SIMONETTA CATTANEO.
(Florence: The Pitti Gallery.)

shoulders; the hair is drawn back and twisted into artificial ropes with pearls and precious stones, and round the neck hangs a medal or order encircled by a snake. The Berlin picture called "The Fair Simonetta," by Botticelli, represents, in startling contrast, a woman of quite a different type, stout and massive. There are, again, certain curious resemblances between one of the allegorical figures in the mysterious "Spring" in the Florence Accademia and Poliziano's *Stanze*, wherein Simonetta Cattaneo, mentioned by name in the act of being transformed into a nymph, is poetically described —although not in a manner to disturb her husband's peace of mind—as the beloved of Giuliano de' Medici. It is probable that this poetic couple is depicted in the misnamed "Venus and Mars" of Botticelli, in the London National Gallery, for the female head bears a strong resemblance to yet another supposed portrait of Simonetta, the other beautiful "Ignota" by Botticelli in the Museum at Frankfort.

Whichever of these various pictures is the true likeness of the fair young wife who died in April 1476, it only concerns us here to recall the fact that amongst the many poets who wrote laments for her, both in Latin and Italian, Poliziano made her the mythological heroine of his *Stanze;* he also dedicated a number of funeral poems to her memory, for several of which Giuliano de' Medici, the " Julio " of the *Stanze*, furnished the ideas. It is a proof, moreover, of the ideal and poetic admiration felt by the two brothers for the beauty of Simonetta, that Lorenzo himself derived from her death the motive for his musings on the subject of the soul's return to the stars. Lorenzo, at that time at Pisa, received daily bulletins concerning the condition of the patient, to attend whom he had sent his own physician. The Archives of Florence also contain some curious reports by Piero Vespucci, Simonetta's brother-in-law.

Thus, on April 18, 1476, we find: "Simonetta is in almost the same condition as when you departed, and there is but little improvement. We do attend upon Master Stefano and all the other physicians with diligence, and shall always do their bidding."

The report of April 20 contains more cheerful news : " A few days ago I did write unto you of the illness of Simonetta, the which, by God's mercy and by the skill of Master Stefano sent by you, hath considerably improved ; there is less fever and less weakness, less hardness of breathing, and she doth eat and sleep better. According to the physicians her sickness will be of long duration, and there is but little remedy for it save good nursing. And seeing that ye are the cause of this improvement, we all, and her mother who

Botticelli.

Accademia, Florence.

PRIMAVERA.

The figure of Flora is a traditional likeness of Simonetta Cattaneo; that of Mercury of Giuliano de' Medici.

is at Piombino, do earnestly give you thanks, and are much indebted unto you for this proof of your friendship on the occasion of her illness. We would not be guilty of ingratitude towards the Master, yet to keep him here so long as the sickness shall endure is neither very necessary, nor would it be possible for us to repay such an obligation with sufficient money. Wherefore do I pray you to send for the aforesaid Master Stefano, and to advise us how much we should give him; he did come upon Good Friday. And we shall always be ready to do everything for the which we have become indebted, and especially shall we endeavour to deserve this and every other honour which ye have done us. I now await your advice, and we do remain . . ."

The improvement was not maintained, however, as Lorenzo was to learn six days later: "*Magnifice ac præstantissime vir, compater honorandissime, etc.* I wrote unto you some days ago of the improvement in Simonetta, yet hath this not continued as I did expect and as we did desire. This night came Master Stefano and Master Moyse to consult together concerning the giving of a medicine unto her; they did decide that she must take it, and so it was done. We cannot tell yet what fruit it will bear, but God grant it be according to our desires! Upon another occasion I did write unto you concerning my difficulty with regard to the rewarding and payment of Master Stefano, but since I have not received any answer from you it hath seemed unto me better to do nothing whatever. Therefore it pleaseth me that he should remain here yet eight days longer, for in that time it should be seen what will be the ending of the sickness. I do not, however, put a limit unto the time of his remaining, unless I know that this is your intention; for which reason I should esteem two lines of reply saying what is your opinion. These physicians are not agreed upon the question of her sickness; Master Stefano declareth that it is neither a hectic fever nor yet a consumption, and Master Moyse holdeth the contrary. I know not which of them is right. I do commend myself unto your Magnificence of Florence, xxij aprelis MCCCCLXXVI. M. tie V. quicquid est Petrus Vespuccius eques."

After her death, an intimate friend wrote to Lorenzo: "The blessed soul of Simonetta hath gone to Paradise, as ye have heard. Truly may it be said that it hath been a second Triumph of Death, for verily, if ye had seen her as she lay dead, ye would have deemed her not less beautiful and graceful than when she was alive. *Requiescat in*

VILLA GUICCIARDINI : POPPIANO.

pace." It is related that after the reception of the news, Lorenzo went out into the calm spring night to walk with a friend, and as he was speaking of the dead lady he suddenly stopped and gazed at a star which had never before seemed to him so brilliant. " See," he exclaimed, " either the soul of that most gentle lady hath been transformed into that new star, or else hath it been joined together thereunto." Walking on another occasion during this same spring in the gardens of one of his splendid villas, he noticed a sunflower, which " at evening remains with its face turned towards the western horizon that hath taken from it the vision of the sun, until in the morning the sun appeareth again in the east," and herein he beheld a symbol of our own destiny when we lose one whom we love, which destiny is to remain " with the thoughts turned towards the last impression of the lost vision " ; but our western horizon, whence the once-set sun never returns, is death.

It is a curious fact that in those times when life was so various, so vigorous, and often so violent, death had power to surround the feminine ideal with such poetry in the eyes and hearts of all. It is true that this poetry was burdened with much use-less mythology, but those disguisings of real women as imaginary nymphs, whereby the artistic present-ment of the truth unhappily lost so much, were withdrawn before the sanctity of the tomb, when, according to Poliziano's imagery on the death of Simonetta, the lover or the poet

> "Beheld his nymph, enwrapped in mournful cloud,
> In cruel wise torn from before his eyes."

One of Messer Angelo's funeral verses on Simonetta, suggested by Giuliano de' Medici, says that "at the point of death the tranquil nymph turned trustingly to God." She was certainly a strange kind of nymph to be thinking about her soul, and it must have been a most singular funeral, for another of these short poems describes how, while Simonetta was being carried to the chapel of the Vespucci in the church of Ognissanti, Love, the son of Venus, in some inexplicable manner joined the company by the way, and from the closed eyes of the dead shot at the mourners arrows of remembrance of their splendour.

The Medicean poet was more happily inspired by the tomb of another young wife, Giovanna degli Albizzi, wife to Lorenzo Tornabuoni and younger sister of Albiera, who died in giving birth to her second child. Poliziano makes her thus lament: "Gentleness of blood, beauty, a son, wealth, conjugal love, wit, good manners and spirit all made me happy, but this happiness the cruel Fates, in order to render death the more bitter to me, did show unto me rather than give." Judged by the light of subsequent events, however, the Fates were

THE MADONNA AND CHILD: A PORTRAIT OF
GIOVANNA DEGLI ALBIZZI.
(Florence: Gallery of the Hospital of Santa Maria Nuova.)

GIOVANNA TORNABUONI.
(Florence: Santa Maria Novella.)

kind to Giovanna, inasmuch as dying at the age of twenty she was spared the grief of seeing her husband beheaded as a Medicean conspirator when only twenty-nine years old, at the time of the Piagnone terror in 1497,[1] nine years after her own death. The universal horror which this execution inspired is shown by Luca Landucci's allusion to it in his *Diario Fiorentino* of : " This—the deaths of the five victims—caused great sorrow unto all the people. They put him to death that same night, and I was not able to restrain my tears when lately I beheld the youth Lorenzo carried to Tornaquinci upon a bier."

Giovanna's features were immortalised by two medals struck in her honour, one having upon the reverse the three Graces as symbolical of her virtues, and the inscription "Chastity, Beauty, Love," the other the effigy of the huntress nymph of Virgil. She is also depicted in the young fair-haired lady, richly dressed in gold brocade, in Domenico Ghirlandaio's " Visitation," in the Tornabuoni chapel in the church of Santa Maria Novella in Florence. Another portrait, also by Ghirlandaio, known as Petrarch's " Madonna Laura," having passed by inheritance from the Tornabuoni into the Pandolfini family, was within the last hundred years to be seen in their palace in the Via San Gallo, but is now in England. The beautiful frescoes, now in the

[1] The Piagnoni were the partisans of Savonarola.

Louvre, discovered only a few years ago in the Villa
Lemmi, in the Pian di Mugnone, near Florence,
once a country house belonging to this family, em-
body portraits of both husband and wife. Injured
as are these, largely, thanks to their removal to
Paris, we may yet obtain from them some idea of
the treasures of the grace and beauty of the Florentine Renaissance once gathered within the walls
of this villa. Owned by the Tornabuoni family
from 1469 till 1541, it was the home of Giovanni
Tornabuoni when he was engaged in building up,
in Florence and in Rome, the commercial and political fortunes of this powerful family. Here he
must have lived when, in 1490, he unveiled his
magnificent chapel, and caused the date to be inscribed there by Poliziano as " the year 1490,
wherein the most beauteous city, noble by reason of
her wealth, her victories, her arts and her buildings,
reposed in the enjoyment of plenty, of health and
of peace," and when, in June 1486, the marriage
was celebrated between his son Lorenzo and the fair
Giovanna. This match had been arranged by Lorenzo de' Medici himself, and the entire city took
part in the rejoicings. The bride arrived at Santa
Maria del Fiore accompanied by a hundred young
girls of the first families, and by fifteen youths all
dressed alike. Both Florentine and foreign knights,
and the Spanish ambassador to the Pope, were
present at the exchange of rings; a Guicciardini and

Botticelli.

Alinari.

ALLEGORICAL FRESCO FORMERLY IN THE VILLA TORNABUONI (NOW LEMMI)
WITH A PORTRAIT OF LORENZO TORNABUONI.

(Paris: The Louvre.)

a Castellani escorted the bride to the Tornabuoni palace ; the neighbouring Piazza di San Michele Berteldi—now Piazza San Gaetano—was converted into a place for dancing. As soon as the bridal couple had returned to the Albizzi palace, the sumptuous supper was served, and the whole night was consumed in dancing in the brightly illuminated ground floor of the palace, and in games and mock tournaments between the men.

The villa in the country offered more tranquil enjoyments to the young couple. Here came to visit them Poliziano, full of almost fatherly affection for young Lorenzo, hitherto his assiduous pupil, in whose triumphs he took the keenest interest, whether they were triumphs in classic literature—he had great hopes of his Greek scholarship —or versifying in Italian, or in the games and jousts in the Piazza Santa Croce. The learned humanist came hither to the quiet villa to pursue his beloved studies, to read his Latin poems, to examine and explain the ancient medals which Lorenzo Tornabuoni was diligently collecting for the Medici palace, and there can be no doubt that either to Lorenzo or to his master was due the medal executed in honour of the young wife. Equally certain is it that the elder Tornabuoni, not content with having his chapel painted by Ghirlandaio, desired that the walls of his villa also should be decorated by the hand of Botticelli. Poliziano probably fur-

M

nished the schemes for these exquisite and immortal allegories and symbols of the beauties of which, as carried out by the artist's genius, the frescoes now in Paris remain to give us a tantalising idea. As Ghirlandajo, in two separate compositions, drew the portraits of the young couple upon the same wall of the chapel, so in like manner Botticelli depicted them upon the same wall in the villa. In one picture, the background of which is a thick wood, reminiscent of Botticelli's other allegory, "Spring," stands Lorenzo Tornabuoni, dressed in the usual Florentine fashion of the time with his hair puffed out round his head, and led by the hand by a lady of modest and gentle mien towards a circle of seven other ladies, all of whom are in fantastic costumes, and carry emblems representing the seven liberal arts. The central figure, who apparently presides over the others, makes Lorenzo a sign of welcome. In the other picture is seen Giovanna, one of the sweetest and most truthful figures ever traced by the brush of a Quattrocento painter, supporting upon her outstretched hands a cloth into which four pretty maidens cast flowers. Giovanna herself wears the dress of the period, but the other four are attired in costumes probably intended to symbolise her special virtues. At the feet, both of husband and of wife, lies an infant supporting a coat-of-arms in gentle allusion to their future hopes.

Such was the position accorded to woman by the

Botticelli.

Alinari

ALLEGORICAL FRESCO FORMERLY IN THE VILLA TORNABUONI (NOW LEMMI)
WITH PORTRAIT OF GIOVANNA TORNABUONI.

(Paris : The Louvre.)

humanistic spirit of Medicean Florence, and in such pictures did the art, inspired by that spirit, represent her. She, in all probability, cared little for this homage unless when it immortalised her—a figure in some religious group, fresco or painting by Masaccio, Benozzo Gozzoli, the Lippis or the Ghirlandajos, Alessio Baldovinetti or Piero di Cosimo ; or in the marble and bronze of Mino da Fiesole, Donatello, Ghiberti, Verrocchio or Poll-aiuolo—set high in the majestic churches raised by Arnolfo and Brunellesco, and bathed in the mysterious light which found a way through the many-hued histories on the great glass windows. Before those figures bowed in prayer, outstretched in the sleep of death, or actively engaged in some episode of Christian story, the souls of brave and pious women sought help and comfort amidst their daily cares, and mingled with the hope of immortality the memorials, affections and mortal glories of the family. To this voiceless poetry of so many silent hearts Antonia Pulci, and Lucrezia Tornabuoni de' Medici, now gave a familiar and homely expression in their Lauds and Sacred Representations. By birth a member of that wholeheartedly Medicean family, the Gianotti, and the wife of, as she was sister-in-law to, a poet, Antonia Pulci was to collaborate with Madonna Lucrezia, own mother of " The Magnificent," in expressing her ascetic aspirations in a form midway between

the dramatic and the epic. These "Sacred Representations" appealed with great success to the
popular love of the concrete, but Madonna Lucrezia
did not therefore stay her hand.   Although without any claim to literary ability, this lady found
time, between listening to Luigi Pulci's recitations
from his *Morgante* and the endless duties of her
high position, to write religious songs for the
Laudesi,[1] or to render the Bible stories into
rhymes which were the delight of her grandchildren
during the long, idle days spent at Fiesole or
Careggi.

Literary, in the strict sense of the word, these
fair ladies could not be called, however closely they
mingled with the learned humanists and scholars
whom the fall of Constantinople had driven over
to Italy.   Unconcerned with deep questions, and
merely regarding the tributes of affection offered to
them by art as pretty flowers by the way, they were
at one with the people in the form with which they
invested their thoughts and ideas, and in seeking
inspiration for their poetry only in real life as the
people saw it.   Yet it was by no means difficult to
find among the princely or noble houses of Lombardy or the Romagna, girls well learned in Latin
and Greek, for were not such accomplishments

---

[1] The *Laudesi* was a religious association, the members of
which went about singing *Lauds* in praise of God and the
Virgin.

courtly, and their existence the honour of that land and age. One downright " marvel of a woman " and humanist, by name Cassandra Fedele, Poliziano found in Venice, and enthusiastically greeted with Virgil's exclamation : *O decus Italiae virgo !* His letter to Lorenzo de' Medici, dated from Venice upon June 20th, 1491, says : " Last evening I did visit that Cassandra Fedele of literary fame, and did salute her in your name. Truly she, Lorenzo, is a thing admirable, and learned in Italian no less than in Latin ; is exceedingly discreet and clever, *et meis oculis etiam* beautiful. I departed much amazed. . . . And, in that she will most surely come visit you one day in Florence, prepare to do her honour." The great citizens of Florence, however, even those belonging to the most exalted oligarchy, Albizzi, Ricci, Strozzi and Rucellai, and, above all, the Medici, remained, amidst all the splendours of humanism, principally and frankly merchants. In their households, therefore, women were always and before all things the consorts of great merchants, good managers and housewives, less interested in books and medals than in their domestic affairs, their bank-book, the pantry and cellar, their poultry and pigeons.

Florence possessed in that century one very learned lady, albeit she has left no books to bear her name. The daughter of a Chancellor of the Republic, not a member of one of the great families, she came of a stock which, like so many others, migrated from the country into the city, and there grew rich and prospered. The beautiful Alessandra was daughter to Messer Bartolommeo Scala, and pupil of the two Greek scholars, Lascaris and Chalcondyles, while a third, Michele Tarcaniota Marullo, who had come to Italy as a humanist and a soldier, became her husband. Notwithstanding all the canonries, priorates, and parish livings with which the Medici had most unsuitably invested him, his crooked neck and squinting eyes, his shapeless nose and his forty years, Poliziano was her ardent adorer, and, for her sake, became the pitiless enemy of her husband and father, whom he slandered cruelly in his terrible iambics. It is not surprising that a passion between two persons of this calibre should have found vent in Greek, or that an account written by Poliziano with all the enthusiasm of a lover, describes Alessandra Scala's performance as heroine of no less a play than Sophocles' *Electra*. The following is a free translation of its six exquisite couplets :—

" An admirable Electra was the youthful Alessandra ; admirable for the manner in which she, an Italian, pronounced the speech of Athens ; in the just intonations of her voice, in preserving the illusion of the scene, in faithfully portraying the character, and regulating the expression, gestures and movements, proper to her part ; in keeping the language of passion within the bounds of decorum, in awakening the pity of the audience by the sight of her tearful face. All were deeply moved, but oh! what envy did I feel within my heart when she clasped Orestes to her breast and cried, 'Do I hold thee in mine arms?' and he replied, 'Oh, mayest thou ever hold me thus!'"

It needed but little more, another Greek epigram or two, for the dramatic critic and enthusiastic admirer to become the declared lover. "At last I have found that which I desired, that which I have always sought, the love long sighed for, the love beheld in my dreams! A maiden of perfect beauty, of grace which is natural and not acquired; a maiden learned in Greek and Latin, excellent in the dance, skilled in music, in which qualities, veiled by her modesty, she is the rival of the Graces. I have found her! But what doth it profit me, if I, who burn for her, can see her scarce once a year?"

Alessandra, no less capable of replying in Greek than of receiving homage in the same language, responded as follows: "There is nothing better than the praises of a man of worth, and with what glory do thy praises cover me! But as for thy dreams, have a care that thou interpret them truly. Thou canst not possibly have found in me all that thou sayest. The divine Homer saith, 'A god should be approached only by those like unto him,'

and between thee and me there is too great difference.   For thou art like unto the Danube, which
floweth from the west unto the south, and then
towards the east, in a mighty stream of water.
Glorious philologist, thou dost disperse the darkness from works in many tongues, Greek, Roman,
Hebrew, Etruscan.   A Hercules of learning, thou
art called upon to show thy strength in labours
upon works of astronomy, physics, arithmetic,
poetry, law and medicine.   My childish writings
are things as light as the flowers and the dew.
Shall I stand by thy side because I have a little
learning, or—as saith the proverb—should we not
be as the gnat beside the elephant, because both
have a proboscis, or the cat beside Minerva on
account of their cœrulean eyes!"   Was ever an
elderly lover put in his place with cleverer excuses
or more refined cruelty!   This time, surely, Messer
Angelo must have heartily cursed all similitudes,
periphrases, symbolisms, and the rest of the
rhetorical armoury, and have wished Greek proverbs, and even the divine Homer himself, at the
devil!   Nevertheless, as elderly lovers often do,
he persevered—but in Greek, which is less common.
"Thou sendest me pale violets, oh Sandra, and I
faint and die for love of thee.   Thou sendest me
flowers and leaves, fair imagery of thy Springtime,
but 'tis the sweet fruit for which I long!"   To
this Alessandra vouchsafed no reply; wherefore

he continued : " I am not permitted either to see thee or to hear thee any longer, oh, Alessandra, but at least thou mightest send me two lines in reply." Finally he sent her a present, of the good taste of which I will leave my readers to judge ! " Accept, oh maiden, this comb of bone for thy locks. I would that I might thus obtain a hair from thy beautiful head."

The hair of this beautiful head was presently cut short on the threshold of that same convent of San Pier Maggiore at the gates of which the like fate had already befallen the head of Albiera, brought thither on her bier ! To this retreat Alessandra came as a Benedictine nun after the death of her Greek husband, and here she died, still young, in 1506.

If art in its various forms does not in itself constitute the poetry of life, its imagery serves to brighten and idealise the hard realities of the latter. But this imagery, being quite distinct from the reality upon which it is based, has its own existence, which is apart from, and even contradictory to, reality. Beatrice, a woman, thus becomes an angel, a symbol, a heavenly being ; Laura, a wife and mother, by poetry regains her freedom, merely to be the heroine of an ideal love. The idealism of the Trecento, natural and Christian alike, was human—in so far, at least, as the spirit is human, but as the materialistic humanism of the Renaissance superseded it, wherever possible, with its mythology, its nymphs and bacchanals, there began to be unwound from the reel of classic antiquity that fine but strong thread which may be traced unbroken throughout all Italian poetry, and embraces not only the *Grazie* of Ugo Foscolo— who, upon the "ethereal heights of Bellosguardo," consecrated a Florentine lady as priestess of the rites of his deities—but even the *Urania* of Manzoni, a work which had already been preceded by the *Inni Sacri* and the *Promessi Sposi*. In the poetry of the Quattrocento, from Boccaccio to Poliziano and Lorenzo, the nymphs Simonetta and Ambra are but two conspicuous figures in the idyll of Fiesole—an idyll in which, under guise of the loves of Affrico and Mensola—the two heroes of the *Ninfale Fiesolano*, tragically metamorphosed into the two streams still called by their names— Messer Giovanni has given a classic and pagan form to a tale of early Florence. From Poggio a Caiano, Careggi and Montughi, to Settignano and Maiano, all these lovely hills are peopled by dryads and hamadryads, naiads and forest nymphs, who with the fauns, their male following, joyously dance in the mysterious light of the full moon, which, shining through the great windows of the Medicean abbey of San Domenico and the old cathedral of Fiesole, glorifies the life-like sculp-

tures of Mino, and lays soft haloes upon the heads
of the virgins and saints of Giovanni Angelico.
The method is nicely exemplified in the case of a
young gentlewoman who died in a villa, probably
at Quarto, of injuries received in saving her child
from beneath the falling roof of a peasant's hut.
The local chroniclers, taking their key from the
Latinists, exalted this maternal devotion by in-
veighing against the household gods for failing
better to support that roof, and against the deities
of the woods and fields for having lured into the
country the fair Alba, whom Venus should surely
have better guarded. Railing against the fates,
they, at the same time, comfort themselves with
the thought that down in the Elysian shades, Alba,
the fairest of all, will usurp the kingdom from
Proserpine. They also give a vivid description of
the victim's mother fainting at sight of the acci
dent, and of the husband's anguish when, returning
from a journey, he finds his wife already buried,
and endeavours to move away the stone from her
tomb in order that he may once more behold her
dear remains.

The famous company of Florentine ladies, whom
Boccaccio imagines as fleeing from the sorrows and
dangers of the pestilence of 1348, and taking refuge
in one of the valleys below Fiesole, have exchanged
the baptismal names given to them in San Giovanni for those of Pampinea or Neifile; their

maids are Misia, Licisca, and Stratilia ; their cook
is Sisisco, and their lovers masquerade under the
names of Panfilo, Filostrato, and Dioneo.   There
is no more truth in the story of their flight than
there is in the calumnious allegation that upon
occasions of great mortality or suffering—whether
in this or any other century—women escape into
the country instead of remaining faithfully at their
posts.[1]   Equally untrue to fact, also, is the quaint
fancy of good Franco Sacchetti of a *Battle between
the Beautiful Women of Florence and the Old*, wherein
the young women are marshalled under the banner
of Venus, and the old ones under that of Proserpine, an idea which is developed in four badly-
constructed cantos, marked by a vulgar disregard
of every noble sentiment, and wanting even in the
good sense so characteristic of his " Tales."   Many
works of a like falsity may be passed over, but another, although little less libellous upon woman,

[1] In the Middle Ages, it is true, public charity seemed almost
to repulse feminine help and pity, and confine it, often most
cruelly, in convents.   At a later period, during the plagues of
1630 and 1633, the only use which the sanitary officials of Florence found for the women was to shut them up in their own
houses, and forbid them to go out unless able to ride in their
own carriages.   In a letter—dated May 14, 1633—addressed to
Galileo, one of them complains of this treatment : " We poor
women are doing quarantine here, of which twenty days are
already passed.   This morning was made the third proclama-
tion for yet another ten days, in the hope that St. John will
deliver us from prison and grant us our liberty.   May it profit
us, and the Lord's will be done."

must be cited, since it is among the finest passages
of prose in the Italian language. In *Le Bellezze
delle Donne*, Don Agnolo Firenzuola imagines
another such company as that described by Boccaccio. For their benefit, one Celso—the author
himself, without his tonsure for the nonce—details
a more or less veiled analysis of the persons of his
hearers, under the feigned names of Monna Lam-
piada, Monna Amorrorisca, Verdespina, and Selvaggia. Æsthetic anatomy of this kind was perhaps
neither unsuitable, nor without its uses in Magna
Græcia, when Zeuxis was painting his famous
Helen; it was distinctly out of place in Prato of
the Cinquecento, before a company of self-respect-
ing women in the abbey garden of Grignano.

Florentine life, from the Trecento to the Cinquecento, could not possibly be reproduced in literature of this kind, a literature which, based upon
books and developed out of books, neither penetrated into, nor in any way approximated to, the
real life of that period. Equally untrue, of necessity, were its portraits of women, posed all against
a mythological background, where everything was
Greek and Roman and nothing mediæval. We
find truth, however, in the descriptions written in
verse or, better still, in pure Florentine prose, of
nuptial banquets, of jousts and tiltings: in these we
have the true woman of the time, gay and valiant,

and supremely contented with herself and the homage of the knights and courtiers around her. Even in these gorgeous surroundings the loves and nymphs have their place, but here they are only extraneous ornaments, sham decorations and incidental apparitions, not mythological symbols of a sentiment or the esoteric expression of a doctrine. The dominant and characteristic figures are those of mediæval chivalry, governors and princes, soldiers, damsels, heralds and pages, ladies cruel and love-lorn servants, behind them the great or gracious memories of the Crusades or Imperial progresses, the saintly deeds of the Paladins, and fair women.

> " The ladies and the knights, the toils and ease,
> That witch'd us into love and courtesy,"
> —*Purgatorio* xiv. 17.

Let us imagine ourselves in the Piazza Santa Croce on February 7th, 1468, spectators of the tournament of which Lorenzo de' Medici writes in his *Ricordi:* "That I might take part in everything, and bear me·like the rest, I did tilt in the Piazza of Santa Croce "—which tilting occasioned an outlay of ten thousand florins—"and although I was very vigorous neither of my years nor of blows, yet was the first prize awarded unto me, namely, a helmet adorned with silver and having a figure of Mars for the crest." Now enter the lists those who are to joust; the Medici, Pitti, Pucci, Vespucci, Benci, Pazzi, and many others, all richly equipped. With more than royal magnificence, Lorenzo appears wearing the device of the golden lilies of France, and with him comes his brother Giuliano, covered with gold and silver, with pearls and every kind of precious stone. Each knight is heralded by trumpets and accompanied by his pages, men-at-arms and young gentlemen on horseback, all splendidly attired and wearing their champion's colours, scarce less than a hundred in each company. Each knight had his banner, upon which, surrounded by various signs and emblems, and usually by flowers and foliage, was embroidered a picture of the lady of his heart. One would be represented lightly veiled in white, with a crown of oak-leaves in her hand, a leopard bound with golden chains crouching at her feet; another was shown attired as a nymph, gathering in her lap the storm-tossed leaves of a beech tree, upon which she fed a deer. Another lady, dressed in white and green, was represented as extinguishing the burning darts of Love in a fountain flowing at her feet. Lorenzo's lady, bathed in sunshine of all the colours of the rainbow, and robed in cloth of Alexandria embroidered in gold and silver, was shown weaving into a garland leaves of laurel plucked from a branch that blossomed upon a dead trunk, while other leaves were strown upon the ground all round her. His motto—*Le Tems Revient*, was lettered in large pearls upon his banner.

Far away from Florence, in the stately Orsini Palace in Rome, was a youthful lady whose thoughts on that day turned often to the resplendent knight of the tournament, but who was not the lady depicted on his banner; nor did she probably regret the fact, for at that time she was already preparing to be his wife and the mother of his children. " Lorenzo is so greatly occupied with this jousting that he hath not written unto me for some while," Clarice had said a month before to one of the Tornabuoni who had come with news of him. Hearing how Lorenzo had taken part in the tournament, and had come out of it safely and with great honours—" had borne himself as worthily as it was possible to relate," and " never had knight done that which his Magnificence had done "—she gently added : " Now that the jousting is over he will have no more excuse to stay him from coming to Rome this Lent." Against this season of Lent the mother of Clarice had ' caused violet cloth be brought from London, to make a petticoat after the Roman fashion." But the faithful Francesco Tornabuoni shall be allowed to give his own news as he wrote it to his patron in Florence on January 4th, 1469 :—

" There is never a day whereon I go not to visit your Madonna Clarice, who hath turned mine head ! For every day seems she more worthy unto me, in beauty, the fullness of all good manners, and in her most admirable spirit. It is now some eight days since she hath begun to learn to dance, and each day she learneth a new dance ; immediately that it is shown unto her she hath learned it. Master Agnolo had prayed her that she would write unto you with her own hand, but by no manner of means will she do it. I have also prayed her so much that for my sake she hath promised to do it; but she telleth me that you show yourself to be so greatly occupied in these days with the tilting that, since the coming of Donnino, she hath received no letters from you. Seeing that you cannot visit her in person, at least be frequent in your letters, for they do give her great consolation. In truth, you have the most worthy companion in all Italy. . . . "

On the eleventh of the same month Francesco again wrote to Lorenzo :—

"In the Name of God, the xj day of February, 1468.[1]

Magnifice vir et honorandissime. This day have we heard in letters from Giovanni Tornabuoni how that you have been at the tilting, and that your Magnificence is come forth

[1] Florentine reckoning.

safely and with very great honour. Immediately that I had heard this I went to tell it unto your Madonna Clarice, and did bring her a letter from Giovanni, and I cannot tell you how great a consolation she had of it. Since iiij days she hath not been joyful until to-day, because she was in constant anxiety about your Magnificence on account of the tilting ; and also she had a little headache. But immediately that she had heard this news her headache did pass away, and she was all joyful. I will not speak of Madonna Madalena, because it would be impossible to tell you how greatly consoled and delighted she is, and there only lacketh one more consolation for her, the which is that you should come hither this Lent, because she doth desire that you should see your merchandise before you take it home, for every day it groweth more valuable." Whether these were the exact words used by the noble matron when speaking of her daughter, or a spontaneous invention of the merchant client writing to his merchant Magnificence, we must not attempt to decide. " Herein is enclosed a letter from her. Madonna Clarice would not write, but biddeth me write unto you for her, and say that she hath a very great secret to tell you which she will not entrust unto any person, nor yet write

B. Gozzoli.   Anderson.

LORENZO I DE' MEDICI.
(Florence : Riccardi Palace.)

it in a letter, for fear that she should be badly served. In short, she calleth you unto her with all her might, and saith that now the tilting is over you have no more excuses for not coming. And she commendeth herself unto your Magnificence, and prayeth you to commend her also unto the Magnificent Piero and to Madonna Contessina, to Madonna Lucrezia, and to Bianca, Nannina and Giuliano. Yesterday I bought violet cloth from London to make a petticoat after the Roman fashion, because Madonna doth desire that this Lent she should go attired after the Roman fashion, which I do think will become her very well—and they shall visit all the churches where there are pardons, and will pray unto God for you."

The letter concludes with congratulations and praises for Lorenzo's success in the tournament, and various greetings from other persons. Clarice finally made up her mind to write to her betrothed, and on January 28th sent the following little letter, which varies greatly in spelling from those written after her marriage :—

"Magnificent consort, greetings. . . . I have received one letter from you and did understand that which you wrote. That you do value my letter is pleasing unto me, as unto one who desireth ever to do that which con-

tenteth you.   Ye do say that ye have written
little: I am content with what doth please
you, holding myself ever in good hope.   Madonna, my mother, sendeth you her blessing.
May it please you to commend me unto your
father and mine, unto your mother and mine,
and unto all others whom ye shall think fit.
Myself do I always commend unto you.   At
Rome, the xxviii. day of January 1469.   Your
Clarice de Ursinis."

On February 25th, in answer to a letter in
which Lorenzo described the tournament, she again
wrote a gentle note, composed as before of congratulations, prayers and greetings.   Characteristic of the manners of the times, and delightful
for the glimpse it affords into family confidences,
is a letter written two years earlier than the fore-
going, namely in March 1467, by Madonna
Lucrezia, wife of Piero de' Medici and mother of
Lorenzo, when she had finally chosen Clarice as a
good match for her son.

"Thursday morning, as I was going to St.
Peter's, I did meet with Madonna Maddalena
Orsini, sister to the Cardinal, and with her was
her daughter, fifteen or sixteen years old.   She
was dressed after the Roman manner, with a
shroud,[1] and thus attired she did appear unto

---

[1] The name given to a large white cloak or drapery, worn
after the fashion of the ancient Romans.

me very beautiful, white and tall ; but since
the maid was all covered I was not able to see
her as I desired. It chanced yesterday that I
went to visit the aforesaid Monsignor Orsini,
who was in the house of his sister aforesaid,
which house doth adjoin and communicate
with his own. When I had paid the necessary visits on your behalf unto his Lordship,
there arrived his sister and her daughter, who
did wear a narrow petticoat after the Roman
fashion without a shroud. We did stay there
a great while in discourse, and I did well observe the maiden. As I have said, she is of
a suitable tallness, and white, and hath very
gentle manners, albeit she is not so pleasing
as our own daughters ; but she is exceeding
modest and can soon be made accustomed unto
our ways. Her hair is not fair, because here
the women are not fair, but is somewhat inclined to red, and she hath of it in abundance.
Her face is somewhat round, but doth not displease me. Her neck is agreeably long, but
seemeth unto me somewhat thin, or rather
slender. We could not see her bosom, because
it is the custom here to go dressed all close,
but she appeareth to be well made. She doth
not bear her head bravely as do our maidens,
but doth carry it a little forward, the which,
methinks, is because she is timid ; but I do

find no sort of defect in her, saving this
timidity. Her hand is long and slender.
Having considered all things, we do judge the
maiden to be far above the ordinary, though
not to be compared with Maria, Lucrezia and
Bianca (her own daughters). Lorenzo himself
hath seen her and will tell thee how much he
is satisfied with her. I should say that both
thou and he will pronounce her to be well
made, and I shall agree with you. God shall
direct us.   Thy Lucrezia."

On June 4th, 1469, the wedding of Lorenzo and
Clarice was celebrated in Florence with great festivities. The first two days were entirely devoted
to the reception in the Medici Palace of gifts from
the villages and towns of Tuscany, among them
one hundred and fifty calves, more than two thousand brace of capons, geese and fowls, casks of
native and foreign wine, and other similar delicacies.
These Lorenzo shared generously with the citizens,
even before announcing five banquets which were
to take place on the Sunday, Monday and Tuesday. At these banquets the loggias and gardens
of the palace in the Via Larga were filled to over-
flowing, and separate tables were set out for the
young women who were the bride's companions,—
" fifty young women with whom to dance," say
the records—and for the older women in company
with Madonna Lucrezia. In the same way, there

were different tables for the "young men who danced," and for those of maturer years. The feasting lasted from the Sunday morning, when the bride—mounted upon the great horse presented to Lorenzo by the King of Naples—left the house of the Alessandri in Borgo San Piero (now Borgo degli Albizzi), and entered her new home followed by a train of nobles, the symbolic olive branch being hoisted at the window to the accompaniment of gay music, until the Tuesday morning, when she went to hear mass at the church of San Lorenzo, bearing in her hand one of the thousand wedding gifts, "a little book of Our Lady, most marvellous, written in letters of gold upon blue paper, and with a cover of crystal and silver work." Thus transported into an atmosphere of youth and beauty, of grace and power ; received in halls which Cosimo, Piero and Lorenzo had adorned with countless treasures of ancient and contemporary art ; surrounded and overwhelmed by the splendour of a wealth the owners of which were so far from being ostentatious that they even sought to conceal its almost embarrassing vastness ; a queen receiving the homage which the finest minds of the whole world paid to this family, whose power lay chiefly in its intellect, Clarice Orsini had ample proof that she had become the wife of the first citizen, not only of Florence, but of all Italy.

From the very first, however, the young wife

showed a distaste for the somewhat unbridled gaiety
of the democratic city, the elegant scepticism of
men who were at once scholars and courtiers, and
those transactions between citizen and client which,
in the service of the patron, could corrupt even old
republican blood. These and other things offensive
to her Roman pride, and her feeling as wife and
mother, drove Clarice into that state of morbid
melancholy which clouded all her life of domestic
virtue. She even succeeded in driving Poliziano
from the house, preferring the society of Ser
Matteo Franco, a worthy chaplain and writer of
humorous sonnets, whose typically Florentine
letters contain vivid descriptions of Madonna Clarice and her children. It is impossible to believe,
however, that as a young bride she failed to
enjoy the general gaiety, the intellectual charm of
those courtly assemblies, of all that appealed so
strongly both to the senses and the imagination in
festivals such as that which took place a short
time before her arrival — February 14, 1464 —
and had filled an entire night of carnival with
sounds of merry - making. Thus runs the
Notizia :—

"The account of a festival made upon a
night of carnival for a lady, daughter to
Lorenzo di Messer Palla degli Istrozi. This
festival was made by Bartolommeo Benci,
lover of the aforesaid lady."

The lady was Marietta degli Strozzi, and her festival shall, as far as possible, be described in the words of the picturesque " Account " which has come down to us. With the aid of eight other youths belonging to the principal families, Bartolommeo Benci had arranged, for the close of carnival, a nocturnal tournament in honour of his own lady-love, and of the respective ladies of his eight companions. Each one of the eight, mounted on a richly-caparisoned horse, was surrounded by thirty young men wearing his colours, and carrying torches in their hands, while eight more walked beside their bridles. Young Benci, bearing the staff of office as " Lord and Captain of the Company," rode a horse —" the noblest horse that ever nature could make, with trappings and saddle and bridle all of crimson, richly embroidered with silver. And he rode upon the said horse wearing a doublet embroidered with pearls and jewels, with two wings upon his shoulders of gold and many other colours. And round the said Lord there did walk fifteen noble youths, dressed in short tunics of crimson satin lined with ermine, with violet hose, which had been given unto them by their Lord. And beside these, the aforesaid Lord was surrounded by one hundred and fifty young men attired, after his own colours, in a green tunic and hose, and upon the breast and the back were embroidered silver falcons whose feathers were scattered all over the tunic ; and these hundred and fifty young men all bare lighted torches in their hands." At the head of the procession, escorted by flute-players, was carried an erection called a "Triumph of Love." This Triumph was "twenty *braccia* high, and was of such a splendour that all were dazzled who beheld it; there were upon it many little spirits of love with bows in their hands, and in some places were the arms of the Benci, and in others was the device of the father of the aforesaid lady, with many little silver bells and divers ornaments. The Triumph was composed of laurel, myrtle, cypress, fir and birch, all things green and warm and belonging unto love. And upon the summit of the Triumph there was a bleeding heart, round the which were flames of fire that did burn continuously." Among the decorations were placed fireworks, to be discharged when the time came. After a splendid supper at Bartolommeo's house, the procession—which must have numbered some five hundred persons—started from the Piazza de' Peruzzi and wended its way to the dwellings of the Strozzi family at Santa Trinità, two Bencis and two Strozzis on horseback going before to regulate the pace. The Signoria had issued orders that nobody was to ride in the streets of the city that night with the exception of those taking part in this tournament, and that should any one be killed by mischance, whoever caused his death should escape punishment or exile. This they termed " a provision against cases of accident " !

When they arrived in front of the lady's house, the parade began. " Each one rode upright in his saddle, according to the custom at tournaments, with a gilded dart in his hand, whereafter did each one run, with a gilded, blunted lance, and break it beneath the window wherein, between four lighted torches, sat the lady. Then were the wings unfastened from the Lord's shoulders and cast upon the Triumph, and order was made that it be set on fire ; and so it burned, with such great shoutings and noise that the sound of them ascended even unto the stars. And the fireworks there set upon the top were devised in such manner that the little spirits of love upon the Triumph appeared, as though in very truth, to shoot them from the bows which they had in their hands. And being thus lighted, they sped through the air near unto the lady ; several of them went into the lady's house, and men said that some had also entered into her heart, there to excite compassion for her lover. And when all this had been done, the aforesaid Lord Love departed with all his company, and in order that he might not turn his back upon the lady, he did make his horse always to walk backwards until he could no longer behold her. And when they were departed from her, they went to break lances, and to show their tilting before the houses of the ladies of each one of the Lord's companions, that is, of the eight aforenamed. After this they did all return unto the Lord's Lady, and, for it was then near day, gave her a morning serenade of much music and great magnificence. Then they departed and did accompany the Lord, this same Bartolommeo Benci, unto his house, in the same manner and order wherein they had set forth at the beginning. And the Lord had ordered many sweetmeats and victuals to be made ready, and he caused them to feast with much magnificence."

If any reader have the curiosity to inquire whether or no those nine tournaments in front of the nine houses inhabited by nine ladies were duly followed by nine weddings, their answer would, at least in so far as some of the loving couples were concerned, be negative, and for the very good reason that the knights were already married ; also, it must be admitted, some of the ladies were likewise provided with husbands. Possibly the other couples arranged a correctly romantic sequel to that gay night, but as the old *Notizia* does not mention their names, their ultimate history is not to be traced. As for the principal couple, however, I am reluctantly obliged to state that, notwithstanding all the tilting and fireworks and lover's homage which concluded the carnival of 1464, Marietta Strozzi, seven years later, married a Calcagnini of

Ferrara, and that in the following year, 1472, the winged and plucked captain, Bartolommeo Benci, wedded Lisabetta Tornabuoni, sister of that Tornabuoni of whom we heard, sending to Lorenzo de' Medici from Rome the news of his lady-love, Clarice Orsini.

Many pleasant memories must the fair Marietta Strozzi have carried away with her from Florence. After the triumph of the Medici, the Strozzi family remained during several generations in exile, her father falling by the sword far from his home, and her mother, the strict and virtuous Alessandra de' Bardi, of necessity sharing her husband's wanderings. Being thus practically an orphan, the girl enjoyed greater liberty than was, perhaps, suitable for her station in life, and, if we are to judge by a letter written in 1469 by Filippo, a son of Alessandra Macinghi negli Strozzi, to his younger brother, Lorenzo, her reputation seems, justly or unjustly, to have suffered. So desperately in love with Marietta had this Lorenzo fallen that he declared he would marry her or none, but the wise elder brother advised him to reflect in time. "She has beauty and a good dowry," he said, "but there are drawbacks which outweigh even these advantages. She was left alone very early, and being without father or mother,[1] and not dwelling in her own house and being very beautiful, it is no

[1] Alessandra de' Bardi had died in 1465.

great matter for surprise if there should be some
fault in her." Poor Marietta! And yet it is only
necessary to read the account of another carnival
adventure which happened to her in the winter
of 1464, a few nights before the tournament already
described, to realise what a Florentine girl could
do in those times and yet create no scandal. The
account is taken from a Latin letter full of youthful confidences and friendly gossip, written by
Filippo Corsini to the eighteen-year-old Lorenzo
de' Medici, then at Pisa :—

"And the whilst I am writing unto thee
almost the whole city is covered with snow,
tiresome for many, and obliging them to stay
within, but for others a cause of much merriment and pleasure. Thou must know that
there were together Lottieri Neroni, Priore
Pandolfini, and Bartolommeo Benci "—the
gay captain of the other adventure—"and
they did say, 'Let us seize upon the occasion
to make some fine diversion.' And immediately, at about two o'clock of the night, they
did present themselves before the house of
Marietta Strozzi, followed by a great multitude assembled from every part, to make sport
with her at throwing snow. They gave her
her portion, and then they began. Ye immortal gods, what a spectacle! How can I
describe it unto thee, my Lorenzo, in this

feeble prose—the innumerable torches, the blowing of trumpets, the piping of flutes, the excited and cheering crowd! And what a triumph when one of the besiegers did succeed in flinging snow upon the maiden's face, as white as the snow itself! But what do I say, flinging snow? It was truly a veritable shooting at a mark, and by most expert marksmen! Moreover, Marietta herself, so graceful and so skilled in this game, and beautiful, as all do know, did acquit herself with very great honour. But the noble youths would not take leave of her until they had bestowed most generous gifts upon her for a remembrance of them. And thus, to the great contentment of all, this pleasant sport came to an end."

One of Poliziano's epigrams—the last quotation from this Florentine of the Quattrocento, who wrote Greek and Latin more often than his native tongue—runs : "Snow art thou, oh maiden, and thou playest with the snow. Play, but see that the snow melt before it be sullied." The scholar who nowadays reads these verses will recall many others on the same theme, both ancient and humanistic, which are contained in the *Anthologia Latina*, and will look upon them as no more than cold-blooded imitations of the classics. But, in this case at least, the scholar's fancy could be illustrated from real life, from a game which, long-forgotten, had been revived—as many another custom of ancient Italy—by the joyous democracy of the Renaissance. And, like many another of these old customs, this also was to disappear, overwhelmed by the growing rigidity of courtly etiquette, the severer code of manners and morals produced, even in Catholic countries, by the Protestant Reformation, and the social philosophy which in the name of universal principles changed the face of the whole world.

But not one of all these public merry-makings, these popular festivals with their fantastic apparatus and their elaborate symbolism, neither wedding procession, breaking of lances in ladies' honour, nor tilting of love-sick knights, could equal in civic pomp and solemnity a certain marriage ceremony widely different from all others, to which allusion has already been made in a preceding chapter of this volume. This was the marriage of the Abbess of San Pier Maggiore, a marriage which for many centuries in mediæval, Renaissance, and even early Medicean Florence, was, with few exceptions, renewed as often as a new bishop was elected, for the bridegroom in this case was—and *honi soit qui mal y pense*—no less a personage than the Lord Bishop himself.

Originally founded in the fourth century, the now vanished church and convent of San Pier

Maggiore ranked among the most ancient of the religious foundations of Florence, and gave a name to a gate and quarter of the city, the quarter which Dante inhabited and cursed. A restoration in the eleventh century strengthened their fabric, in that the second circle of the city walls was then built against them. About the middle of the fourteenth century the church was re-decorated, but during the " barocco " period of bad taste and vandalism it was despoiled of its marbles and other treasures to build the private chapels of noble families. Now, not only does no vestige of it remain,[1] but Time, which " changes alike man and his tombs," [2] has with difficulty resisted the modern craze for re-naming, and preserved the ancient designation in the Arco di San Piero—a mere passage-way, under shelter of which flower-sellers and fruit-stalls congregate without a thought of the ruins and bones below. Of those whom we have met in these pages, the two fair Albizzi sisters rest beneath that spot in peaceful company with the nun, once a learned Greek scholar, whose early death, ere time could dull her hair or wrinkle her brow, made her a fit bride for that strange episcopal marriage. Immured within the convent walls, she could, indeed, no longer use her worldly learning upon the immortal pages of Homer and Sophocles,

[1] The church of San Piero was destroyed in a great fire.
[2] Foscolo, " Sepolcri."

O

but had, nevertheless, ample opportunity for exercising it upon the rude legal Latin of the authentic
documents and privileges connected with those
mystical espousals, which, as these documents de-
clare, date from times "earlier than the memory
of man."

The new spouse of the Florentine Church made
her state entry through the gate of San Pier Gat-
tolini, now the Porta Romana.   There he was
met not only by a procession of the secular clergy
of the town, and of the monastic orders, but by
the Podestà and the Captain of the People, with
all their knights and justices, attended by musicians
and a crowd of people.   Waiting for him at the
gate were also the two families of the Visdomini
and the Tosinghi.   These families enjoyed important hereditary rights over the administration
of the episcopal revenues, and were accused by
Dante of having enriched themselves at the expense
of the Church.[1]   As *vicedomini*, or regents of the
vacant see, they were privileged to receive the
Bishop at the gate of the city, and thence to accompany him to the convent and the waiting Abbess,
representing the Florentine Church.   The Bishop,
therefore,—in full ecclesiastical vestments, cope
and mitre—was no sooner entered the town than
he was met by four of these, on foot and under a
canopy of cloth of gold stretched upon four spears

[1] *Paradiso*, xvi., 112-114.

or lances, while two others placed themselves at
his horse's bridle. The whole company having
moved on to San Pier Maggiore, the Bishop dis-
mounted at the gate, the *vicedomini* " received him
in their arms, and attended him to the altar,"
and assisted him to robe for the final ceremony.
When the Abbess knelt before him, praying him
" with a cheerful countenance, to be united spiritu-
ally unto her," and he gave her the ring, a member of the Albizzi family was privileged to hold
the bride's finger while this was put on. Still supported by the *vicedomini*, the Bishop then retired
to the Abbess's own chamber, where he found a
magnificent bed on which to repose at leisure. For
twenty-four hours the Abbess yielded possession of
her room to the Bishop, and when, on the following
morning, he departed thence to his induction, the
vicedomini again conducted him to the Cathedral.
Needless to say, the entire city always crowded to
witness this marriage. Besides the two already
mentioned, other leading families of the city held
privileges and rights connected with this or that
part of the ceremony. These not infrequently led
to protests, quarrels and lawsuits; after the ceremony of 1301 the syndic and the procurator of
the convent complained because the two families
of the *vicedomini*, and the canons, had admitted
more persons to the wedding feast in San Piero
than they had any right to do; in 1383 the cere-

mony was the occasion of a disturbance for which
some were afterwards punished. The Abbess
retained possession of the horse ridden by the
Bishop on his entry into the city ; the right to the
saddle, at one time the perquisite of the Bellagi,
was subsequently acquired by the Strozzi, to the
great triumph of the whole of that family. Thus
the city enjoyed a great festival, and the Florentine
Church obtained her Bishop, by a ceremony the
essential part in which was played by a woman.

These old-time ceremonies and festivals of the
city are picturesque and interesting, but the purpose of these pages is to discover the real life behind all the ideal transformation and glorification
with which contemporary art invested the women
of that age ; we want to learn what manner of
women, in the privacy of their homes, were the
wives and mothers, the sisters and daughters, of
the Florence of that time.

A certain personage called *Le Diable Boiteux*—
advanced by Le Sage to be the occupant of the
chair of one of the greatest and most malicious
professors of moral philosophy yet known to this
world—was until recently held possessed of the
exclusive right to uncover the roofs of quiet
homes, and, without any introduction, to surprise
the inmates who were quietly attending to their
own affairs. A few years ago, however, as I was

carefully and patiently examining papers bearing on the early history of the Medici, I chanced to discover a forerunner of Le Sage's *Diable Boiteux* in the person of a favourite courtier of Lorenzo and his sons, who, when one of those sons became Pope Leo X., was advanced to be a Cardinal of Holy Church. Francesco Dovizi—surnamed Bibbiena after his native town—author of the *Calandria*, in an unpublished prologue to that famous comedy, makes an imaginary pilgrimage from one woman's room to another. Rendered invisible by sorcery, he describes the series of strange scenes brought to his eyes in various houses in which the womenfolk are preparing to attend a dance. But I have no desire to make a third with the cardinal and the devil; moreover, I think that this place has already been taken by Messer Guido Biagi, who has initiated us so learnedly into the secrets of the private life of the old Florentines.[1]

I must, here, pause for a moment to give a necessary warning. Numerous as are the portraits of women contained in Florentine tales and comedies of the Quattrocento and Cinquecento, in my opinion they are far too greatly indebted to the classics, and to Boccaccio, and are too satirical in character, for us to accept them as accurate representations of the women of the period. That period

---

[1] *The Private Life of the Florentines of the Renaissance*, by Dr. Guido Biagi.

possessed no historical novelist, as did the Trecento in Sacchetti. It would be difficult to say, for instance, of what period in the history of Florence the personages of Niccolo Machiavelli's *Mandragola* might safely be accepted as types; and most assuredly there was nothing in good Marietta Corsini [1] to warrant her comparison, poor soul, with the woman in *Belfagor* whose marriage with the devil drove him to such desperation that he fled helter-skelter back to the peace of hell.

That the great historian could at times speak with the utmost reverence of a woman, is seen in his touching tribute to the memory of Annalena Malatesta, the hero of a story which, were it not too true a drama of grief and bloodshed, might seem one of the most pathetic legends of wifely and maternal love. To the house of Annalena, where beyond the Arno her name still lives among the people, there came one day a messenger from Florence. "Lady," he cried, "they have stabbed your husband, Messer Baldaccio, to death in the Palace of the Signori; they have flung his body from the window, and have cut off his head for a traitor and a criminal." And she, in whose veins ran the proud blood of that Paolo Malatesta, whose love and sorrow—the guilty kiss and the embrace in hell—are immortalized in Dante's verse; who, a fifteen-year-old bride, pledged her heart and faith

[1] Machiavelli's wife.

Donatello.   Alinari

A BUST CALLED GINEVRA CAVALCANTI, BUT NOW GENERALLY
SUPPOSED TO BE A PORTRAIT OF ANNALENA MALATESTA.

(Florence: Museo Nazionale.)

to the rough soldier of Anghiari, the brave and
brutal condottiere, and was now the mother of his
child ; ran, poor lady, to the Signori, to the cruel
judge who had made her a widow, and by her tears
and prayers saved her husband's possessions to his
son. But soon the child, her little Guidantonio,
to whose sole care she had meant to devote her
life, followed her husband, and she, hardly more
than a child herself, was left alone. Then Annalena, turning her house of sorrow into a convent,
and for ever enclosing within its walls the short
romance of her youth, her marriage and her motherhood, her memories of love and death, of a cradle
and two graves—in the very chambers in which she
had known a mother's joys and sorrows—gave herself as a virgin to God, and there, as a mother of
virgins, spent her long and gentle life. An affectionate mother she must have been, with sympathy
and compassion for worldly splendours and flat-
teries, for Naldo Naldi, one of the humanists
who celebrated the beauty of Albiera, addressed to
the fifty-year-old Annalena a Latin elegy imploring the prayers of herself and her nuns for the soul
of "that youthful lady whom thou didst love as a
tender mother loveth her only child." It is hard
to say whether there was not more cruelty than
piety in these words, which the Latinist probably
wrote without thinking, but which must have
brought the young mother's tears back to the eyes

of the aged nun.   Annalena died when she was
sixty-four, and commended her convent to the
care of Lorenzo de' Medici. That powerful family
early took especial interest in the institution, and
the rooms once inhabited by the foundress, the
widow of a soldier of fortune, afterwards afforded
refuge and safety—in times unpropitious for all
who bore the name of Medici—to a boy who was
destined to become the prince and chief of those
men of war, Giovanni delle Bande Nere himself.

Seeking the woman whom no envious Fortune
robbed of her husband and children—the woman
who was her family's ornament and comfort,
example and inspiration, strength and providence,
the housekeeper, wife and mother—we shall find
numberless types. These types, idealised indeed
but not too far from actual life, exist in the many
books of feminine "government, manners or discipline" produced in the Middle Ages — the
treatises on the *Governo della Famiglia* of the
fifteenth century; books of a secular cast, such as
that adorned by the names of Agnolo Pandolfini
and Leon Battista Alberti; the delightful pages of
Vespasiano the paper-seller, and those in which
the religious sentiment predominates, like the *Cura
Familiare* of the pious Giovanni Dominici, dedicated
to an excellent lady, Bartolommea degli Alberti.
The ideal, or rather traditional type of woman was
certainly derived from the remembrance of those

"good and dear," or "beloved, perfect and honest" women whose presence counted for so much of sweetness and virtue in the domestic chronicles of the Trecento.

Among the illustrious figures of his own times, depicted with something of that rhetorical colouring characteristic of him, Vespasiano gives a long account of Alessandra de' Bardi, wife of Lorenzo di Messer Palla Strozzi, and mother of the lively Marietta. He describes Alessandra as "of exceeding great beauty and comeliness of body, more than any other in the city of Florence." She was so tall that she could afford to despise " pianelle," a kind of high slipper dear to ladies less favoured by nature. Her mother educated her " with all diligence," more perhaps, than her husband's exile and other family circumstances enabled Alessandra herself afterwards to bestow upon the education of her own daughter ; she was brought up in the love and fear of God to lead a virtuous life, taught that she must " never lose time by lacking occupation," never "speak with the servants of the house save in her mother's presence," and be " the first in the house to arise in the morning." She also learned " all those things which it is meet that a woman should know, to have the care of a family, and above all she learned to make everything, both of silk and other stuffs, that belong unto a woman." She also learnt " all that whereby, if needful, she might be able to live, and herself to do all things and likewise to teach them unto others," from reading down to the smallest detail of household management. " Very rarely was she seen either at the door or at the window, both because she took no pleasure in this, and because she did occupy her time with laudable matters. Upon most days her mother did conduct her at a very early hour to hear mass, always with her head covered so that it was nearly impossible to see her face." But this girl, brought up almost like a nun, had learnt other things besides her domestic duties, and when after her marriage the Imperial Embassy came to Florence in 1432, she knew how to do the honours not only of her own house but of the city also—that city of Florence which " in those times," says Vespasiano, "abounded in virtue and riches, and the fame of which had gone out through the whole world"; which " unto those ambassadors did seem to be another world by reason of the great number of noble and worthy men who were at that time in it, and not less by reason of its women, beauteous in body and in mind, because—be it said with respect unto all the women of other cities of Italy— Florence did at that time possess the most beautiful and the most virtuous women that were in all Italy, and their fame was spread throughout the whole world." Vespasiano describes a ball given in honour of the gentlemen of the Embassy by the

Signoria, which took place in the Piazza, upon a scaffolding or terrace built out from the side of the Palace towards the Via Condotta, with a great display of arm-chairs, benches, tapestries and festoons of flowers. The principal young men of the city were all dressed alike in rich green cloth, with kid boots reaching up to their thighs, and the girls and young married women wore splendid dresses, high to the throat and adorned with jewels and pearls. Of the ladies, two of whom were deputed to do the honours to each Ambassador, Alessandra— newly married and aged barely eighteen—and one Francesca Serristori were assigned to the chief guest. After the dancing refreshments were carried round, and Alessandra herself waited on the ambassadors "with a fine embroidered napkin over her shoulder, . . . with infinite courtesy doing reverence, and courtesying almost to the ground in a manner so natural that it did seem as though she had never done aught else." More dancing followed until, when it became time to accompany the ambassadors to their lodgings, and each one gave an arm to two fair Florentines, upon either side one, Alessandra took the right arm of her guest. At the door of his lodgings the chief ambassador presented two magnificent rings from his finger—the first to Alessandra, the other to her companion, and thus, after the usual formal salutations, the ladies were conducted to their own homes.

The Quattrocento biographer who, towards the end of the century, wrote of these and other Florentine women of the preceding generation— Alessandra died in 1465—draws endless comparisons between them and the Florentine women of his own day, deploring the deterioration of their once strict and virtuous manners. These are sometimes no more than the customary regrets of the past in which writers of all ages find it necessary to indulge, but more often they are due to Vespasiano's cynical temperament. He would, for example, have women " learn not to speak, but especially in church, nor "—a small addition—" in any other place either." But with these exceptions and in all seriousness, his lamentations, especially when they take the form of definite charges, seem to be evoked by the actual condition of affairs. He particularly regrets the change in that domestic life which women control, the real condition of which betrays itself in their acts and conduct. This change was gradually brought about by the increasing splendour of the Medici, whose power was now absorbing, voluntarily or involuntarily, not only the interests and fortunes of the lesser families, but also their affections, their hopes and their plans. The most eager acceptance, and pursuit, of this influence, on behalf of their families, came as usual from the women. " Do thou remember that the adherents of the Medici have

always prospered : not so those who adhere unto
the Pazzi, for they have always been undone."
Thus wrote in 1461, seventeen years before the
bloodthirsty conspiracy, another Alessandra who
had married into the Strozzi family. As wife and
as mother, she like Alessandra de' Bardi suffered
much, alike from the exile of this family, but
had the consolation before she died of seeing her
children, restored to their native land, largely
through her own efforts, laying the foundations of
that splendid palace which is the lasting monument
of their greatness. This was Alessandra Macinghi
negli Strozzi, to whom another memorial has been
raised in our own day by the publication of those
letters to her exiled children, mentioned in the in-
troductory chapter to this book, which have been
given to the world by Cesare Guasti, a writer and
scholar well able to appreciate and interpret the
tales of joy and sorrow that they contain.[1]

Alessandra Macinghi Strozzi was a matron whose
manner of life, and whose piety, would have agreed
alike with the goodness of Archbishop Antonino and
the austerity of Girolamo Savonarola. Remembering this, we must look indulgently on a certain
hardness of character for which the age, rather than
Alessandra herself, is to be blamed, while the very
fact that the Medici could attract to their party
such individuals—and such families as, for ex-

[1] See also the final chapter of the present volume.

ample, the Rucellai—proves that their work was less one of corruption than of acquiring power among the citizens, of taking as much of the State —the words are Machiavelli's—as was conceded to them bit by bit, so that their strength invincibly surmounted all obstacles, overcame all resistance, and crushed all opposition. The wisdom of her advice to follow the Medici and not the Pazzi was tragically justified only a few years later—in May, 1478—by another woman's voice, and the agony of a daughter's heart, when the murder of Giuliano de' Medici and the wounding of Lorenzo were avenged as national crimes in the blood of the conspirators, and of all suspected of assisting them in any way. One of these, Piero Vespucci, a man of little judgment or wisdom, had been at one time devoted to Lorenzo, had tilted with him in the tournament at Santa Croce in 1464, and had been one of the gay youths who rode with Benci beneath Marietta's windows. He now possessed a married daughter named Ginevra, some twenty years old, and sister-in-law to the fair Simonetta. This daughter addressed to Lorenzo the heart-broken words contained in the following letter, now for the first time printed :—

"Beloved, on behalf of a good father. The reason of these mournful lines is because yesterday I was not able to speak with you as I did desire, to implore you, and to recall unto you the love and goodwill ye bore unto this house, the words spoken and the promises made unto me, and the kindness shown unto me when ye did call me sister. Wherefore I pray you now to give ear unto my prayers, and remembering in this matter all your love and promises, to have mercy and compassion upon us all. I would that it should please you to consider the condition of my father, and to look at him through mine eyes, and not to consider that which he doth in all his affairs, for he is not alone in this matter. And I do pray you with all mine heart that ye grant me this grace, to restore him unto me without further hurt, and that the punishment he hath already suffered for this offence shall suffice. For when I remember me of his age and of how that he is in feeble health ; that he hath had the fever a good while and hath it now again ; of where he is, and how that he hath chains upon his feet ; at thought of this my heart doth break. Do these lines bring weariness, have patience I pray you : remember how that to them which do mercy shall mercy be shown, and send me good answer by him which beareth this. I pray God move your heart that my father be restored to me this night. Surely this should be so were I with you, for then should ye suffer my persistence even there-

unto. Now hear I again that he is tortured :
I conjure you keep us no more in despair.—
Ginevra the Unfortunate.

Caesare Guasti's valuable work is at one with
many newly recovered documents in proving not
only the entire devotion with which the women of
this period gave themselves up to their families,
but also that such powerful families as the Medici,
Strozzi, Rucellai, Guicciardini, Soderini, and Ridolfi, owed no small part of their success to the like
loyalty. Fully aware of this, Savonarola counted
largely upon the solidarity of Florentine family interests when he made his attempt to replace the
decaying Medicean supremacy by sound democratic
institutions. Endeavouring first to reform manners and customs, and rally the women under this
standard, he called upon the mothers and matrons
rather than the mystics and devotees. The ready
response of these last was but natural, nor is it
surprising either that these mystical ladies—as one
of the Visdomini, a Gianfigliazzi and two Rucellai
—having played the part of veritable "Jacobins" in
the Piagnone "Terror," found final refuge in a convent, and were there—in one case at least—hailed as
saints, or that Fra Domenico's appeal for volunteers to suffer the trial by fire in attestation of
Savonarola's doctrine was answered by an astound-
ing number—lay and religious, youths and women
—the last in particular pressing eagerly forward

with cries of "Take me! take me!" Of such enthusiasts Monna Bartollomea Gianfigliazzi had "her devotions and her spirits, as she herself did say," but, according to Villari, Savonarola placed no great faith in her "madness." The friar's two Rucellai disciples were Camilla, who belonged to the Bartolini Davanzi family, and Marietta, the wife of an Albizzi. Camilla had left her husband and become a Dominican tertiary under the name of Sister Lucia, and that she was zealously "Jacobin" is proved by a page in the Savonarola trial which refers to the dark episode of the execution of the five Medici adherents in 1497: "Filippo Arrigucci, who was then one of the Signori, desired to throw Bernardo del Nero, the Gonfalonier of Justice, out of the windows of the Palazzo. Wherefore the aforesaid Filippo sent unto Madonna Camilla de' Rucellai to ask of her what he should do, and she did send unto him the answer that it had been revealed unto her in a vision that Bernardo del Nero should be thrown from the window."

To the mothers, then, the women and children, Savonarola first addressed himself, and it may be said that he relied on the power of maternal affection as a political instrument with as much faith as his adversary, Pope Borgia, relied on the sword and dagger of his son Valentino. "Oh women and children," he cried in one of his sermons, "your reform is not yet accomplished. Say unto

P

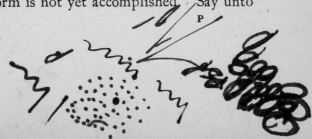

your Magnificent Signoria from me that this is not a thing of men, but of God : And bear unto them this message, that they remedy all those things which are not right, and make them perfect. But if they do not this, but do mock at the works of God and speak against them, then shall the King punish them. And say unto them that they themselves are not lords, but the ministers of Christ, our Lord and King. Unto you I speak, ye fathers and mothers : repeat and confirm this matter unto your children, for it leadeth only to good living. Otherwise hath God prepared a punishment for them who do contrary to His commandment. These things I tell you of a surety ; lay them therefore to your hearts." Fruit of such admonitions is to be seen in a letter in the *Documenti e Studi* of Gherardi, written to her husband by a certain Guglielmina della Stufa. He was Commissioner for the Republic in Arezzo. The writer relates how Fra Girolamo had that very morning assured them of the happy time at hand, when they would lack nothing, but had also warned them that evil times would precede the good. "And in order that the evil may be less, he hath bidden us fast and pray from now until the day of the Holy Spirit ; and we must not doubt that God is pitiful and will lighten the troubles that shall fall upon us. All here do trust in Him that He shall so do by us, and herein also it behoveth us now likewise to do, that God may deliver us from the sorrows and tribulations which shall come upon this city, or rather upon the whole world." A more curious document yet, first printed by Guido Biagi in 1898, is a letter from a nun addressed to Fra Girolamo himself, wherein the writer's prayer for the reform of her sex is touched with a feeling akin to jealousy lest the Friar may busy himself with the men and children rather than with the women.

" We are, most reverend and beloved father in Christ Jesus, debtors not unto the flesh, but to mortify the works of the flesh in spirit and in manner of living. And this is desired by very many persons, but chiefly by the maidens, who are zealous and fervid that the honour of God be magnified in them, and have many times received counsel and teaching from you in your preaching, that they should reform unto an honest and simple life. With a burning love and marvellous fervour ye do urge them to reform, but it seemeth unto them that ye do mostly urge that the men and children should begin to reform, and that ye do give no care unto the women. And although we be but little worthy, we are, nevertheless, greatly beloved of God, seeing that He was willed to be born of a woman, and the Church saith *Intercede pro devoto femineo sexu*. These do desire, therefore, that for the sake of justice ye should be prayed to notify and make public this reform, in order that their desire may be fulfilled. Ye must know that there is not less virtue in the preserving of what hath been gained than in the gaining, but rather the more, as saith Jovanni Cassiano in his writings. And since ye have already laboured and sown for a great while, it is needful to make sure that the enemy do not come and sow tares. But the chief matter is that the time of summer is at hand, when the maidens will clothe themselves anew, and they desire to know what fashion and shape of dress they shall wear. Ye know that their judgment will lead them astray, and if ye do not provide for them by means of this reform they will be too long delayed. Wherefore, of your charity, let it please you to make it manifest as quickly as possible. No more. May Christ Jesus keep you alway. Our sister and myself, your spiritual daughters, we do pray you always to remember us in your prayers; and all our house is likewise ever at your commands. On the 2nd day of May, in the year of grace mccclxxxxvi. On behalf of your spiritual daughter in Christ,

Margarita di Martino."

The great-souled friar was burnt, and the prophet belied by facts; but a large part of the gene-

A MARBLE FIREPLACE FORMERLY IN A HOUSE BELONGING
TO THE BORGHERINI FAMILY.

(Florence : Museo Nazionale.)

ration which had listened to his inspired words remained faithful to the old battle-cry of the glorious Commune—*Popolo e Libertà*, when the children who had danced round the Burning of Vanities at the Carnival of the Piagnoni, now grown to manhood and defending the walls of their besieged Florence, fought against Pope and Emperor the last battles of Italian freedom.

During the thirty-five years between the revolution of 1494 and the fall of the Republic in 1530, both sides—the heirs and avengers of overthrown liberty, and the heirs and supporters of the splendid ambitions of those who desired its overthrow—were animated by an equal courage of opinions and of deeds, and an intensity of moral energy so great that it may be said to have regulated their conduct in practical matters almost as fully as it inspired them in their struggles for the mastery. Art and the development of thought were, so to speak, arrested by anxiety for the unknown future. Deserted now was the Medicean garden at San Marco, where Poliziano instructed painters and sculptors in the myths of Hellas, Luigi Pulci in Carlovingian history, and where Ficino sought in Plato for bonds of union between pagan civilisation and the faith of Christ. It was now the turn of Machiavelli, who, in the Oricellari gardens, so idealised the toga-draped figures of ancient Rome that, fired with a new enthusiasm, young men conspired against the

Medici, while from the great events of Roman history he drew those lessons in State-craft destined
for the guidance of that Prince, who, by desperate
methods in desperate times, should save Italy
through the triumph of a generous idea. But the
Medici, upon whom he founded his portrait of
the Prince, all died young, and upon their tombs
Michael Angelo sculptured his figures of the sad
Thinker and of Night. Very different, and by no
means generous, was the other triumph prepared
for their family by Leo X. and Clement VII., who
made use of their sacred office for the purpose.
During this period of strife and resistance, in which
defence and attack, alternating with conspiracies
and expulsions, found their conclusion in that
downfall of heroes so vividly set out by the war-
rior-merchant, and defender of Florence besieged,
Francesco Ferruccio,[1] domestic life neither was,
nor could remain, the gay and assured existence
by which, from the time of Cosimo to that of
Lorenzo, Florence was reconciled to the loss of
her liberty. The carnivals arranged by the magnificent Lorenzo de' Medici the Elder—as he was
called by the contemporaries of his nephew Lorenzo,
Duke of Urbino, who in his Duchy forestalled

---

[1] Francesco Ferruccio, who fought against the Imperial army
at the siege of Florence, fell at Gavinana—in the Pistoiese
Apennines—in 1530. Already *in articulo mortis*, he was stabbed
by Fabrizio Maramaldo, captain of the Imperial troops.

the title with which the family in Florence were about to crown their boundless covetousness—had passed away beyond the possibility of revival even by the Companies of the *Broncone* and the *Diamante* into which, imitating the undertakings, devices and example of those past splendours, the younger generation of Medicean adherents had for their amusement formed themselves. In that life, now no more than an incessant warfare of dark schemes and interests, the women of Florence kept tireless watch over their hearths and homes, the mothers, as always, bearing the greater share in this watching. " I have lost not only my mother," writes the *Magnifico* himself, " but my one refuge from many of my troubles, a comfort in my labours, and one who did save me from many of those labours." " Return unto your mother, who awaiteth you with such great longing," wrote Alessandra Macinghi Strozzi, and the voice of the brave old woman sounded to her exiled children as the voice of their beloved fatherland, once more opening to them the arms so long and so cruelly closed.

Both Lucrezia and Alessandra may be said to have themselves arranged the marriages of their sons, sharply scrutinising with jealous maternal eyes every detail of a proposed daughter-in-law— her personal appearance, mind, manners, relations, and dowry. Alessandra, it may be remembered, had not looked with much favour upon the fair

Marietta of the tilting and the snow.   Maria Salviati, widow of the great captain Giovanni delle
Bande Nere, foresaw the future exalted position
of her son Cosimo, who, unexpectedly called to be
Duke of Florence when only eighteen years of age,
was yet, thanks to the training of this high-minded
woman, able to vanquish or crush such enemies as
Filippo and Piero Strozzi, and to foil or repulse
the dangerous ambition of a partisan like Francesco
Guicciardini.   Maria Soderini vainly devoted herself to her unfortunate son Lorenzino de' Medici,
trying first to lead him into better ways, and then
to save his life.   She and her beautiful daughters,
Laudomia and Maddalena, and Maria, daughter
of Filippo Strozzi, the greatest gentleman of the
century, who had married a Ridolfi, shared bravely
in the fruitless, but not ungenerous, endeavours
of the exiles to prevent the establishment of the
Medicean princedom.   Against the violence and
treachery upon which this princedom was founded
brave protest was also made by Giulia, daughter
of the exiled Messer Salvestro Aldobrandini, who,
when she was invited to dance at the court of
Urbino by Fabrizio Maramaldo, replied : " Out of
my sight, base murderer of Ferruccio ! "   One of
the fairest of that fair company, however, Luisa
Strozzi, fell a victim to the new prince, and this
mysterious tragedy, to which only a few years
later was added the death of her father Filippo,

G Vasari   Alinari.

MARIA SALVIATI.

(Florence: Palazzo Vecchio.)

recalls darkly the warning of her far-seeing grand-mother that "those who are against the Medici shall be undone." To these words, however, no attention had been paid even by one of the Medici —Clarice, a daughter of the Magnificent Lorenzo's son Piero, and mother of Luisa, who married Filippo Strozzi, and was the zealous participator in his manifold ill-fated ambitions. In mind a man rather than a woman, she is to be counted among the proudest souls even of the proud Cinque-cento. On the eve of the expulsion of the Medici in 1527, this woman caused herself to be carried in a litter to the Medici palace, and there bitterly reproached the two illegitimate members of the family, Ippolito and Alessandro, as unworthy bearers of the name, and misusers of the power derived from the favour of the people by those forefathers in whose name she—a true Medici, and in the palace of their race—now pointed out to them, and almost drove them down, the road to exile.

They were strong women, these, to whom the men whose names they bore might safely entrust their domestic affairs, the care of children and fortune, of house and estate. Thus did Messer Luigi Guicciardini, during his absence as Commissioner for the Medici, entrust everything to his wife, Monna Isabella, whom I have the good fortune to make known through her letters, written from the country, included in this volume. Thus, too, did Pierfrancesco Borgherini commit the custody of his palace, and the honour of his family, to his wife, Madonna Margherita, sure that she would give him entire satisfaction. And when a certain Della Palla, agent and buyer of treasures of Florentine art for King Francis of France, presented himself at the house of Monna Margherita, armed with an order from the Priori to bargain for the decorations of one of her rooms, a marvellous work by Jacopo da Pontormo, that truly great lady received him with these words :—

"So thou dost actually dare, Giovambattista, thou base broker, thou twopenny pedlar, thou darest seize upon the ornaments of gentlemen's chambers, thou darest rob this city of its richest and most valuable things, as thou hast constantly done, in order to adorn therewith the strange countries of our enemies. . . . I do not marvel at thee, thou low-born man, enemy of thine own country, but I do marvel at the magistrates of this city who abet thee in this abominable wickedness. This bed, which thou dost seek to obtain for thine own particular interests and thy greed of money, although out of thine evil mind and thy false piety thou dost allege another reason,"—*i.e.* to conciliate the King and obtain his favour for the besieged city—"is the

bed given unto me at my marriage, in honour
of which Salvi, my father-in-law, did provide
all this magnificent and stately furniture, the
which I who revere for his memory's sake,
and for love of mine husband, shall defend
with my very blood and even with my life
itself. Get thee forth of this house with
these thy ruffians, Giovambattista, and unto
those who sent thee with the order that these
things should be taken away from the place
whereto they do belong, say that I am she
who will not permit that any one thing be
moved hence, and that if they—who do believe in a vile and worthless man like thee—
desire to make a gift unto King Francis of
France, then they shall despoil their own
houses of the ornaments and the beds in their
chambers, and shall send them. And if ever
again thou dost dare to enter this house upon
such an errand, then shall I teach thee, with
most serious hurt unto thyself, the respect due
from thy like unto the houses of gentlemen."
Vasari's preservation, amplification though it
may be, of this outburst of a woman's righteous
anger should surely go far towards reconciling us
with the oratory of the Cinquecento. Florentines
of to-day, pausing amidst the treasures of the
Bargello to admire the wonderful fireplace by
Benedetto da Rovezzano, once actually adorning a

room in the house of the Borgherini, and now an
inalienable heirloom of the Italian nation, must
surely feel proud of their townswoman whose
pride preserved so many things of value from
being carried out of the city.

But if Margherita and Isabella upheld, and
Maria Salviata Medici herself powerfully represented, that Medicean party from which, at least
in the dark ending to all its ambition, all our
sympathies have fled ; if in the breasts of Clarice
Medici Strozzi, and other women—relatives of
banished citizens, there burned the interests and
rancours of ambitions less fortunate than those of
the Medici ; heroines were, nevertheless, not lacking in the cause of dying liberty, or among that
people who fought for liberty without a thought, or
an aim, beyond it—nameless heroines, for the most
part, such as are found in the lower classes, usually
as generous with its names as with its blood ;
nameless heroines who figured in the legends
told in lonely huts during the long melancholy
winter evenings. Such was Lucrezia Mazzanti of
Figline, who sought refuge in the waters of the
Arno from the brutal violence of the Imperial and
Papal soldiery. Married and middle-aged she was,
perhaps, but popular tradition has reinvested her
with the poetry of youthful maidenhood, and the
last humanists of the Renaissance dedicated their
Latin verses to this Roman Lucretia, while they

acclaimed a new Brutus in Lorenzino de' Medici. Another popular heroine of this period has been depicted in more modern times by Guerazzi, who, during the hard years of Italian servitude, wished to pose as the Homer of Florentine liberty. This woman, whom in *The Siege of Florence* he calls Monna Chita, the silk-spinner of Borgo San Friano, does not seem to have been attractive. He says she was " tall of stature, thin, and so sunburnt that she was almost copper-colour ; the muscles of her neck were thick and prominent, her veins swollen, her lips scarlet and always moving, even when she was not speaking ; her nostrils quivered and her eyes shone brightly, constantly turning from one side to the other, and her face was square and bony "—a prototype, indeed, of Michael Angelo's " Fates." To the defence of her native city, this poor widow gave not only the gold earrings which had been her husband's wedding gift to her, but also her only son—" my Ciapo, aged but sixteen years and eight months, seeing that he will not be seventeen until the Feast of San Zanobi "—causing him to swear upon the Crucifix the oath with which the Spartan youth received his first shield : " With this or upon this." Patriotism this was, indeed, which could stir these mothers of the people to sacrifice their sons to the love of country. The times were not far off when the Italian people was forced to forget that it had ever

possessed a fatherland, must search the public pla-
cards, whereon the Government made known its
laws, to learn whether it even had the right to
rear families; when under the oppression of that
double tyranny, political and social, no voice was
heard save that of Lucia [1] bidding farewell to her
native hills.

Republican liberty had fallen, and upon its ruins
peace had been made between the Church of Rome
—which had preserved its unity despite secular
corruption and pagan refinement—and the Holy
Roman Empire, the mediæval ideals of which had
been materialised under the oppressive rule of
Charles V., that monarch upon whose dominions
the sun never set. Amidst the dark and shameful
conjugal dramas of the Medicean dukes and grand
dukes, and their courtiers, the last figure invested
with the ancient glory of the Florentine woman,
beautiful, widely read, skilled in music and poetry,
instructed in many languages and with a deep
knowledge of her own—was the gentle and unfortunate Isabella Medici Orsini, Duchess of Bracciano.[2] Other gentle souls found refuge in the con-

[1] The heroine of Manzoni's famous novel, *I Promessi Sposi*.
[2] Isabella Medici Orsini, Duchess of Bracciano, the third and
favourite daughter of the Grand Duke Cosimo I., was born in
Florence in 1542. She married Paolo Giordano, Duke of Bracciano, who neglected and abandoned her, but immediately after
her father's death in 1574 sought her out, accused her of infidelity, and strangled her.

vent. Sometimes voluntarily sought and chosen, this was but too often the prison-house in which the wickedness or cowardice of nobles confined such unconscious maidenhood as is immortalised in Manzoni's Geltrude.[1] Thus, hurrying her from one convent to another, the Florentine republicans concealed Caterina de' Medici during the siege, regarding as a useful hostage the woman whom they preserved for a very different position. "Go, tell those my fathers and masters that I will to become a nun, and for ever to remain with these my reverend mothers," was a message sent to the Signoria by her who was to sit upon the throne of France, and to witness the Wars of Religion and the Massacre of Saint Bartholomew.

Sweet hours of silence, spent in pious meditations on human sin and sorrow, on God's goodness and the terrors of His judgment, seemed, on the contrary, the fitting destiny of Caterina de' Ricci, whose early entry into the Convent of San Vicenzo at Prato occurred at a time when, in intervals of battling for the national freedom, her countrymen were waging duels for the unworthy favours of another member of her family, Marietta Ricci Benintendi, while wild bloodshed and wilder orgies were dragging in the dust the name of yet a third kinswoman, Cassandra Ricci.[2] Within her

[1] Also a character in *I Promessi Sposi*.

[2] Cassandra de' Ricci, a daughter of Federigo Ricci, fell into evil courses, and was the nominal, if not the actual, cause of

convent Caterina was a focus for the last traditions
and affections of Fra Girolamo's followers, and
consecrated his faith and martyrdom before that
altar over which she was herself one day to preside
as a saint. She did not, for all this, forget her
family according to the flesh, nor yet her greater
family—the world of Florence. To her relations
she wrote letters full of the words of peace, of love,
and of consolation. If need were, her superiors,
and the prelates of the Church, she rebuked in
terms of respect; strengthened those in business,
or troubled with the cares of city government, with
words of encouragement in their honest labours,
bidding them fix their thoughts on heaven; re-
minded princes of justice, women of love and
gentleness; and to the two wives of Francesco de'
Medici sent—her love to the unhappy Joan of
Austria, her prayers to Bianca Cappello. In the
ever-increasing darkness of these times, when domestic and foreign tyranny alike weighed heavily
upon political and intellectual liberty, the convents
did not, indeed, lack women like Caterina, whose
love and pity were still devoted to those who remained in the world. Whether they had entered
their prisons of free will, or driven by the world's
unkindness, these devotees still felt and made their

the death of Piero Buonaventuri, the husband of Bianca Cappello. After her marriage with Simone Bonciani in 1553, she
became the heroine of many scandalous stories.

own all the sorrows of the families to which they belonged.

To the Villa del Gioiello—the name of which still we hold sacred—upon the hill of Arcetri, came to die, himself almost a prisoner, the great liberator of modern thought, Galileo, and from the neighbouring convent of San Matteo there watched over him the affection and prayers of a saintly creature —his child through love, against whom he had committed the further sin of condemning her to a life of vicarious expiation. This daughter Virginia —by his wish now sister Celeste—might not visit him in person, but could write to her father those letters through which she survives to the present day, letters that share his sorrows, tremble at his illness, and reverently worship the divine intellect which " penetrated the heavens." Sending him a rose in winter, she desired him to find therein a symbol of " the Spring of Eternity which shall follow the short, dark winter of our present life." She took upon herself the spiritual penances imposed on him by the Holy Office ; rejoiced when she received one of his books, or heard of honours paid to him ; to give him more liberty would cheerfully have " dwelt in a prison even more narrow than that wherein she now dwells," and regretted the profession of her veil once only since then it forbade her to visit and nurse him in sickness. When, in common with all other nuns, she

Q

must choose the saint of her especial "devotion," with the sublime profanity of a daughter she chose her father, whom she prayed God to preserve in life, because "after him there remaineth unto me in this world naught of good." And when the martyrdom of imprisoned filial love came to its early end— she died at the age of thirty-three—her old father, in his poverty and his glory, felt that with her death was sundered the dearest link which bound him to this earth. Surely she found her reward, for in the lives of how many women is written a page worth the one half of Galileo's dying cry, when, more and more cruelly crushed by that unworthy warfare against the rights and the future of humanity as represented in himself—blind and sick, insulted with humiliating concessions granted as though to a pardoned criminal, in receipt of charity and permissions bestowed upon him as upon one merely tolerated by the great ones of the earth —he, who had revealed the mysteries of the heavens, felt but a little later the coming of death to himself also, and cried: "Now hear I my beloved daughter calling continually unto me!"

The fall of the Free Republics was followed by a season of hapless servitude. But in the third century after that fall the grave was opened, and Italian liberty rose from the dead. And to that resurrection the women of Florence, as of every other city, village and hamlet in all Italy, offered the sacrifice of grief and martyrdom, of anxiety and trembling hopes, the thoughts and labours of men whom they loved and inspired, their own lives and the blood of their children. From Eleonora Fonseca to Teresa Confalonieri, from the mother of the Ruffini to the mother of the Cairoli; women whose names were Guacci, Turrisi Colonna, Ferrucci, Brenzoni, Paladini, Percoto, Milli, Mancini Fusinato—all gave to Italy of their dearest and their best. The traditions re-told in this story of the brave women of past ages have been nobly carried forward by the mothers and wives, the sisters and daughters of Tuscany, the gentle ladies and good women of the people who, from Curtatone and Montanara to the conquest of Rome, stood for the cause of Liberty, and shrank not though in that long pursuit their dearest fell before their eyes.

CHAPTER V

A MATRON OF THE CINQUECENTO

Being certain letters written by Isabella Sacchetti Guicciardini

I

FLORENCE, *July* 5, 1535.

MOST DEAR LUIGI, I have received your two letters, to the which I will reply very briefly, seeing that I am busy; for to-morrow morning, so God will, we shall pass into the country very early, and I am hindered on account of Simona.[1] And so we go to Popiano,[2] in the name of God, and may it please

[1] This daughter, who was ill, was the youngest of six, the others being : Margherita, married first to a Tornabuoni in 1519, and secondly to a Bini in 1533 ; Piero, who died young in 1527 ; Guglielmetta and Lorenzo, who died in infancy in 1509 ; and Messer Niccolò, a well-known lawyer and a lecturer at the College of Pisa, a senator in 1554, orator to Pope Paul IV., and ducal commissioner at Pisa, where he died in 1557.

[2] Poppiano, or Popiano, in the Val di Pesa, is a village with a noble villa, or country mansion, and a parish church. The patrician Florentine family of the Guicciardini were formerly lords of Poppiano, and still own the fortified castle now used as a country house, with the surrounding land ; they are also patrons of the parish church. There is a tradition that the Guicciardini originally came from Poppiano, and at a farm belonging to the Foundling Hospital here stayed Don Vincenzo Borghini, the famous Florentine scholar, who assisted in the revision of the *Decamerone* about 1572, and initiated the earliest critical studies of ancient Italian literature.

Him to be merciful unto us and keep us in good health there.   And from thence I will write unto you according as I am able ; and as soon as I shall have put the most necessary things in order I will send the man unto you with the things for which ye have asked ; but ye must send him back speedily that he may attend unto his business.   And if ye send me another good ass, I will despatch oats and other things into Florence, as much as I can, for the winter.

No more.   I commend myself unto you.   May Christ keep you.   The 5 day of July, 1535.—
ISABELLA in Florence.

The family of Messere hath notified that they will arrive upon Saturday week.[1]

[Addressed on the outside to]
    THE MAGNIFICENT SIGNORE,
      THE COMMISSIONER OF AREZZO,
LUIGI GUICCIARDINI, *my honoured consort in Arezzo.*

II

POPPIANO, 6 *August*, 1535.

yhs.

MOST DEAR LUIGI, I have received with pleasure your letter of the 29th of last month, for

---

[1] The *Messere* here mentioned was Luigi's son Niccolò, but the title was also applied to his brother Francesco, the great historian and statesman.

methought I had been too long without any letter from you.   The sojourning here is pleasing, and delighteth us ; but it is sometimes exceeding hot, and it is impossible to go out of the house when there is sun, or to go even a short way without perspiring greatly.

The wheat hath been for the most part put in the store-places underground, because it was beginning to grow hot.   For the selling of it, a sample hath been sent to Florence, and it shall be dealt with according as you did write.   I hope to God that the greater part will be sold, for I do not think that we can ourselves use it.   As for the asses, I will use all diligence to see that they be well fed, and will do mine utmost to order it that they and the man shall lose no time, and that their burdens be only such as they can bear with ease. The wooden vessels will be useful, if ye can procure several for the cellars here and in Florence. Of wooden chests we have sufficient for the present.

Ye do well to think first of Simona before all other business, and ye can believe that I have no other desire than to see her established in the position which should be hers while you and I are still alive ; and if God help us to place her in such position, we shall be comforted.   If we have time and money after this business is concluded, we shall not fail to make good use of it."

VILLA TORNABUONI (NOW LEMMI): PIAN DI MUGNONE, NEAR FLORENCE.

On this subject of Simona's marriage, Luigi
wrote as follows to his son Niccolò:—" Concerning Simona I will only say that I am much
inclined to Bernardo Vettori, because there is
none other who pleaseth me so greatly for all
reasons as doth he.   Ridolfi seemeth to have
his mind fixed upon a large dowry, and more
than is right, seeing that he is very rich.   If
Pier Francesco Ridolfi had been alive, I would
have prayed his good offices in the matter,
since he was a friend of his grandfather Lionardo; but he being dead I must think of other
means. I do think that if I were there it would
be an advantage ; nevertheless, my being here
should not be an hindrance unto the matter.
The important thing is to make a decision,
and not to grudge 300 scudi more in order
to establish her well, she being the last.
Wherefore do thou look about thee for someone who belongeth to a less great and notable
family, providing only that he be rich, not unworthy, and possessing brains. For seeing that
thou art on the spot, and canst speak of the
matter with Piero Bini, it cannot be that ye
will not find either one of the two aforenamed, or Nerli, to be suitable."   As will be
seen later, Simona married Pierantonio di Pierfrancesco de' Nobili, a member of one of those
lesser families looked down upon by Luigi

and those who, like himself, belonged to the greater families.

"Ye must be sure that I will remind the labourers [1] of everything the which I know to be useful, but I cannot greatly go about to overlook them on account of the heat. Ye must remember that something is due to old age. This next week will I see if a man may be obtained, and will commence the repairing of some of the small things in the lanes and the pond.

Simona saith that she will write unto you. Her eyes are not yet wholly healed; of a morning they are red, and swollen more than ordinarily round their rims, and I do think this is caused by a superfluity of blood.

No fish have yet been caught in the baskets, because it seemed unto me that the labourers were so busy from morning until night that I desired not to give them further fatigues. So soon as they shall have finished mending the barns, methinks I shall set them to the emptying of the stone basin and its cleansing; and they shall take out the largest fish and put in smaller ones, since truly, as ye say, danger is that they be stolen by other persons. Last Friday morning they did seem to be greatly agitated, and I was not able to discover the wherefore. Early in the morning one of our

---

[1] The peasants, or the hired labourers, who did agricultural and farm work on the estate.

maids went thither, who found them all outside
the fountain, and so much upon the edge that they
gasped for want of water. I went myself to see
them, and methought they were fine fish ; we took
of them about two pounds' weight, the which were
excellent. I did scold mightily, and asked the
reason of the labourers, and it seemed that they
were all astonished, and said that fish did sometimes
leap out of the water when it was very hot, because
there was much stuff at the bottom of the basin,
and they were afraid when washing was done there.[1]
This may be true, and I would believe thus did the
fish leap out every time that washing is done
there ; but they have not done it since, nor had
they ever done it before.

Piero saith that one of the pistachio nut trees
hath taken root ; one of the pines began to grow,
but afterwards was eaten by a worm. The figs
and peaches he saith are doing well.

I do most certainly think that had I and the
family come to stay with you in Arezzo, ye would
have saved many a ducat, if only the cost of our
being here. For the keeping open house, as we
must here, cannot be done without expense, as ye
will see. And the excuse of your house there I
do accept as I have heard it from others, albeit that,
as hath been told me, ye are a more numerous company than we. Wherefore this take I for one of

[1] Apparently linen was washed or rinsed in the fish-pond !

your good customs, seeing ye have, as hath ever been, most ample space, both for the household and for other things.[1]   Therefore, in this case, I grieve and make complaint both of nature and of fortune —of nature, firstly, which gave not unto me the qualities which should suffice you ; and of fortune, secondly, in that it made us one.   Yet, howsoever matters turn, so God hath ordered all things, and may it please Him that all end with the salvation of your soul and mine.   Little, methinks, it matters unto any save Simona that now I find myself near unto the time when I must render an accompt of this, my journey, which draweth to its end.

We must wait until this terrible heat is past, and meanwhile the garnering of the wheat will be finished.   To-morrow will the last be measured, and I do think that Andrea's crop shall prove 12 or 13 moggia.   Then, first, I shall be able to give you the whole tale.

I turn now to the vintage.   I must cause new hoops to be put round several vats, and must order the vinegar casks to be repaired, for I have found them all spoiled, and know not the reason thereof. And the cherry-tree must be sawed down, for though this hath been many times so ordered, yet hath it never yet been done.   I will now arrange and give

[1] This was not the first time that Luigi had invented excuses for leaving his wife and family behind when appointed as Commissioner to other places, and she was annoyed.

orders for all these matters if I can. But I fear
that my departure will be an hindrance, because to
order a thing and not be there to see it carried out
doth never succeed; and if I had foreseen and
thought of many things the which I now see must
be done, I know not if I would have arranged for
this visit to Arezzo. I see that ye do desire it, and
my will is to content you. And if I must let all
things here go to perdition, and ye decide that I
must come, I will do it ; but I return before 15
days because of many things undone. That which
doth trouble me more than aught else is that I
have here no elderly woman whom to leave in
charge for 15 days. Messere doth not seem willing that Caterina should remain here, and she herself doth not wish it, because she thinketh that she
would be too much alone when Messere is no more
here.[1] If I come unto you, they will all leave before my departure. Messere's [2] daughter, Simona,
considered it too hot, and is not yet come hither ;
and I do not think that she will come either hither
or to you. I can find no person suitable to leave
here for the necessary affairs.

The best of the cheese, the first making that is,
hath been sent into Florence ; the remnant here is

---

[1] This was her son Niccolò and Caterina Jacopi, his wife.
[2] One of the three daughters of Messer Francesco the historian. Both brothers had named a daughter after their own
mother, Simona di Bongianni Gianfigliazzi.

not very good. I should like to know how many couple of cheeses ye do desire to have, and how many pounds altogether, so that I may choose the best.[1]

I did think no more of that sickness, because ye did not speak of it again. And according to what Master Lionardo[2] telleth me, there is no need for anxiety.

It grieveth me that ye have so much annoyance with the servants. It is a wearisome thing, but ye are not alone in it, it is the same for all. Something must be endured sometimes. Since ye have had Ottaviano, I do think there hath always been some bother; he did behave badly in the house, he hath an evil tongue, and doth occasion scandals, and he is stupid and doth never think of aught. But we are all full of faults ; we must bear one with another until we die.

I have given your message unto the labourers. There are now no worms in the figs ; they be gone. A good many orange-trees below the grotto have begun to sprout. There are 2 nut-trees, the others have dried up; I have had them watered several times.

I will say no more now. I commend myself unto

---

[1] Cheese is now sold in shapes or forms, but at that time they spoke of a " pair of cheeses," or a couple of curd cakes, &c.

[2] One of the numerous doctors consulted by Monna Isabella.

you. May Christ keep you. The 6 day of August, 1535.—ISABELLA at Poppiano.

[On the cover]
To THE MAGNIFICENT SIGNORE,
THE COMMISSIONER OF AREZZO,
LUIGI GUICCIARDINI, *mine honoured consort in Arezzo.*

III

POPPIANO, 30 *November*, 1542.

yhs.

DEAREST LUIGI, I have received your three letters, of the 7th, the 13th and the 18th, and I will now reply unto those things which seem unto me of most importance.

Firstly, with regard to the wine ; there hath been very little here or anywhere. We could obtain no more from Ripalto and Mulino for the reason which I have already written unto you : both the one and the other are very poor. The peasants there seem unto me to be helpless and irresolute people, and methinketh that Giovanni hath no mind to abide in that place. A few days since he did tell me that the land did in no wise please him, that he worked very hard, but being by the roadside, he did suffer much hurt through the shepherds ; he did say he would help me to find labourers if I would help him to find

another estate.[1]   He asked me to write unto you, in
order that ye might arrange matters at your leisure.
I answered that I would not write unto you, because
I desired not to have the trouble of finding another
estate, and that he must await your arrival.   Since
then I have not seen him again.

The vines here gave promise better than elsewhere.   Still, I know not how they did turn out ;
we used the greatest care, however.

Read my letter again; ye will see that I told you
how that the hoops upon the casks of old wine had
burst.   It would have been much better if I had
only sold it all, but I kept it as long as I judged
right, and did succeed in keeping it until after
Easter ; and I had a small cask of half-wine,[2] the
which I had intended for the maidservant's drink-
ing until February, and there remained 12 barrels
of it.   But fate willed that the last hoop of the
cask should burst, and in the morning the wine was
found to have flowed all over the floor.   Think if
I grieved, for it was good wine, and now we shall be
obliged to buy a little ; I have bought several flasks
of old wine, and some I have had from Florence.

---

[1] The Italian word, *podere*, used here has no equivalent in
English ; it means a field or farm land usually planted with
various sorts of produce, vines, olives, vegetables, and often
wheat.   In this case it was clearly a *podere* planted with vines
amongst other things.

[2] Half-wine, *mezzo-vino* or *stretto*, is a very inferior quality of
wine produced by watering the crushed grapes and pressing them
again.

It grieveth me sorely that ye are in such discomfort and trouble, as ye did write unto me. Ye must do as ye have bidden me to do—look upon these matters as pleasures, and weary yourself as little as possible, and hope for the time to come. Wheresoever there is man in this world, there also are discontented people, and chiefly at our age when everything doth weary us. After all, we shall have repose in a future life.

I have not yet caused the firewood to be cut on account of the weather; it hath done naught but rain this long time, and the roads be so heavy it hath been impossible to cart the wood hither. I have used some belonging to Casini, and also of their charcoal without becoming too much the debtor of this family, and with the oak by the roadside and some other dry things we do live sufficiently well. I have had no washing done, and the flax must wait to be bleached. If the weather should improve for some days, the wood shall be cut as ye have written.

The price of oil fell 20 soldi last Monday, as ye will have heard from Messere, to whom I did write of it. According to report, the water hath risen so high that it hath not been possible to cross over the Pesa,[1] so I think there will have been no market at San Casciano. Ye must say for certain :

[1] A small river which flows into the Arno near Montelupo. San Casciano is a village higher up the same stream.

"When prices have risen so far, sell!" for prices do vary greatly with each market, and two markets will have been held before we can have your answer. I did tell the overseer—*i.e.* of the labourers making olive oil—that which ye wrote, and when the time doth serve he will do his best; he hath never yet been able properly to use his hand, and often it paineth him greatly. I did speak to Tozo concerning the vine stakes, and he saith they will be ready in a month. The canal and sluices at the Mill were finished on the 21 of this month, after which came two floods;[1] I am told that the work done stood the test exceeding well. But, according to what is told me, the miller is so useless a man that I doubt whether he will keep the place in due order for you. For the canal must be often repaired, and he doth nothing. Ye will have heard what Bastiano of Empoli judged fit to be done concerning the pond and the ditch.

With regard to having brought the labourers with me, so far I cannot complain more than in past years. They have each bought three pigs; Piero hath spent 31 lire, and the Casini family 35, and, according to what these peasants say, the pigs be full grown and fit to fatten. I have told them all that you did write concerning the ditch and the other things, and they say that they will do every-

---

[1] *i.e.* floods on the swift stream Virgignio, on the right bank of which stands Poppiano.

thing; it seemeth that they do desire to depart from here in good friendship with you. There are very few acorns anywhere; near the oak at Mal Fastello,[1] where are usually so many that they cover all the ground, I saw scarce an hundred, and it is the same thing with the oak near to the capers. They are worth a *grosso* the bushel, or more. I have bought a small pig which did cost me 9 lire and 12 soldi,[2] and shall kill it this carnival, seeing how that we shall be here. It happeneth that very many apples have gone rotten, so that I shall gain nothing by them; they have become so useless and strange that they are only fit to give unto the pigs. I do think they will consume them all, together with several bushels of acorns which I had. The meat shall be salted here; for that which is in Florence ye can arrange, if it be well, to salt it there.

The roofs must be mended in August. Since I have been here it hath done naught save rain ever since the vintage, and the weather hath never yet served for making the repairs. When first I did come hither I was not able to get the carpenter; then methought that as the days were so short, and little work could be done, it was not worth the cost to bring a carpenter from Castelfiorentino or from Florence. Also those benches must be made, a

[1] The name of one of the places on their estates.
[2] Roughly, about seven shillings and ninepence.

R

doorway opened into the large courtyard, all these windows must be covered with cloth,[1] and many other things if we would live here in comfort. But for so small a matter as mending the doors I cared not to spend money in bringing hither a master carpenter through such bad weather. If we be all in good health this next summer, and foresee that we shall be able to sojourn here in peace, then may we bring hither a good carpenter and cause all the work to be done. So for the present we must be patient, as we have been before. Ye write that ye are sending me a list of these creditors who say that they must have money from you ; I shall be glad of it, because I will not pay without ye tell me what they ought to have. The man from Vanozzo saith he hath not been paid for the vines that we did have from him. I see that from Benedetto Canbi ye had some beam or other for the house for which he is unpaid ; Meo Giorli saith that he did help you in some work and hath not yet been paid. Wherefore it would please me if ye would look over everything, if so able, and the sooner the better, so that I may settle all these matters.

Ye will remember that when that physician came, when ye were here, I did say unto you that I deemed him to be a man of worth ; and I do think it certain that if the doctors had bled Messere at

---

[1] Cloth or thick paper was often used to fill up windows instead of glass, especially in country houses.

the beginning, it would have done him great good,
because his face was very red, especially when he
was eating. Master Marcantonio was doubtful,
and would not do it. Of mine own ailments I have
no need to tell you, because ye know them exactly.
Master Giovanbatista caused me to take an elec-
tuary, the which is called *mitridato*,[1] mingled with
Malmsey wine. It did me much good, although
the taking of syrops and medicines hath generally seemed hurtful unto me at the time. The
mitridato I do take in the winter, but not in the
summer.

In answer to your letter of the 12th, there is
nothing else to tell you, save that the wheat hath
been taken up from the store-place, and is in good
condition. I have caused it all to be sifted, and
disposed in the loft of the house, the old apart from
the new. If ye desire that it be sold tell me. The
old would fetch 33 soldi, the new 35. There is
but little spoiled of the old ; methinks the sifting
did it good, it now looketh much better. I have
only seen Francesco Caradori once since I have been
here. I did speak with Tozo concerning the stakes,
as ye bade me, and he did promise to see concerning
them. The white wines have fermented as usual,
and the *vernaccia*[2] is almost clear. I do not think

[1] A remedy alleged to have been invented by Mithridates,
believed to be an antidote to every kind of poison.
[2] A special kind of white wine.

it is very good this year; other years it was much better. The *greco*[1] will be good; it is not yet clear.

If Cavalcante[2] should come hither, I shall welcome him heartily that so I may have news of your condition. Albeit, considering what ye do write me, my mind may be at peace, and from the news I have of Messere I learn that the improvement hath continued; so that methinketh ye are all free from sickness, and may it please God thus to preserve you. Truth it is that the times are averse to the obtaining of relief, and especially of aged persons; but, as ye say, ye do find it go slowly, the which is natural.

When Messere desireth to have from the nuns that concerning which ye wrote unto me, I will do that is needful. I cannot imagine who hath hindered you from carrying out this business in your own way, if it be as profitable as ye write.

I did receive your letter of the 18th by the lad who was going to San Casciano. It pleased me greatly to hear that your improvement had continued so well that ye do think yourself almost restored to your customary state of health. I will endeavour with the best of my power to carry out all the things of which ye remind me. Later, I

---

[1] Another kind of wine.

[2] Cavalcante Cavalcanti, a firm adherent of Luigi and his family; he is frequently mentioned in these letters.

did receive another letter from you of the 18th, announcing the departure of Cavalcante upon the 19th ; I fear, however, that he did not depart by reason of the bad weather, because I have not heard of his arrival.

The pond and the ditch are not yet begun by reason of the weather, and of the opinion of Bastiano of Empoli, as I do think ye will have heard already from Messere and from himself. I did tell all your orders unto the labourers, concerning the open ditches and the olives to be gathered and looked over ; but we have had such wet and rotting weather that the olives have not yet been touched, nor the trunks examined on account of the gathering. To-day, which is the end of the month, the weather is beautiful, and a good wind blows. We shall see if it doth now improve, but I have no great faith in it, seeing that the moon is in its last quarter.[1] If this weather should continue until the new moon, methinks we may have good hopes of it ; and if it do but stay fair during December and January, many things can be sown, and perchance the price of corn and oats will not be changed. Here I have received several requests for grain, and in this weather I could have sold some bushels. I did not sell, however, because Messere and Gregorio did advise me to wait for some market, and

[1] Isabella was a great observer of the moon, both in arranging the affairs of her house and estate, and in the care of her health.

so I did.   I shall be glad to know your opinion as
quickly as possible, because Christmas is at hand,
and the time of our departure from here draweth
nigh.   I have sold beans, and am still selling a few
bushels ; at first I did sell them for 22 soldi, and
now for 29, but only a few bushels.

Ser Antonio[1] must be excused, because he hath
an infirmity so cruel that it would draw pity from
a stone ; he is ofttimes heard to cry aloud like
unto a woman in travail, and his suffering is such
that often he doth pray for death.   Sometimes he
can say mass, and get about the house ; he hath no
sign of fever.   He hath caused himself to be examined, and they did tell him that he hath not the
stone but a fistula, and is like to live some while yet
in this martyrdom.   May God grant him patience
and strength to support such great suffering as he
seemeth bond unto.

This time I will say no more, for I have been
writing several days.   This much writing doth op-
press me, for I write to Messere and to Simona,[2]
and for the works and the grain ; there is so much
of it that mine own affairs do fall into disorder, and
I grow too weary.   Wherefore ye must hold me
excused if I write not so often unto you as perchance ye might desire, and as I should also wish ;

---

[1] The parish priest of Poppiano, who looked after the affairs
of his " honoured patron," as he called Luigi.

[2] Her daughter, now married to Pierantonio de' Nobili.

but I cannot perform so much. I do commend myself unto you. May Christ keep you. The 30 day of November 1542.

ISABELLA at Poppiano.

[Addressed to]

THE MAGNIFICENT COMMISSIONER
OF CASTRACARO,
LUIGI GUICCIARDINI, *mine honoured consort in Castracaro.*[1]

IV

POPPIANO, 12 *and* 13 *December,* 1542.

yhs.

MOST DEAR LUIGI, I have received yours of the 23rd of last month and one of the 5th of the present, and herein will I reply to both as far as be needful.

With regard to your first letter, we must thank God that ye be well and quickly recovered from the sickness whereof ye told me, which seemeth to have been of no little importance. May God be ever thanked for it, to Whom have prayers for you not lacked, if so be that He will ever to accept them. But your own help is needed, and without that I do think that little else will avail.[2]

---

[1] A small place in the Tuscan Romagna, now the province of Florence.

[2] Simona also wrote to her father on this occasion, expressing her grief and anxiety at his illness, and saying that she had

Concerning the canal and the sluices, I have not
been thither and cannot tell you precisely where
they are. I can only tell you that I sent to fetch that
miller of Castelfiorentino who did often come to
see you in Florence—his name is Michele, but he is
nicknamed Gold Thorn—whom I hold to be a person very clever with these rivers, and of some im-

ordered prayers to be said for his recovery at several convents.
From his son, Messer Niccolò, came the following philosophical
epistle, an example of the learning attributed to him by his contemporaries:—"With regard to your sickness, Master Marcantonio saith—for Master Giovanni Batista is not yet returned—
that he attacheth no great importance unto the pulse, because
neither Galen nor the ancients did pay any attention unto it ; and
the other things can ye more easily regulate by means of a good
life than with medicine. And unto me it seemeth a wise counsel,
considering your age and that of the physician who doth advise
you ; for I would not that he should make experiments upon your
case out of his own imagination. I do trust more in your prudence than in his learning, for a physician hath need of experience and prudence besides science. But of this I will say no
more, save that your weariness of mind and body will be greatly
lessened if you do look upon business as pleasure, and above all
if you do read something sacred, which reading hath of all times
greatly profited me, and especially the Bible. And Cornelius
Tacitus saith of Tiberius, *quod sumebat solatium a negociis*.
Have not too great desire to grow young again with remedies
which all cause you to grow old. If ye do possess Marcus
Tullius *De Senectute*, read it ; it did delight me greatly when I
did read it in my boyhood, and I do think that it will please and
delight you greatly ; but endeavour to understand it well." After
certain passages on domestic and public affairs, Messer Niccolò
ends his letter with these words : "Every animal doth beget its
like, as saith the Song of Daniel ; " a sentence the deep learning enshrined in which must have been immensely gratifying
to the Magnificent Commissioner !

portance. He did furnish the plans for the canal
and the sluices, and saith that for this year there is
no need to fear danger ; and, during two or three
floods which have since happened, the sluices resisted well, and I am told they are exceeding useful
and have prevented such damage as it seemed the
water threatened. It is true that Bongianni,[1] having viewed the place, maintained it better to make
another sluice between the two already built, and
since I did receive your letter of the 5th of the present month I have spoken with him concerning the
matter, for methought ye did desire that another
should be made. Perchance he hath written unto
you concerning it ; he doth think that for the present there is nothing to be done, so we must wait
to see at another flood. Yet hath the water made
great eddies there even in these days, when it is
lowest of all the year, and the need is clear that such
works should have been made. The master from
Empoli went there and did approve the fitness of all
done, nor did he advise that aught else were needful. I have not been there since the roads have been
so bad, and it was too far for me to go thither on
foot. I did pay out six ducats of gold for the work,
and the irons, and all that was needful. Before that I
did pay twelve lire in two sums—all money thrown
away ; when engaged upon such works there can be

[1] The one amongst the Guicciardini brothers who gave his
whole attention to domestic affairs. He was never married.

no mistake in having the opinion of those who are skilled in judging of that which others do need. This miller is exceeding weak both in soul and mind, in brain and in body ; he ought to keep there someone who should ever be repairing, now the stakes and now the marble, but I do not know how he could pay him for I am told that he is very poor. I will do the best I can with him.

Concerning the wheat in the full store-place,[1] I caused this to be opened some fifteen days past, and took out only so much that Pieretto could enter in. He turned the straw over and over and found it quite dry ; then he probed with a stick even to the bottom, and found it dry everywhere. I kept it open three or four days and then examined it again, and finding it dry everywhere I did put back that which had been taken out, and closed it again ; and so it is left. The wheat in the store-place which is not full, I did take out and did have sifted, and it is in the loft over the chamber in the little house. I have not sold any, because I had no need of money and because I did not think I should lose aught by waiting for a while ; I shall get 32 or 33 soldi for it. I have sold several bushels of beans, and they do fetch 22, 28 and 26 soldi.

Ye remember how I wrote unto you that Francesco di Ser Cione could give you no money, but

[1] Grain was often stored in holes or places dug out in the earth, and covered with straw to keep it in good condition.

that he would give you some land ; read my first letter again. I had 6 lire from Pogna ; from Gregorio I have had 87 lire ; from Ser Antonio I had 27 lire which he had collected from Francesco di Ser Cione, and the rest he did tell me as I have written above.

The white wines are good ; the worst evil is that there is not much, and that this is not as good as usual. I gave your message unto the labourers, who affirm that the water-channels, and all else, be in good condition, and that they are careful that the cattle shall not pasture where ye do not wish that they should go. They are now gathering the olives. Since St. Andrew's Day we have had very good weather, but before that we had rain, fog, and wet, as ye wrote that ye likewise had.

The new labourers did come on St. Simon's Day, when Messere was here. The man from the Lotti hath not been since ; Pieretto's man hath been twice, the last time being at St. Nicholas, when they did tell me that they would wrap up the large plants in order that they might not be hurt by the cold. After the vintage they will sow certain grain used at this season, to wit, the oats. They are now gathering the olives, since they cannot, at this present, do aught else on the old land. There be but few pears ; yet shall we have two tubs full after that some of the autumn ones have been sold. I did reckon that from all the fruit which hath been sold I have gained 34 lire and 10 soldi. I have about 40 tubs full of apples, but they are so poor and bad that I shall gain but little by them; I have sold a great quantity at 8 soldi the tub, but have not yet measured the remainder. Perchance we shall get some money from the miller, but I desire not to enter into this matter when ye are not here, and so have I said unto Giovanni of Ripalto. The labourer who is come in place of Piero seemeth unto me full of promise, and desirous of doing all things well; [1] if his deeds do fulfil his promise, he will do well. By that time ye will be with us, if so God please. If he doth succeed, I shall be greatly pleased. The man from the Lotti speaketh little, and I have seen him only a few times; he seemeth to be a man of sense. We must judge of them according to their deeds; as saith the proverb, "I do not know thee unless thou dost work for me"; it is not easy to judge of a person until he hath been proved. There are not many olives; the overseer doth think that the two *poderi* will yield some thirty barrels of oil. I did give your message unto Ser Antonio, who was well pleased. He doth live in great torments, poor soul. If Francesco Caradori should come hither I will tell him what ye do write; I have seen him but once since I have been here.

[1] Several peasants had quitted Isabella's service, and here she is alluding to those who had replaced them.

Concerning your letter of the 5th, it did please
me to hear that ye have almost recovered from
your stomach, and from your other ailments; I
had much gladness of the news. May it please
God to keep you in health, and may ye understand
how to take care of yourself. I have not seen
Cavalcante, albeit I did hear that he remained fifteen days in Florence. Ye can imagine how gladly
I would have seen him. Methinks ye do greatly
dislike your office, and this sojourning in Castracaro, for ye did go there so unwillingly and with
such displeasure, and I do fear ye have regretted
it all this time. But I would that ye should, as
ye have bidden me, look upon business as pleasure.
Think ye that I find it greatly pleasing or divert-
ing this sojourning here with two maids, and
none other to see or speak with, and to spend my
time in writing, in paying workmen and in keeping of accounts? These matters weigh sore upon
persons of advanced age. Those who would be contented in this world must find their pleasure in the
things which do displease them, for otherwise they
would be always in grief and weariness; and remember that time doth fly, and that we approach the end
of this journey. I do go often to visit Ser Antonio,
and when I behold him in such pain, I feel myself
greatly privileged seeing that I am able to sleep, to
eat and to take some rest. Wherefore, being in
this condition, let us return thanks unto God.

The men are sowing seed all over the earth of the ditch, as ye bade them. The well doth not fill because the land, which should supply it, hath been sown over. Had I had my way, I should have filled up that hole, but since ye did order that the ditch should be made the wheat must be let go. The fountain throweth out much water, with a jet of almost half a barrel, and the washing place runneth ever over; it doth seem strange that this is built so low, seeing there is always a plenty of water, and the pond full. It were better, I think, to divert the water into one stream, when there is not so great an abundance.

Write unto me when Bongianni shall cause the store-hole to be made, and I will pay for the work. The stakes have not yet been brought: Tozo did tell me that he would provide them, but that they cannot be cut before January, and I do hear the same from Cavalcante's bailiff who is bound to provide of these for Bongianni. I have bought no wood; when they did cut stakes for the Vergignio [1] there remained some over with which, and that ye did write unto me I might take for the fire, I have sufficient, for the weather at present is such that we can go forth to walk. I have caused some of the wine of Paterno be brought hither from Florence, which was excellent, and other have I bought from Montagnana. I shall endeavour to lack as little as possible.

[1] The river at Poppiano.

In this letter will I say no more, for the hour waxeth and I have not supped. I commend myself unto you. May the Lord keep you in health. The 12 day of December, 1542.—ISABELLA at Poppiano.

The reckoning for the pigs which have been sold did agree with your sending. In your letter of November 7th ye wrote unto me that, seeing ye did feel yourself in better health, ye were sending me the list of such as allege you do owe them money. Here, therefore, is Vanozo's reckoning on account of the vines, and I do understand that ye have to pay for a piece of wood obtained from Benedetto Canbi, which was put in the little house; Meo Giorli saith that ye do owe him for some work which he did; the blacksmith saith that ye have to pay for 2 pounds of nails, and for certain wine afforded unto Maria, but I did think that this was paid this some while. I should be glad to know from you if all these persons are to receive the sums here written down. They are small matters and I will satisfy every one; I do think they are all matters forgotten, but those to whom they are owing probably think otherwise, and that is not well. Wherefore I should be glad if ye would inform me on this subject as quickly as possible, because presently it will be time to return into Florence; it is nigh unto Christmas and the business here is almost concluded. The roofs will be finished mending by Saturday ; they were damaged in such manner that it will cost me three ducats or more, with the lime, tiles, bricks and labour ; but they are well done. Ser Antonio hath felt somewhat better since Sunday ; he did say mass this morning, and commendeth himself unto you.

I did add this upon the 13th.

[Addressed to]
THE MAGNIFICENT SIGNORE,
THE COMMISSIONER OF CASTRACARO,
LUIGI GUICCIARDINI, *mine honoured consort in Castracaro.*

V

FLORENCE, 9 *January*, 1543.

yhs.

DEAREST LUIGI, I have received three letters from you, but will not reply unto them at this time. I will only say that it will be eight days to-morrow since I did return from Poppiano. Up there I did take care of myself, with rest and good living, and did eat chickens pounded and made into broth ; I did so greatly improve that Messere and Bongianni judged it advisable for me to come to Florence, considering that if mine ailment had returned I should have been in a condition worse than before.[1] Had Ser Antonio been in health, or had there been another good priest at hand, I should have risked abiding there a few days longer; but there was none, and I did let myself to be persuaded. Ye can well believe that the fatigues of departure, the change of air, and the many visits, did arrest the improvement. And here do I sit all sadly in my chamber, as many a time ye have seen me sit, with an headache, and a depression at mine heart which naught may overcome, so that body and legs and heart do all seem weary with weakness upon this left side. I have little taste for my food, but wine do I like, and much strength do I derive from it. The wines are good, as Cavalcante will have told you, for he did taste all, both from the country and from Florence, the white and the red. I was very well when he did arrive at Poppiano, and feeling better than I had done for a long time, as he will have told you, so much so that methought often that nature was putting forth all her strength at this late age. I could walk a little, I did sleep and eat very well, and in every way was I much better than I had been the previous year. The morning after Cavalcante was arrived everything did begin to go amiss. It is true that the weather changed, becoming exceeding cold; although I had

---

[1] During the last days of her stay in the country Isabella had suffered from an illness, that seems to have grown worse with each succeeding attack, of which she gives a detailed account in letters to her children.

S

warm clothing, I did feel it greatly in mine head, and in all my body.

I did send to call Master Giovanbatista that I might describe mine ailments unto him. But when he was come, he said that he did desire to see me more at leisure, and that he was then very busy; he would pay no heed to me at that moment on account of being so busy. Since then I have not seen him, and did not care, but abode some days in bed in order that he might judge better of mine ailments. I will oblige him to come, and if ye do see your physician there, inquire of him what is his opinion. Likewise ye should speak unto him concerning Simona and Pierantonio, for I did find her grown so fat that I am convinced the water of Porretta doth not help her to grow lean. Pierantonio is just as he always is.

Ye bid me tell you how much the meat is worth. I did speak with Cecco, the gate-keeper,[1] concerning it; he saith that it will cost me $10\frac{1}{2}$ lire to bring it from the butcher. Wherefore I think it would be well to salt there four pieces more than were to be salted for you, of value as ye did write to me. It doth seem unto me better economy to do thus. For the villa I will have that pig salted which I did buy, and which will be about 150 pounds.

The old wheat hath not been sold; it will not fetch more than 24 or 25 soldi the bushel, because

[1] Cecco was probably a collector of duty at the city gate.

the price of all things hath gone down. Messere did sell 20 barrels of oil, for 7 lire and 2 soldi.

I will say no more now. I commend myself unto you. May Christ preserve you and keep you in health. The 9th day of January, 1542.[1]—ISABELLA in Florence.

I did keep this back until this evening when I have received your letter of the eighth ; this hath rejoiced me greatly.   It doth only grieve me to hear that ye have had a chill for two nights. Let me hear frequently how it is with you. Cavalcante will inform you of my condition. Simona and Caterina have been to visit me since my return hither. I do not intend to have meat salted here, as Cavalcante will tell you ; he will likewise tell you of the wood-cutting at Poppiano, and ye must inform him what ye do desire should be done, and when. I will say no more.   Have a care of yourself ; so will I of myself. God grant us that we may meet again in good health.

[Addressed to]
THE MAGNIFICENT SIGNORE,
THE COMMISSIONER OF CASTRACARO,
LUIGI GUICCIARDINI, *mine honoured consort in Castracaro.*

---

[1] According to the Florentine reckoning, *i.e.*, but 1543 by ordinary reckoning.

These letters, full of domestic cares and womanly affection, written with simple dignity not untinged here and there with melancholy, reveal as in a mirror what manner of woman was this noble matron—the wife of Luigi, and sister-in-law to Francesco Guicciardini, the statesman and historian who was one of Italy's greatest ornaments, and whose fame time has not dimmed.

Isabella Sacchetti Guicciardini may be regarded as having been a living example of the ideal woman described by the old writers of books on family management. These good men "held it to be the most joyful of all things properly to attend unto their own affairs," but they did not, on that account, neglect their duty in public matters. Believing strongly in a division of labour and responsibility, man, in their opinion, "should leave the management of the house and of all smaller matters unto the woman, keeping for himself all manly business, and the things proper unto men." "A man must bring all things into the house, the woman must preserve and defend both them and herself, with fear and with suspicion; the man must defend his house, his wife and family and his country, not sitting idly down, but exerting mind and body, with courage giving of his sweat and of his blood." Thus did Madonna Isabella manage her domestic affairs on behalf of her husband, absent as commissioner in Arezzo, in Romagna, Pisa or Pistoia, writing him letters concerning which our only regret must be that so few have survived to the present day. How welcome her letters were to that husband, a man not easily satisfied, is to be seen in his replies. " After thou hast been some days at Poppiano," we read in one of these, " thou must write and tell me how things are there, and if the fowling-place planted this year grows well, and the capers and nut trees planted this year . . . and how the olives and the vines do promise. . . ." And she excused herself for not writing as often " as perchance ye might desire, and as I should wish to do."

Widely different were the ways of life depicted in these letters from those of the present day. Laws, customs, and institutions have changed in course of time ; other sentiments, ideas, and affections rule social relations, civilisation has acquired the advantages and blemishes of old age ; life has been made easier by the glorious triumphs of human intelligence over nature, and minds and bodies alike are differently tempered. The ladies of to-day would assuredly not return from the country into the city in the manner in which their ancestresses performed the journey ; Isabella, feeble health and advancing years notwithstanding, rode upon a mule, considering a litter unnecessary luxury. Yet, despite of all differences and the little light which we are able to throw upon the glories of those bygone times, it is not impossible that a lady of the

present day may find both profit and pleasure in
learning what were the interests and occupations of
one who lived four hundred years ago.

If the history were to be written of the five sons
of Piero Guicciardini, of whom Francesco was the
eldest and Luigi the youngest, it would show in
what way and through what influences the love of
liberty, of country and of possessions, was in the
minds of some of the worthiest citizens combined
with devotion to the fortunes of the descendants
of Cosimo and Lorenzo de' Medici. Such a book
would also show reasons for, if it could not morally
justify, deeds which to-day would seem almost to
deserve the name of high treason, deeds not done
by Messer Francesco Guicciardini alone, but by
other men of equal rank and fame. The principal
personage in that book would be Luigi; the most
important documents would be the correspondence between him and his son Niccolò, in whose
degree of Doctor of Laws contemporary opinion
saw the family's return to the greatness of his
uncle. A more probable successor to this, by
virtue of some of his qualities at all events, was
Luigi Guicciardini himself, a proud man and a
strong, and with plenty of opportunities to prove
himself. Thus, when as Gonfalonier of Justice,
in April 1527, he had to enforce order in the city
which had risen against the Medici, his firmness
and bravery earned general praise. When Medi-

GENEALOGY OF THE GUICCIARDINI

PIERO
di Jacopo di Piero di Luigi,
1454–1513,
married Simona di Bongianni Gianfigliazzi.

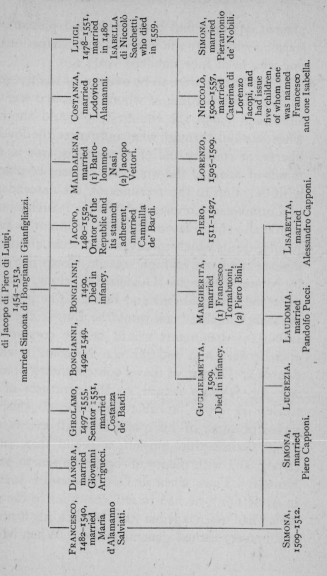

FRANCESCO,
1482–1540,
married
Maria
d'Alamanno
Salviati.

DIANORA,
married
Giovanni
Arrigucci.

GIROLAMO,
1497–1555,
Senator 1551,
married
Costarza
de' Bardi.

BONGIANNI,
1492–1549.

BONGIANNI,
1490.
Died in
infancy.

JACOPO,
1480–1552,
Orator of the
Republic and
its staunch
adherent,
married
Cammilla
de' Bardi.

MADDALENA,
married
(1) Barto-
lommeo
Nasi,
(2) Jacopo
Vettori.

COSTANZA,
married
Lodovico
Alamanni.

LUIGI,
1478–1551,
married
in 1480
ISABELLA
di Niccolò
Sacchetti,
who died
in 1559.

SIMONA,
1509–1512.

SIMONA,
married
Piero Capponi.

LUCREZIA.

GUGLIELMETTA,
1509.
Died in infancy.

LAUDOMIA,
married
Pandolfo Pucci.

MARGHERITA,
married
(1) Francesco
Tornabuoni,
(2) Piero Bini.

LISABETTA,
married
Alessandro Capponi.

PIERO,
1511–1527.

LORENZO,
1505–1509.

NICCOLÒ,
1500–1557,
married
Caterina di
Lorenzo
Jacopi; and
had issue
five children,
of whom one
was named
Francesco
and one Isabella.

SIMONA,
married
Pierantonio
de' Nobili.

cean Commissioner at Pisa in 1530, however, he was reproached for cruelty because, having taken over the city from his Republican predecessor, he caused the latter to be tortured to death. Such of his letters, written to his brother after the days of freedom were over, as have been published are quite in accordance with his actions. In his description of the *Sack of Rome*, for instance—a description dedicated to Duke Cosimo—he shows himself averse to that "barbarian" foreign power with whose aid the Medici would willingly have dispensed, had it been possible, in their subjugation of the state. Such of his dialogues and treatises as deal with politics would undoubtedly repay study. Certain of these were designed as a revenge against Machiavelli, in whose book, the *Asino d'Oro*, he figures amongst the other Medicean adherents: other productions of his pen, preserved amongst the Magliabechiana manuscripts, are entitled *The Game of Chess*. "Luigi is at his country house," Busini wrote to Varchi, in 1527, in a budget of city news during the days of freedom, "where he is writing his *Game of Chess*, comparing this game to a good father." This treatise, dedicated to the Duke, is, however, a *Comparison between the Game of Chess and the Military Craft*.

As historical witnesses, the written word probably carries greater moral weight than any other means by which a man is able to place his thoughts

and feelings upon record, and this in no less degree when it preserves the peculiarities and idioms
of past centuries all uncorrupted by the faults of
daily speech. A hundred years later, the letters of
a Florentine woman would hardly have contained
such a charming and accurate picture of country
life as that drawn by Madonna Isabella—the active
housekeeper whom we see amidst maids and farm
labourers, millers, masons, overseers and workmen, arranging their duties, settling their work,
paying bills and conferring with her brother-in-law
Bongianni, the one of all the brothers who might
be called the squire of the family. These long
and detailed letters to her husband, full of questions, reminders and practical suggestions, come
fresh from her mind as she pauses for rest between
active hours spent upon problems of the crops and
fish-ponds, the wine and oil and wood, San Casciano
market, the beasts of burden and the men who
tended them. She has arranged for the winter provisions, including a pig for salting, repairs in the
house, the mill and the care of the fields ; she has
settled money matters and engaged labourers, and
found time to comfort the poor priest afflicted with
a hopeless malady; she has her own difficulties with
servants. Yet she advises her husband to be patient
in his own troubles, and all these things she describes
in language so simple and vivid that we seem ourselves to see and hear the whole.

It is not surprising that, with all this on her hands, Isabella complained that with so much work and writing to do her own "little affairs" got into disorder.　But she was a woman who always found time and leisure for everything. She arranged a suitable marriage for her daughter Simona, and corresponded with her when she had left home, as also with her son, Messer Niccolò, the most important person in all the world to her; she advised her husband about his health, or admonished him concerning heavenly things, and although she reproached him with a separate establishment, and not taking her with him to the cities whither he was sent as Commissioner—as he would have done, she bitterly added, had she been a more worthy wife—the selfsame letter protests the difficulty that would follow did she leave home for even a fortnight.

Traces of ill-humour are often visible in these letters, for the writer "took things greatly to heart when they did not go well with her," as Luigi wrote of her to her son; and she said of herself that her mind was never at rest, because she was ever expecting the worst.　She constantly discussed her ailments, but they did not prevent her from living almost into her eightieth year—1559, eight years after the death of her husband and two after that of her son—nor did her restless nature allow her to abate anything of her activity as housekeeper and mother of a family. From Luigi's own letters, also, it is easy to see that the austerity of their characters in no way excluded affection between husband and wife.

" Although it be true," he once wrote from the Romagna, " that I am here called lord by all, and that every one doth stand uncovered in my presence ; that I have as many servants as I may desire, and that, according to the usage of the place, I nothing lack in reason, thou must nevertheless take it for certain that I have suffered infinite trouble of mind because of the affairs both of there and of here, that I have never an hour of repose or consolation whatsoever, seeing that satisfaction there is none in those who do ordinarily converse with me, and that it would give me an incomparably greater delight might I see the things which be mine own—as thee and mine household, my friends and mine own villa— than do all these lordships, uncovered heads, and other things which be here and which I can have. Wherefore doth every hour seem unto me a thousand years until I am able to go thither, even for only eight days."

Another time, when as a good wife and mother she lamented certain heavy domestic expenses, the still absent Commissioner affectionately reassured her :—

"Concerning the great expenses which we have this year had, and shall yet have, in order to finish the walls and furnish the houses, ye say very true; but without the monies that mine office doth bring we could not have commenced anything, and still less have concluded everything. Wherefore I do think that all things can be accomplished, and the houses furnished well, and some money remain to lay aside. Therefore consider no more of difficulties, nor yet of the things of perchance. And even if I have not found a gold mine, as ye write unto me, I have found here a certain stream which both flows pleasantly and sufficeth for the time. So be ye of good cheer, for everything will easily be arranged. Be merry, and remember that this time we have come forth out of the mire, and that in future we shall have no cause to complain of our fortunes; for we shall lack nothing that is reasonable, and I think that the stream which is now flowing will provide abundantly for everything. May it please God to let us enjoy ourselves together, and keep us in good health."

Luigi's entire correspondence with "dearest Isabella," and other letters in which he mentions her, are full of respect, affection, and the utmost confidence and admiration. With these feelings

mingle other strange subjects—astrological super-
stitions, according to which he frequently points
out to her the days and hours, or the aspects of
moon or stars that are to govern her comings and
goings, even the times when she is to change her
rooms, empty the cellar, or have medicaments
prepared by the apothecary.

Madonna Isabella's letters are written in a forcible yet flowery Italian, reminiscent of the language
used by the dramatists and novelists of that century, and a lexicographer might well find in it
new words and sayings, especially in reference to
country life, which are singularly apt and expressive. This descendant of the kindred of Franco
Sacchetti, and sister-in-law to Francesco Guicciardini, certainly followed in the footsteps alike of her
own and her husband's race, for, limited as her voca-
bulary may be, the words never fail vividly to bring
the things she would describe before our mind's eye.
The worthless miller, weak in spirit and brain and
body, who inspired but little confidence in the judi-
cious lady; the tiresome servant, the cause of so
much annoyance to the Magnificent Commissioner
of Arezzo, who had an evil tongue and gave rise to
scandal; the farm labourers, one of whom made
many fair promises, while the other said little but
seemed a sensible man—both to be judged according
to their deeds; the fishpond tampered with by some
unknown person; the cask of old wine that burst,

and over which she mourned with all the regret of
a thrifty housewife, and the picture of herself, sitting sick and sad in her chamber, are sketches that
no elaboration could make more lifelike. In other
as yet unpublished letters, Isabella recognises her
own anxious and apprehensive nature, ever too
ready to believe the worst, especially where the wel-
fare of those dear to her was concerned. From these
needless terrors she often sought refuge in prayer,
" but fear was the more potent, because methought
I did deserve every ill," until, at last, she realised
with joy and gratitude that " God is more merciful
than just."

When she chose, both her thoughts and words
could rise to higher things. Not only were domestic and material cares perpetually interwoven with
family affections and ambitions, but she tempered
her occasional outbursts of impatience or bitterness
with self-reproaches and moral reflections. Thus
the sinister portrait of the servant Ottaviano concludes with the remark : "We be all full of faults ;
we must bear one with another until we die."
When discontented with anything, she consoles
herself with the hope that God will presently send
better things : " Please God we may choose the
better part, which doth not seem our general custom." The name of God begins and ends all her
letters, and her deep religious feeling, strict sense
of duty, and fearless outlook on death and eternity,

brighten and ennoble all the lesser qualities of her character. An unpublished letter of the year 1537, written to her husband at Pistòia, whither he had been sent as Commissioner on account of the struggles between the Cancellieri and the Panciatichi, is a good example of these traits.

"May it please God to end all these discords and tribulations that have been cause of the dangers through which ye have passed. Ye may comfort yourself that ye were so prompt and quick-witted with those hot-headed ones, and bethink yourself of all that might have happened because of them. But consider likewise what was the cause of all their misery. And above all things, commend yourself unto God, that He may show us the way and the true light, for in these times we have much need of His help."

Such was this noble matron of the Guicciardini, a type of many a Florentine woman of her own and other times. Names and memories change and are renewed from generation to generation, but with many are associated traditions and examples that are a joy and benefit to all. No quality of all the many that men evince was dearer to our forefathers, or more gladly recorded by them, than family "piety." Of Isabella Sacchetti Guicciardini it may truly be said that she is "of them which have left a name behind them that their praises might be reported." This record is of her own unconscious making, and has come down to us through the happy chance of the survival of her letters. It is, then, surely our duty to remember her, whose personality has thus happily re-arisen from among the silent multitude of those "that have left no memorial, but are perished as though they had never been born." Of all the heathen gods the Lares and Penates alone have survived, and as long as the world endures family love and pride will keep alive the flame on the altar of this immortal myth.

CHAPTER VI

A LETTER OF ALESSANDRA MANCINGHI STROZZI

THE pages of this book contain more than one allusion to the letters written by Alessandra Mancinghi Strozzi to her children in exile. One, however,[1] an autograph original preserved in the Florentine State Archives, and by some means overlooked when Cesare Guasti collected and printed these letters in 1877, seems a fitting pendent to this study of the women of Florence. It is one of the best and most maternal of all those written by the brave lady who remained faithfully at her post in Florence, opposing to party proscription that patient constancy and trustful hope, which having sustained her through days of misfortune, carried her to ultimate triumph. The letter is addressed to her eldest son, Filippo, and the persons mentioned are Lorenzo, her second son; Matteo, who died young; Niccolò Strozzi, a cousin of her dead husband, who played a father's part towards the orphans; Jacopo, Niccolò's brother; Caterina, who was married to Marco Parenti, and Alessandra, who afterwards married Giovanni Bonsi.

---

[1] Received in Naples on November 28.

T

To FILIPPO DEGLI STROZZI *in* NAPLES.

In the name of God, the 8th day of November 1448. Upon the 6th day of this month I did receive from thee a letter written upon the 16th of last month, whereunto I will herewith reply.

Thou dost tell me of Matteo's doings, how that he hath written thee a letter concerning our condition. And it is true; it is even worse than he did say. God be praised for all things. Thou didst well to show the letter unto Niccolò. Seeing that our condition is known unto strangers, it should be known likewise unto those who are our kinsmen, and do continually assist us. Neither hath Niccolò waited until now to show his goodwill towards us, but hath been ever ready to do good unto us; this do I well know by experience, and thou shouldst know it even better than I. Thou dost tell me that Matteo being still here, Niccolò is desirous that I should make him ready and send him unto thee, partly because of the pestilence which doth render it dangerous to abide here, and partly because he hath no occupation and wasteth his days. It is true that the pestilence hath commenced here, and that all who could go unto their villas have departed thither; some have already died in the country, and in almost every place in the neighbourhood one or another is dying of it. The family is still at the

Benedetto da Maiano

Äinai

FILIPPO STROZZI

(Paris : The Louvre.)

villa, but if there be no further peril, I do think
they will presently return to Florence. It is believed that for this winter the pestilence will do no
more hurt, but that in the springtime it will cause
great destruction. May God help us! Matteo
hath heard me say that now the pestilence is come
I have no money to give away, and it is true. I
know not how I can send him away from me, for
he is little and hath need of my care, nor know I
how that I may live without him. Of my five
children how shall I abide with one only, and she
Alessandra whom I do expect to marry at any time?
The utmost that I can keep her with me is less than
two years, and at thought thereof must great grief
fall upon me so to remain alone. A while ago Matteo went unto Marco's villa, and there sojourned
six days; methought I should not live until his
return. I had none to do me a service, and I was
greatly hindered without him, for he writeth all my
letters. Moreover, he had a grievous sickness this
summer, and I did think he would die; but good
nursing saved him. And when I took counsel with
the physician concerning the sending of him away,
he said, "An ye hold him dear, send not him
away, for he is of a delicate nature, and should he
fall sick without your care, then surely were he
like to die. Wherefore, if ye hold him dear, send
him not away from you so young." For this reason,
and because I have need of him, I may think no

more of it. True it is that about a year ago I was desirous of sending him ; but then was Caterina at home, so that I felt not so lonely. But when I heard of the ill-health of Lorenzo, I grieved so deeply for them both that if they had been dead, I could not more have grieved. And, between one thing and another, I did determine not to send him away saving there were great need of it. I have taken counsel with Marco and with Antonio degli Strozzi. They did both advise me not to send him away for the present, but that if there should be a great pestilence in the spring, as they do expect, and if the pestilence have abated at Siena, and upon all that road even unto Rome, then might I send him. Truly it were madness in me to send him now, wherefore, though I do determine to send him, it will not be yet awhile. Therefore think ye no more upon it at this present. I am acquainted with your needs better than anyone, and if ye are not able to earn money for yourself ye must not be put to the charge of other persons. For my part, I will use all mine endeavour—and if the Commune take it not from me, for I am no longer able to defend myself—by good management and every other means to preserve for you the little that I have. God will be mine aid, and unto you may He give virtue and health according to my desires.

Concerning the flax, I will trust in thy judgment. If thou sendest it, set within it 10 lbs. of almonds against Lent; they will travel well within the bale of flax. I ask them of thee because I hear that in Naples they cost but little, and here are they dear. See that thou send them, for so shall the expense be small.

Concerning Marco Parenti, I can inform thee that he is a good youth, and doth treat Caterina exceeding well; also dealeth he fairly with all men, which doth much content me. He is of good character, but the contributions he is forced to pay are too heavy, for he hath been taxed at eleven florins. Hitherto he hath paid everything, and so be he doeth no worse, I am content with him. May God bestow His grace upon him. Caterina is not yet with child, at which, considering these times of pestilence, I do rejoice. She is lean in her body, and herein resembles she her father. May God give her strength.

I did write unto thee upon the 4th of this month, and did enclose my letter in one from Marco, and since the messenger departed more soon than I did expect, I think that thou wilt receive it at the same time as this. Therein write I unto thee concerning the little house of Niccolò Popoleschi, which hath been sold unto Donato Rucellai; it standeth close by ours, adjoining our court, so that on no account will we lose it out of our hands. Filippo, answer me quickly, for I must write unto Jacopo in Bruges.

No more at present.   God guard thee from evil.
Thine Alessandra, widow of Matteo degli Strozzi
in Florence.

See that thou art obedient unto Niccolò, and do
thy duty towards him, showing thyself grateful for
the good he doeth thee.   For if thus thou do, I
shall likewise be satisfied.   May God in His mercy
grant thee grace.   A few days since hath Matteo
written a letter unto Lorenzo in Avignon.

INDEX

THE END

Printed by BALLANTYNE, HANSON & Co.
Edinburgh & London